C-215 CAREER EXAMINATION SERIES

This is your PASSBOOK for...

Associate Traffic Enforcement Agent

Test Preparation Study Guide Questions & Answers

NLC®
NATIONAL LEARNING CORPORATION®

212 Michael Drive, Syosset, NY 11791
(516) 921-8888 • www.passbooks.com
E-mail: info@passbooks.com

PASSBOOK® SERIES

THE *PASSBOOK® SERIES* has been created to prepare applicants and candidates for the ultimate academic battlefield – the examination room.

At some time in our lives, each and every one of us may be required to take an examination – for validation, matriculation, admission, qualification, registration, certification, or licensure.

Based on the assumption that every applicant or candidate has met the basic formal educational standards, has taken the required number of courses, and read the necessary texts, the *PASSBOOK® SERIES* furnishes the one special preparation which may assure passing with confidence, instead of failing with insecurity. Examination questions – together with answers – are furnished as the basic vehicle for study so that the mysteries of the examination and its compounding difficulties may be eliminated or diminished by a sure method.

This book is meant to help you pass your examination provided that you qualify and are serious in your objective.

The entire field is reviewed through the huge store of content information which is succinctly presented through a provocative and challenging approach – the question-and-answer method.

A climate of success is established by furnishing the correct answers at the end of each test.

You soon learn to recognize types of questions, forms of questions, and patterns of questioning. You may even begin to anticipate expected outcomes.

You perceive that many questions are repeated or adapted so that you can gain acute insights, which may enable you to score many sure points.

You learn how to confront new questions, or types of questions, and to attack them confidently and work out the correct answers.

You note objectives and emphases, and recognize pitfalls and dangers, so that you may make positive educational adjustments.

Moreover, you are kept fully informed in relation to new concepts, methods, practices, and directions in the field.

You discover that you are actually taking the examination all the time: you are preparing for the examination by "taking" an examination, not by reading extraneous and/or supererogatory textbooks.

In short, this PASSBOOK®, used directedly, should be an important factor in helping you to pass your test.

ASSOCIATE TRAFFIC ENFORCEMENT AGENT

JOB DESCRIPTION

This class of positions encompasses supervisory work of varying degrees of difficulty in the traffic enforcement area. All personnel perform related work.

Under supervision, performs the following: Supervises a squad of Traffic Enforcement Agents; assigns, trains, and evaluates subordinate employees; monitors productivity; prepares reports; prepares and serves summonses for vehicles and pedestrians when required; investigates complaints and patrol problems; recommends disciplinary action; assists traffic enforcement personnel when injured or when involved in a conformation; operates portable and vehicle radios; operates a motor vehicle; performs related work.

EXAMPLES OF TYPICAL TASKS

Allocates available personnel in accordance with priority areas when not all personnel are present. Changes post assignments on weekly roll call when necessary. Prepares daily field patrol report. Prepares absence control form. Signs radios and other vehicles out or in. Inspects uniforms, appearance, and equipment at roll call. Instructs subordinates about departmental rules and, regulations and daily field conditions. In the field, determines whether subordinates are following departmental rules and regulations. Prepares written reprimands to subordinates who do not follow rules and regulations. Reviews summonses at subordinates' work location. Checks field patrol report for accuracy and completeness. Attempts to resolve problems between subordinates and irate citizens. Helps subordinates with difficulties on the job. Responds to an emergency situation where an agent has been hurt or assaulted and takes appropriate action. Observes and reports traffic hazards and field conditions. Helps citizens with various problems, such as directions. Reviews all subordinates' summonses daily and takes appropriate action. Fills out forms at the end of the day. Inspects departmental vehicles to determine whether they are in the proper working condition. Determines proper codes to use for radio transmission. Uses radio to properly transmit various types of information. Gives oral reprimands when necessary. Counts and bags summonses daily. Responds to and investigates citizens' complaints. Evaluates employees' performance. Recommends disciplinary action. Conducts "one on one" supervision. Recommends commendations and awards for district office at the end of tour. Checks and reviews subordinates; attendance records.

WRITTEN TEST

The written test will be of the multiple-choice type and may include questions on:

1. Rules and regulations;
2. Properly filling out summonses;
3. Checking field reports for accuracy and completeness;
4. Responding to emergency situations where an agent has been hurt or assaulted;
5. Using radio to properly transmit various types of information;
6. Preparing daily field patrol reports;
7. Absence forms and other forms;
8. Signing radios and/or vehicles out and in;
9. Changing post assignments on weekly roll call;
10. Inspecting uniforms, appearance, and equipment at roll call;
11. Allocating available personnel in accordance with priority areas when all personnel are present;
12. Instructing subordinates about departmental rules and regulations and daily field conditions;
13. Reviewing subordinates' summonses and taking appropriate action;
14. Preparing written reprimands to subordinates; and
15. Standards of employee conduct.

HOW TO TAKE A TEST

I. YOU MUST PASS AN EXAMINATION

A. WHAT EVERY CANDIDATE SHOULD KNOW

Examination applicants often ask us for help in preparing for the written test. What can I study in advance? What kinds of questions will be asked? How will the test be given? How will the papers be graded?

As an applicant for a civil service examination, you may be wondering about some of these things. Our purpose here is to suggest effective methods of advance study and to describe civil service examinations.

Your chances for success on this examination can be increased if you know how to prepare. Those "pre-examination jitters" can be reduced if you know what to expect. You can even experience an adventure in good citizenship if you know why civil service exams are given.

B. WHY ARE CIVIL SERVICE EXAMINATIONS GIVEN?

Civil service examinations are important to you in two ways. As a citizen, you want public jobs filled by employees who know how to do their work. As a job seeker, you want a fair chance to compete for that job on an equal footing with other candidates. The best-known means of accomplishing this two-fold goal is the competitive examination.

Exams are widely publicized throughout the nation. They may be administered for jobs in federal, state, city, municipal, town or village governments or agencies.

Any citizen may apply, with some limitations, such as the age or residence of applicants. Your experience and education may be reviewed to see whether you meet the requirements for the particular examination. When these requirements exist, they are reasonable and applied consistently to all applicants. Thus, a competitive examination may cause you some uneasiness now, but it is your privilege and safeguard.

C. HOW ARE CIVIL SERVICE EXAMS DEVELOPED?

Examinations are carefully written by trained technicians who are specialists in the field known as "psychological measurement," in consultation with recognized authorities in the field of work that the test will cover. These experts recommend the subject matter areas or skills to be tested; only those knowledges or skills important to your success on the job are included. The most reliable books and source materials available are used as references. Together, the experts and technicians judge the difficulty level of the questions.

Test technicians know how to phrase questions so that the problem is clearly stated. Their ethics do not permit "trick" or "catch" questions. Questions may have been tried out on sample groups, or subjected to statistical analysis, to determine their usefulness.

Written tests are often used in combination with performance tests, ratings of training and experience, and oral interviews. All of these measures combine to form the best-known means of finding the right person for the right job.

II. HOW TO PASS THE WRITTEN TEST

A. NATURE OF THE EXAMINATION

To prepare intelligently for civil service examinations, you should know how they differ from school examinations you have taken. In school you were assigned certain definite pages to read or subjects to cover. The examination questions were quite detailed and usually emphasized memory. Civil service exams, on the other hand, try to discover your present ability to perform the duties of a position, plus your potentiality to learn these duties. In other words, a civil service exam attempts to predict how successful you will be. Questions cover such a broad area that they cannot be as minute and detailed as school exam questions.

In the public service similar kinds of work, or positions, are grouped together in one "class." This process is known as *position-classification.* All the positions in a class are paid according to the salary range for that class. One class title covers all of these positions, and they are all tested by the same examination.

B. FOUR BASIC STEPS

1) Study the announcement

How, then, can you know what subjects to study? Our best answer is: "Learn as much as possible about the class of positions for which you've applied." The exam will test the knowledge, skills and abilities needed to do the work.

Your most valuable source of information about the position you want is the official exam announcement. This announcement lists the training and experience qualifications. Check these standards and apply only if you come reasonably close to meeting them.

The brief description of the position in the examination announcement offers some clues to the subjects which will be tested. Think about the job itself. Review the duties in your mind. Can you perform them, or are there some in which you are rusty? Fill in the blank spots in your preparation.

Many jurisdictions preview the written test in the exam announcement by including a section called "Knowledge and Abilities Required," "Scope of the Examination," or some similar heading. Here you will find out specifically what fields will be tested.

2) Review your own background

Once you learn in general what the position is all about, and what you need to know to do the work, ask yourself which subjects you already know fairly well and which need improvement. You may wonder whether to concentrate on improving your strong areas or on building some background in your fields of weakness. When the announcement has specified "some knowledge" or "considerable knowledge," or has used adjectives like "beginning principles of..." or "advanced ... methods," you can get a clue as to the number and difficulty of questions to be asked in any given field. More questions, and hence broader coverage, would be included for those subjects which are more important in the work. Now weigh your strengths and weaknesses against the job requirements and prepare accordingly.

3) Determine the level of the position

Another way to tell how intensively you should prepare is to understand the level of the job for which you are applying. Is it the entering level? In other words, is this the position in which beginners in a field of work are hired? Or is it an intermediate or advanced level? Sometimes this is indicated by such words as "Junior" or "Senior" in the class title. Other jurisdictions use Roman numerals to designate the level – Clerk I, Clerk II, for example. The word "Supervisor" sometimes appears in the title. If the level is not indicated by the title, check the description of duties. Will you be working under very close supervision, or will you have responsibility for independent decisions in this work?

4) Choose appropriate study materials

Now that you know the subjects to be examined and the relative amount of each subject to be covered, you can choose suitable study materials. For beginning level jobs, or even advanced ones, if you have a pronounced weakness in some aspect of your training, read a modern, standard textbook in that field. Be sure it is up to date and has general coverage. Such books are normally available at your library, and the librarian will be glad to help you locate one. For entry-level positions, questions of appropriate difficulty are chosen – neither highly advanced questions, nor those too simple. Such questions require careful thought but not advanced training.

If the position for which you are applying is technical or advanced, you will read more advanced, specialized material. If you are already familiar with the basic principles of your field, elementary textbooks would waste your time. Concentrate on advanced textbooks and technical periodicals. Think through the concepts and review difficult problems in your field.

These are all general sources. You can get more ideas on your own initiative, following these leads. For example, training manuals and publications of the government agency which employs workers in your field can be useful, particularly for technical and professional positions. A letter or visit to the government department involved may result in more specific study suggestions, and certainly will provide you with a more definite idea of the exact nature of the position you are seeking.

III. KINDS OF TESTS

Tests are used for purposes other than measuring knowledge and ability to perform specified duties. For some positions, it is equally important to test ability to make adjustments to new situations or to profit from training. In others, basic mental abilities not dependent on information are essential. Questions which test these things may not appear as pertinent to the duties of the position as those which test for knowledge and information. Yet they are often highly important parts of a fair examination. For very general questions, it is almost impossible to help you direct your study efforts. What we can do is to point out some of the more common of these general abilities needed in public service positions and describe some typical questions.

1) General information

Broad, general information has been found useful for predicting job success in some kinds of work. This is tested in a variety of ways, from vocabulary lists to questions about current events. Basic background in some field of work, such as sociology or economics, may be sampled in a group of questions. Often these are principles which have become familiar to most persons through exposure rather than through formal training. It is difficult to advise you how to study for these questions; being alert to the world around you is our best suggestion.

2) Verbal ability

An example of an ability needed in many positions is verbal or language ability. Verbal ability is, in brief, the ability to use and understand words. Vocabulary and grammar tests are typical measures of this ability. Reading comprehension or paragraph interpretation questions are common in many kinds of civil service tests. You are given a paragraph of written material and asked to find its central meaning.

3) Numerical ability

Number skills can be tested by the familiar arithmetic problem, by checking paired lists of numbers to see which are alike and which are different, or by interpreting charts and graphs. In the latter test, a graph may be printed in the test booklet which you are asked to use as the basis for answering questions.

4) Observation

A popular test for law-enforcement positions is the observation test. A picture is shown to you for several minutes, then taken away. Questions about the picture test your ability to observe both details and larger elements.

5) Following directions

In many positions in the public service, the employee must be able to carry out written instructions dependably and accurately. You may be given a chart with several columns, each column listing a variety of information. The questions require you to carry out directions involving the information given in the chart.

6) Skills and aptitudes

Performance tests effectively measure some manual skills and aptitudes. When the skill is one in which you are trained, such as typing or shorthand, you can practice. These tests are often very much like those given in business school or high school courses. For many of the other skills and aptitudes, however, no short-time preparation can be made. Skills and abilities natural to you or that you have developed throughout your lifetime are being tested.

Many of the general questions just described provide all the data needed to answer the questions and ask you to use your reasoning ability to find the answers. Your best preparation for these tests, as well as for tests of facts and ideas, is to be at your physical and mental best. You, no doubt, have your own methods of getting into an exam-taking mood and keeping "in shape." The next section lists some ideas on this subject.

IV. KINDS OF QUESTIONS

Only rarely is the "essay" question, which you answer in narrative form, used in civil service tests. Civil service tests are usually of the short-answer type. Full instructions for answering these questions will be given to you at the examination. But in case this is your first experience with short-answer questions and separate answer sheets, here is what you need to know:

1) Multiple-choice Questions

Most popular of the short-answer questions is the "multiple choice" or "best answer" question. It can be used, for example, to test for factual knowledge, ability to solve problems or judgment in meeting situations found at work.

A multiple-choice question is normally one of three types—

- It can begin with an incomplete statement followed by several possible endings. You are to find the one ending which *best* completes the statement, although some of the others may not be entirely wrong.
- It can also be a complete statement in the form of a question which is answered by choosing one of the statements listed.

- It can be in the form of a problem – again you select the best answer.

Here is an example of a multiple-choice question with a discussion which should give you some clues as to the method for choosing the right answer:

When an employee has a complaint about his assignment, the action which will *best* help him overcome his difficulty is to
A. discuss his difficulty with his coworkers
B. take the problem to the head of the organization
C. take the problem to the person who gave him the assignment
D. say nothing to anyone about his complaint

In answering this question, you should study each of the choices to find which is best. Consider choice "A" – Certainly an employee may discuss his complaint with fellow employees, but no change or improvement can result, and the complaint remains unresolved. Choice "B" is a poor choice since the head of the organization probably does not know what assignment you have been given, and taking your problem to him is known as "going over the head" of the supervisor. The supervisor, or person who made the assignment, is the person who can clarify it or correct any injustice. Choice "C" is, therefore, correct. To say nothing, as in choice "D," is unwise. Supervisors have and interest in knowing the problems employees are facing, and the employee is seeking a solution to his problem.

2) True/False Questions

The "true/false" or "right/wrong" form of question is sometimes used. Here a complete statement is given. Your job is to decide whether the statement is right or wrong.

SAMPLE: A roaming cell-phone call to a nearby city costs less than a non-roaming call to a distant city.

This statement is wrong, or false, since roaming calls are more expensive.

This is not a complete list of all possible question forms, although most of the others are variations of these common types. You will always get complete directions for answering questions. Be sure you understand *how* to mark your answers – ask questions until you do.

V. RECORDING YOUR ANSWERS

Computer terminals are used more and more today for many different kinds of exams.

For an examination with very few applicants, you may be told to record your answers in the test booklet itself. Separate answer sheets are much more common. If this separate answer sheet is to be scored by machine – and this is often the case – it is highly important that you mark your answers correctly in order to get credit.

An electronic scoring machine is often used in civil service offices because of the speed with which papers can be scored. Machine-scored answer sheets must be marked with a pencil, which will be given to you. This pencil has a high graphite content which responds to the electronic scoring machine. As a matter of fact, stray dots may register as answers, so do not let your pencil rest on the answer sheet while you are pondering the correct answer. Also, if your pencil lead breaks or is otherwise defective, ask for another.

Since the answer sheet will be dropped in a slot in the scoring machine, be careful not to bend the corners or get the paper crumpled.

The answer sheet normally has five vertical columns of numbers, with 30 numbers to a column. These numbers correspond to the question numbers in your test booklet. After each number, going across the page are four or five pairs of dotted lines. These short dotted lines have small letters or numbers above them. The first two pairs may also have a "T" or "F" above the letters. This indicates that the first two pairs only are to be used if the questions are of the true-false type. If the questions are multiple choice, disregard the "T" and "F" and pay attention only to the small letters or numbers.

Answer your questions in the manner of the sample that follows:

32. The largest city in the United States is
    A. Washington, D.C.
    B. New York City
    C. Chicago
    D. Detroit
    E. San Francisco

1) Choose the answer you think is best. (New York City is the largest, so "B" is correct.)
2) Find the row of dotted lines numbered the same as the question you are answering. (Find row number 32)
3) Find the pair of dotted lines corresponding to the answer. (Find the pair of lines under the mark "B.")
4) Make a solid black mark between the dotted lines.

VI. BEFORE THE TEST

Common sense will help you find procedures to follow to get ready for an examination. Too many of us, however, overlook these sensible measures. Indeed, nervousness and fatigue have been found to be the most serious reasons why applicants fail to do their best on civil service tests. Here is a list of reminders:

- Begin your preparation early – Don't wait until the last minute to go scurrying around for books and materials or to find out what the position is all about.
- Prepare continuously – An hour a night for a week is better than an all-night cram session. This has been definitely established. What is more, a night a week for a month will return better dividends than crowding your study into a shorter period of time.
- Locate the place of the exam – You have been sent a notice telling you when and where to report for the examination. If the location is in a different town or otherwise unfamiliar to you, it would be well to inquire the best route and learn something about the building.
- Relax the night before the test – Allow your mind to rest. Do not study at all that night. Plan some mild recreation or diversion; then go to bed early and get a good night's sleep.
- Get up early enough to make a leisurely trip to the place for the test – This way unforeseen events, traffic snarls, unfamiliar buildings, etc. will not upset you.
- Dress comfortably – A written test is not a fashion show. You will be known by number and not by name, so wear something comfortable.

- Leave excess paraphernalia at home – Shopping bags and odd bundles will get in your way. You need bring only the items mentioned in the official notice you received; usually everything you need is provided. Do not bring reference books to the exam. They will only confuse those last minutes and be taken away from you when in the test room.
- Arrive somewhat ahead of time – If because of transportation schedules you must get there very early, bring a newspaper or magazine to take your mind off yourself while waiting.
- Locate the examination room – When you have found the proper room, you will be directed to the seat or part of the room where you will sit. Sometimes you are given a sheet of instructions to read while you are waiting. Do not fill out any forms until you are told to do so; just read them and be prepared.
- Relax and prepare to listen to the instructions
- If you have any physical problem that may keep you from doing your best, be sure to tell the test administrator. If you are sick or in poor health, you really cannot do your best on the exam. You can come back and take the test some other time.

VII. AT THE TEST

The day of the test is here and you have the test booklet in your hand. The temptation to get going is very strong. Caution! There is more to success than knowing the right answers. You must know how to identify your papers and understand variations in the type of short-answer question used in this particular examination. Follow these suggestions for maximum results from your efforts:

1) Cooperate with the monitor

The test administrator has a duty to create a situation in which you can be as much at ease as possible. He will give instructions, tell you when to begin, check to see that you are marking your answer sheet correctly, and so on. He is not there to guard you, although he will see that your competitors do not take unfair advantage. He wants to help you do your best.

2) Listen to all instructions

Don't jump the gun! Wait until you understand all directions. In most civil service tests you get more time than you need to answer the questions. So don't be in a hurry. Read each word of instructions until you clearly understand the meaning. Study the examples, listen to all announcements and follow directions. Ask questions if you do not understand what to do.

3) Identify your papers

Civil service exams are usually identified by number only. You will be assigned a number; you must not put your name on your test papers. Be sure to copy your number correctly. Since more than one exam may be given, copy your exact examination title.

4) Plan your time

Unless you are told that a test is a "speed" or "rate of work" test, speed itself is usually not important. Time enough to answer all the questions will be provided, but this does not mean that you have all day. An overall time limit has been set. Divide the total time (in minutes) by the number of questions to determine the approximate time you have for each question.

5) Do not linger over difficult questions

If you come across a difficult question, mark it with a paper clip (useful to have along) and come back to it when you have been through the booklet. One caution if you do this – be sure to skip a number on your answer sheet as well. Check often to be sure that you have not lost your place and that you are marking in the row numbered the same as the question you are answering.

6) Read the questions

Be sure you know what the question asks! Many capable people are unsuccessful because they failed to *read* the questions correctly.

7) Answer all questions

Unless you have been instructed that a penalty will be deducted for incorrect answers, it is better to guess than to omit a question.

8) Speed tests

It is often better NOT to guess on speed tests. It has been found that on timed tests people are tempted to spend the last few seconds before time is called in marking answers at random – without even reading them – in the hope of picking up a few extra points. To discourage this practice, the instructions may warn you that your score will be "corrected" for guessing. That is, a penalty will be applied. The incorrect answers will be deducted from the correct ones, or some other penalty formula will be used.

9) Review your answers

If you finish before time is called, go back to the questions you guessed or omitted to give them further thought. Review other answers if you have time.

10) Return your test materials

If you are ready to leave before others have finished or time is called, take ALL your materials to the monitor and leave quietly. Never take any test material with you. The monitor can discover whose papers are not complete, and taking a test booklet may be grounds for disqualification.

VIII. EXAMINATION TECHNIQUES

1) Read the general instructions carefully. These are usually printed on the first page of the exam booklet. As a rule, these instructions refer to the timing of the examination; the fact that you should not start work until the signal and must stop work at a signal, etc. If there are any *special* instructions, such as a choice of questions to be answered, make sure that you note this instruction carefully.

2) When you are ready to start work on the examination, that is as soon as the signal has been given, read the instructions to each question booklet, underline any key words or phrases, such as *least*, *best*, *outline*, *describe* and the like. In this way you will tend to answer as requested rather than discover on reviewing your paper that you *listed without describing*, that you selected the *worst* choice rather than the *best* choice, etc.

3) If the examination is of the objective or multiple-choice type – that is, each question will also give a series of possible answers: A, B, C or D, and you are called upon to select the best answer and write the letter next to that answer on your answer paper – it is advisable to start answering each question in turn. There may be anywhere from 50 to 100 such questions in the three or four hours allotted and you can see how much time would be taken if you read through all the questions before beginning to answer any. Furthermore, if you come across a question or group of questions which you know would be difficult to answer, it would undoubtedly affect your handling of all the other questions.

4) If the examination is of the essay type and contains but a few questions, it is a moot point as to whether you should read all the questions before starting to answer any one. Of course, if you are given a choice – say five out of seven and the like – then it is essential to read all the questions so you can eliminate the two that are most difficult. If, however, you are asked to answer all the questions, there may be danger in trying to answer the easiest one first because you may find that you will spend too much time on it. The best technique is to answer the first question, then proceed to the second, etc.

5) Time your answers. Before the exam begins, write down the time it started, then add the time allowed for the examination and write down the time it must be completed, then divide the time available somewhat as follows:
   - If 3-1/2 hours are allowed, that would be 210 minutes. If you have 80 objective-type questions, that would be an average of 2-1/2 minutes per question. Allow yourself no more than 2 minutes per question, or a total of 160 minutes, which will permit about 50 minutes to review.
   - If for the time allotment of 210 minutes there are 7 essay questions to answer, that would average about 30 minutes a question. Give yourself only 25 minutes per question so that you have about 35 minutes to review.

6) The most important instruction is to *read each question* and make sure you know what is wanted. The second most important instruction is to *time yourself properly* so that you answer every question. The third most important instruction is to *answer every question.* Guess if you have to but include something for each question. Remember that you will receive no credit for a blank and will probably receive some credit if you write something in answer to an essay question. If you guess a letter – say "B" for a multiple-choice question – you may have guessed right. If you leave a blank as an answer to a multiple-choice question, the examiners may respect your feelings but it will not add a point to your score. Some exams may penalize you for wrong answers, so in such cases *only*, you may not want to guess unless you have some basis for your answer.

7) Suggestions
   a. Objective-type questions
      1. Examine the question booklet for proper sequence of pages and questions
      2. Read all instructions carefully
      3. Skip any question which seems too difficult; return to it after all other questions have been answered
      4. Apportion your time properly; do not spend too much time on any single question or group of questions

5. Note and underline key words – *all, most, fewest, least, best, worst, same, opposite,* etc.
6. Pay particular attention to negatives
7. Note unusual option, e.g., unduly long, short, complex, different or similar in content to the body of the question
8. Observe the use of "hedging" words – *probably, may, most likely,* etc.
9. Make sure that your answer is put next to the same number as the question
10. Do not second-guess unless you have good reason to believe the second answer is definitely more correct
11. Cross out original answer if you decide another answer is more accurate; do not erase until you are ready to hand your paper in
12. Answer all questions; guess unless instructed otherwise
13. Leave time for review

b. Essay questions
1. Read each question carefully
2. Determine exactly what is wanted. Underline key words or phrases.
3. Decide on outline or paragraph answer
4. Include many different points and elements unless asked to develop any one or two points or elements
5. Show impartiality by giving pros and cons unless directed to select one side only
6. Make and write down any assumptions you find necessary to answer the questions
7. Watch your English, grammar, punctuation and choice of words
8. Time your answers; don't crowd material

8) Answering the essay question

Most essay questions can be answered by framing the specific response around several key words or ideas. Here are a few such key words or ideas:

M's: manpower, materials, methods, money, management
P's: purpose, program, policy, plan, procedure, practice, problems, pitfalls, personnel, public relations

a. Six basic steps in handling problems:
1. Preliminary plan and background development
2. Collect information, data and facts
3. Analyze and interpret information, data and facts
4. Analyze and develop solutions as well as make recommendations
5. Prepare report and sell recommendations
6. Install recommendations and follow up effectiveness

b. Pitfalls to avoid
1. *Taking things for granted* – A statement of the situation does not necessarily imply that each of the elements is necessarily true; for example, a complaint may be invalid and biased so that all that can be taken for granted is that a complaint has been registered

2. *Considering only one side of a situation* – Wherever possible, indicate several alternatives and then point out the reasons you selected the best one
3. *Failing to indicate follow up* – Whenever your answer indicates action on your part, make certain that you will take proper follow-up action to see how successful your recommendations, procedures or actions turn out to be
4. *Taking too long in answering any single question* – Remember to time your answers properly

IX. AFTER THE TEST

Scoring procedures differ in detail among civil service jurisdictions although the general principles are the same. Whether the papers are hand-scored or graded by machine we have described, they are nearly always graded by number. That is, the person who marks the paper knows only the number – never the name – of the applicant. Not until all the papers have been graded will they be matched with names. If other tests, such as training and experience or oral interview ratings have been given, scores will be combined. Different parts of the examination usually have different weights. For example, the written test might count 60 percent of the final grade, and a rating of training and experience 40 percent. In many jurisdictions, veterans will have a certain number of points added to their grades.

After the final grade has been determined, the names are placed in grade order and an eligible list is established. There are various methods for resolving ties between those who get the same final grade – probably the most common is to place first the name of the person whose application was received first. Job offers are made from the eligible list in the order the names appear on it. You will be notified of your grade and your rank as soon as all these computations have been made. This will be done as rapidly as possible.

People who are found to meet the requirements in the announcement are called "eligibles." Their names are put on a list of eligible candidates. An eligible's chances of getting a job depend on how high he stands on this list and how fast agencies are filling jobs from the list.

When a job is to be filled from a list of eligibles, the agency asks for the names of people on the list of eligibles for that job. When the civil service commission receives this request, it sends to the agency the names of the three people highest on this list. Or, if the job to be filled has specialized requirements, the office sends the agency the names of the top three persons who meet these requirements from the general list.

The appointing officer makes a choice from among the three people whose names were sent to him. If the selected person accepts the appointment, the names of the others are put back on the list to be considered for future openings.

That is the rule in hiring from all kinds of eligible lists, whether they are for typist, carpenter, chemist, or something else. For every vacancy, the appointing officer has his choice of any one of the top three eligibles on the list. This explains why the person whose name is on top of the list sometimes does not get an appointment when some of the persons lower on the list do. If the appointing officer chooses the second or third eligible, the No. 1 eligible does not get a job at once, but stays on the list until he is appointed or the list is terminated.

X. HOW TO PASS THE INTERVIEW TEST

The examination for which you applied requires an oral interview test. You have already taken the written test and you are now being called for the interview test – the final part of the formal examination.

You may think that it is not possible to prepare for an interview test and that there are no procedures to follow during an interview. Our purpose is to point out some things you can do in advance that will help you and some good rules to follow and pitfalls to avoid while you are being interviewed.

What is an interview supposed to test?

The written examination is designed to test the technical knowledge and competence of the candidate; the oral is designed to evaluate intangible qualities, not readily measured otherwise, and to establish a list showing the relative fitness of each candidate – as measured against his competitors – for the position sought. Scoring is not on the basis of "right" and "wrong," but on a sliding scale of values ranging from "not passable" to "outstanding." As a matter of fact, it is possible to achieve a relatively low score without a single "incorrect" answer because of evident weakness in the qualities being measured.

Occasionally, an examination may consist entirely of an oral test – either an individual or a group oral. In such cases, information is sought concerning the technical knowledges and abilities of the candidate, since there has been no written examination for this purpose. More commonly, however, an oral test is used to supplement a written examination.

Who conducts interviews?

The composition of oral boards varies among different jurisdictions. In nearly all, a representative of the personnel department serves as chairman. One of the members of the board may be a representative of the department in which the candidate would work. In some cases, "outside experts" are used, and, frequently, a businessman or some other representative of the general public is asked to serve. Labor and management or other special groups may be represented. The aim is to secure the services of experts in the appropriate field.

However the board is composed, it is a good idea (and not at all improper or unethical) to ascertain in advance of the interview who the members are and what groups they represent. When you are introduced to them, you will have some idea of their backgrounds and interests, and at least you will not stutter and stammer over their names.

What should be done before the interview?

While knowledge about the board members is useful and takes some of the surprise element out of the interview, there is other preparation which is more substantive. It *is* possible to prepare for an oral interview – in several ways:

1) Keep a copy of your application and review it carefully before the interview

This may be the only document before the oral board, and the starting point of the interview. Know what education and experience you have listed there, and the sequence and dates of all of it. Sometimes the board will ask you to review the highlights of your experience for them; you should not have to hem and haw doing it.

2) Study the class specification and the examination announcement

Usually, the oral board has one or both of these to guide them. The qualities, characteristics or knowledges required by the position sought are stated in these documents. They offer valuable clues as to the nature of the oral interview. For example, if the job involves supervisory responsibilities, the announcement will usually indicate that knowledge of modern supervisory methods and the qualifications of the candidate as a supervisor will be tested. If so, you can expect such questions, frequently in the form of a hypothetical situation which you are expected to solve. NEVER go into an oral without knowledge of the duties and responsibilities of the job you seek.

3) Think through each qualification required

Try to visualize the kind of questions you would ask if you were a board member. How well could you answer them? Try especially to appraise your own knowledge and background in each area, *measured against the job sought*, and identify any areas in which you are weak. Be critical and realistic – do not flatter yourself.

4) Do some general reading in areas in which you feel you may be weak

For example, if the job involves supervision and your past experience has NOT, some general reading in supervisory methods and practices, particularly in the field of human relations, might be useful. Do NOT study agency procedures or detailed manuals. The oral board will be testing your understanding and capacity, not your memory.

5) Get a good night's sleep and watch your general health and mental attitude

You will want a clear head at the interview. Take care of a cold or any other minor ailment, and of course, no hangovers.

What should be done on the day of the interview?

Now comes the day of the interview itself. Give yourself plenty of time to get there. Plan to arrive somewhat ahead of the scheduled time, particularly if your appointment is in the fore part of the day. If a previous candidate fails to appear, the board might be ready for you a bit early. By early afternoon an oral board is almost invariably behind schedule if there are many candidates, and you may have to wait. Take along a book or magazine to read, or your application to review, but leave any extraneous material in the waiting room when you go in for your interview. In any event, relax and compose yourself.

The matter of dress is important. The board is forming impressions about you – from your experience, your manners, your attitude, and your appearance. Give your personal appearance careful attention. Dress your best, but not your flashiest. Choose conservative, appropriate clothing, and be sure it is immaculate. This is a business interview, and your appearance should indicate that you regard it as such. Besides, being well groomed and properly dressed will help boost your confidence.

Sooner or later, someone will call your name and escort you into the interview room. *This is it.* From here on you are on your own. It is too late for any more preparation. But remember, you asked for this opportunity to prove your fitness, and you are here because your request was granted.

What happens when you go in?

The usual sequence of events will be as follows: The clerk (who is often the board stenographer) will introduce you to the chairman of the oral board, who will introduce you to the other members of the board. Acknowledge the introductions before you sit down. Do not be surprised if you find a microphone facing you or a stenotypist sitting by. Oral interviews are usually recorded in the event of an appeal or other review.

Usually the chairman of the board will open the interview by reviewing the highlights of your education and work experience from your application – primarily for the benefit of the other members of the board, as well as to get the material into the record. Do not interrupt or comment unless there is an error or significant misinterpretation; if that is the case, do not hesitate. But do not quibble about insignificant matters. Also, he will usually ask you some question about your education, experience or your present job – partly to get you to start talking and to establish the interviewing "rapport." He may start the actual questioning, or turn it over to one of the other members. Frequently, each member undertakes the questioning on a particular area, one in which he is perhaps most competent, so you can expect each member to participate in the examination. Because time is limited, you may also expect some rather abrupt switches in the direction the questioning takes, so do not be upset by it. Normally, a board member will not pursue a single line of questioning unless he discovers a particular strength or weakness.

After each member has participated, the chairman will usually ask whether any member has any further questions, then will ask you if you have anything you wish to add. Unless you are expecting this question, it may floor you. Worse, it may start you off on an extended, extemporaneous speech. The board is not usually seeking more information. The question is principally to offer you a last opportunity to present further qualifications or to indicate that you have nothing to add. So, if you feel that a significant qualification or characteristic has been overlooked, it is proper to point it out in a sentence or so. Do not compliment the board on the thoroughness of their examination – they have been sketchy, and you know it. If you wish, merely say, "No thank you, I have nothing further to add." This is a point where you can "talk yourself out" of a good impression or fail to present an important bit of information. Remember, *you close the interview yourself.*

The chairman will then say, "That is all, Mr. ______, thank you." Do not be startled; the interview is over, and quicker than you think. Thank him, gather your belongings and take your leave. Save your sigh of relief for the other side of the door.

How to put your best foot forward

Throughout this entire process, you may feel that the board individually and collectively is trying to pierce your defenses, seek out your hidden weaknesses and embarrass and confuse you. Actually, this is not true. They are obliged to make an appraisal of your qualifications for the job you are seeking, and they want to see you in your best light. Remember, they must interview all candidates and a non-cooperative candidate may become a failure in spite of their best efforts to bring out his qualifications. Here are 15 suggestions that will help you:

1) Be natural – Keep your attitude confident, not cocky

If you are not confident that you can do the job, do not expect the board to be. Do not apologize for your weaknesses, try to bring out your strong points. The board is interested in a positive, not negative, presentation. Cockiness will antagonize any board member and make him wonder if you are covering up a weakness by a false show of strength.

2) Get comfortable, but don't lounge or sprawl

Sit erectly but not stiffly. A careless posture may lead the board to conclude that you are careless in other things, or at least that you are not impressed by the importance of the occasion. Either conclusion is natural, even if incorrect. Do not fuss with your clothing, a pencil or an ashtray. Your hands may occasionally be useful to emphasize a point; do not let them become a point of distraction.

3) Do not wisecrack or make small talk

This is a serious situation, and your attitude should show that you consider it as such. Further, the time of the board is limited – they do not want to waste it, and neither should you.

4) Do not exaggerate your experience or abilities

In the first place, from information in the application or other interviews and sources, the board may know more about you than you think. Secondly, you probably will not get away with it. An experienced board is rather adept at spotting such a situation, so do not take the chance.

5) If you know a board member, do not make a point of it, yet do not hide it

Certainly you are not fooling him, and probably not the other members of the board. Do not try to take advantage of your acquaintanceship – it will probably do you little good.

6) Do not dominate the interview

Let the board do that. They will give you the clues – do not assume that you have to do all the talking. Realize that the board has a number of questions to ask you, and do not try to take up all the interview time by showing off your extensive knowledge of the answer to the first one.

7) Be attentive

You only have 20 minutes or so, and you should keep your attention at its sharpest throughout. When a member is addressing a problem or question to you, give him your undivided attention. Address your reply principally to him, but do not exclude the other board members.

8) Do not interrupt

A board member may be stating a problem for you to analyze. He will ask you a question when the time comes. Let him state the problem, and wait for the question.

9) Make sure you understand the question

Do not try to answer until you are sure what the question is. If it is not clear, restate it in your own words or ask the board member to clarify it for you. However, do not haggle about minor elements.

10) Reply promptly but not hastily

A common entry on oral board rating sheets is "candidate responded readily," or "candidate hesitated in replies." Respond as promptly and quickly as you can, but do not jump to a hasty, ill-considered answer.

11) Do not be peremptory in your answers

A brief answer is proper – but do not fire your answer back. That is a losing game from your point of view. The board member can probably ask questions much faster than you can answer them.

12) Do not try to create the answer you think the board member wants

He is interested in what kind of mind you have and how it works – not in playing games. Furthermore, he can usually spot this practice and will actually grade you down on it.

13) Do not switch sides in your reply merely to agree with a board member

Frequently, a member will take a contrary position merely to draw you out and to see if you are willing and able to defend your point of view. Do not start a debate, yet do not surrender a good position. If a position is worth taking, it is worth defending.

14) Do not be afraid to admit an error in judgment if you are shown to be wrong

The board knows that you are forced to reply without any opportunity for careful consideration. Your answer may be demonstrably wrong. If so, admit it and get on with the interview.

15) Do not dwell at length on your present job

The opening question may relate to your present assignment. Answer the question but do not go into an extended discussion. You are being examined for a *new* job, not your present one. As a matter of fact, try to phrase ALL your answers in terms of the job for which you are being examined.

Basis of Rating

Probably you will forget most of these "do's" and "don'ts" when you walk into the oral interview room. Even remembering them all will not ensure you a passing grade. Perhaps you did not have the qualifications in the first place. But remembering them will help you to put your best foot forward, without treading on the toes of the board members.

Rumor and popular opinion to the contrary notwithstanding, an oral board wants you to make the best appearance possible. They know you are under pressure – but they also want to see how you respond to it as a guide to what your reaction would be under the pressures of the job you seek. They will be influenced by the degree of poise you display, the personal traits you show and the manner in which you respond.

ABOUT THIS BOOK

This book contains tests divided into Examination Sections. Go through each test, answering every question in the margin. We have also attached a sample answer sheet at the back of the book that can be removed and used. At the end of each test look at the answer key and check your answers. On the ones you got wrong, look at the right answer choice and learn. Do not fill in the answers first. Do not memorize the questions and answers, but understand the answer and principles involved. On your test, the questions will likely be different from the samples. Questions are changed and new ones added. If you understand these past questions you should have success with any changes that arise. Tests may consist of several types of questions. We have additional books on each subject should more study be advisable or necessary for you. Finally, the more you study, the better prepared you will be. This book is intended to be the last thing you study before you walk into the examination room. Prior study of relevant texts is also recommended. NLC publishes some of these in our Fundamental Series. Knowledge and good sense are important factors in passing your exam. Good luck also helps. So now study this Passbook, absorb the material contained within and take that knowledge into the examination. Then do your best to pass that exam.

EXAMINATION SECTION

EXAMINATION SECTION
TEST 1

DIRECTIONS: Each question or incomplete statement is followed by several suggested answers or completions. Select the one that BEST answers the question or completes the statement. *PRINT THE LETTER OF THE CORRECT ANSWER IN THE SPACE AT THE RIGHT.*

1. When Lt. Stern opens the District Office every morning at 4:45, he must call the Office into service. 1.____
   In order to report *in service,* the Lieutenant should radio

   A. or telephone a 10/98 to Control
   B. or telephone a 10/60 to Control
   C. a 10/7 or call Control by Landline
   D. a 10/61 or call Control by Landline

2. On Monday, Traffic Enforcement Agent Jones submits a Leave Request Form (TCD-105) and a doctor's note to Lt. Vorhees for his absence the previous Friday. 2.____
   When Lt. Vorhees reviews the doctor's note, which one of the following must be included for the note to comply with departmental procedures? The

   A. doctor's telephone number
   B. doctor's diagnosis
   C. date of the follow-up appointment
   D. doctor's signature

Question 3.

DIRECTIONS: Question 3 is to be answered on the basis of the following form.

TRAFFIC CONTROL BUREAU

TCD-404

To: District Commander Capt . Emma Barnes Date: May 29
From: TEA William Hill Subject: Requestfor Tour Change

I request approval for a tour change from 7:00 to 9:00
on the following date(s) June 15, - July 3
The reason for this request is to drive my daughter to Day Care
This is/ is not to be a mutual exchange with
Signed William Hill
Squad Leader____________
District Commander____________

3. Traffic Enforcement Agent Hill, who is in Lt. Walker's 7:00 - 3:00 squad, gives the Lieutenant the above memo. He tells Lt. Walker that he would like to change his schedule for three weeks and has already spoken with Lt. Baker, who said he would be welcome on her 9:00 - 5:00 tour. 3.____
   After reviewing the memo, Lt. Walker should tell Agent Hill to

A. record the ending times for the tours
B. enter Lt. Baker's name on the memo
C. indicate the date when he would like to return to the 7:00 - 3:00 assignment
D. present the memo directly to Captain Barnes since it does not require the Lieutenant's signature

Question 4.

DIRECTIONS: Question 4 is to be answered on the basis of the following form.

DEPARTMENT OF TRANSPORTATION
TRAFFIC CONTROL DIVISION

WITNESS STATEMENT OF ACCIDENT

ANSWER ALL QUESTIONS FULLY. THIS IS YOUR NOTICE TO YOUR EMPLOYER OF WITNESS OF INJURY ON THE JOB. PRINT OR WRITE LEGIBLY.

1. Full name of witness MARY (first) LEE (middle) MILES (last)
2. Address Cabrini Hospital
3. Witnessed accident sustained by TEA Ella McCloud (name of injured)
4. Date of Accident May 1
5. Description of accident Hour 10:12 A.M. ___ P.M. ___
Agent hit head on file cabinet while performing routine duties in the District Office

Dated: May 1 (Sign here) Mary Lee Miles

4. While working in the District Office, Traffic Enforcement Agent Ella McCloud was filing papers in the bottom drawer of a file cabinet. When Agent Mary Lee Miles asked if she had any *Wite-out*, Agent McCloud stood up and hit her head on the top drawer, which had been left open. After Agent McCloud is taken to Cabrini Hospital for x-rays, Lt. Williams directs Agent Miles to complete a Witness Statement of Accident form.
In reviewing the form shown above, Lt. Williams realizes that it is incomplete because it fails to include 4._____

A. any reference to the role of Agent Miles in causing the accident
B. the address of the witness
C. a statement concerning Agent McCloud's carelessness
D. the extent of the injury and the type of treatment given

5. Upon reviewing his current paystub, Lt. Swain notices that he has accrued ten days of annual leave when he is entitled to twenty days.
In this situation, Lt. Swain should 5._____

A. submit an MP-147 to D.O.T. Timekeeping with paystubs to verify the problem
B. submit a memo to D.O.T. Timekeeping explaining the problem
C. go to D.O.T. Timekeeping with paystubs and explain the problem to them in person
D. have the Staff Lieutenant check her time records and submit a memo to the Captain explaining the problem

Question 6.

DIRECTIONS: Question 6 is to be answered on the basis of the following information.

It has come to Lt. Small's attention that several radios in his command have serious mechanical problems. Radios #1210, #1212, #1216, and #1226 are able to receive messages but the sound *breaks up* when the operator attempts to transmit a message.

Lt. Small has arranged to send these units to Radio Repair and takes the following actions:

1. Records the radio numbers in the District Office log.
2. Lists the radio numbers in the Equipment Distribution and Log form (TCD-504).
3. Writes a memo to the Captain to document the radio numbers and reason for repair.
4. Logs the radio numbers on the Roll Call Sheet (TCD-201) in the appropriate column.

6. Which one of the following choices CORRECTLY classifies the above actions into those that are correct and those that are not? 6._____

   A. 1 and 2 are correct, but 3 and 4 are not.
   B. 1 and 3 are correct, but 2 and 4 are not.
   C. 2 and 3 are correct, but 1 and 4 are not.
   D. 2 and 4 are correct, but 1 and 3 are not.

7. Traffic Enforcement Agent Lipton was standing by the table in the muster room when a chair was overturned and fell on his foot. He refused medical attention. As his supervisor, Lt. Bell should do which of the following in this situation? 7._____

   A. Ask the agent if he is all right and make a notification of the incident on Agent Lipton's TCD-210.
   B. Have the agent walk around the room to make sure that his foot is not injured, and note the incident on the Lieutenant's own TCD-321.
   C. Fill out Workers' Compensation papers and have the agent write a memo refusing medical aid.
   D. Direct the agent to go to his family doctor and submit a doctor's note.

Question 8.

DIRECTIONS: Question 8 is to be answered on the basis of the following form.

SUMMONS REFUSAL REPORT

TCD-304

Parking Enforcement Agent	Shield #	District Office	Date
Holly, Albert	5869	T-117	05 28 09

Attached Summons Number	Location of Violation	Time of Issuance
89-609079-4	618 Ave. T	11:35 AM

The motorist drove off after you advised him that he was being served a summons.

Yes [X] No [ ]

The motorist physically prevented you from issuing the summons.

Yes [ ] No [X]

Other circumstances: ______

8. On May 28, 2009, Traffic Enforcement Agent Holly wrote Summons #89-607097-4 at 11:35 A.M. in front of 618 Avenue T. However, the motorist jumped into his car and drove away before Agent Holly could put the summons on the car. Agent Holly then completed the Summons Refusal Report (TCD-304) shown above. 8.___
Lt. Mack reviews the form to check for errors in the following sections:

1. Date of Issuance
2. Attached Summons Number
3. Location of Violation
4. Time of Issuance

Lt. Mack should notice that there
A. is an error in 1, but not in 2, 3, or 4
B. is an error in 2, but not in 1, 3, or 4
C. are errors in 1 and 3, but not in 2 and 4
D. are errors in 2 and 4, but not in 1 and 3

5. Captain Roberts of the T1404 command has ordered street enforcement at bus stops along Main Street between 5 PM -7 PM Monday and Friday. This is to continue for a period of two weeks. 5.___
In order to carry out this assignment, Lt. Jones should make a notification

A. to all agents assigned to that area on Monday
B. on the Conditions Board under the appropriate area as soon as possible
C. to the early Conditions Car Agent on each day during the two-week period
D. at the next day's Roll Call to alert all of the Early Squad Leaders

Question 10.

DIRECTIONS: Question 10 is to be answered on the basis of the form appearing on the following page.

Election of Rate Of Charge Against Annual and/or Sick Leave Balances
for Absence Due To Injury Sustained in the Performance of Official Duties

(Pursuant to Regulation 7.0 of the Leave Regulations for employees who are under the Career and Salary Plan)

INSTRUCTIONS: The injured employee, or an authorized person acting in his behalf, should submit this election notice (in duplicate) to the head of his department or agency within the first seven calendar days of absence due to injury sustained in the performance of official duties.

I, ______________________ (Print name of injured employee), employed in ______________________ (Print name of city department or agency) in a position which is subject to the Leave Regulations for employees who are under the Career and Salary Plan, or my authorized agent, do hereby elect the option designated below, subject to the conditions attached thereto, as the one to be applied in determining the charge, if any, to be made against my annual and/or sick leave balances for absence due to injury sustained in the performance of my official duties:

(Check one option only)

☐ OPTION 1: I elect to receive the difference between the amount of my weekly salary and the compensation rate, subject to the following conditions:

(a) A pro-rated charge shall be made against my sick leave and/or annual leave balances equal to the number of working days of absence less the number of working days represented by the Worker's Compensation payments, and;

(b) My accrued sick leave and/or annual leave balances, or such leave credits advanced to me in accordance with the Career and Salary Plan Leave Regulations, are adequate to meet the charges made against them for supplementary pay, and;

(c) The injury sustained by me was not the result of my willful gross disobedience of safety rules or my willful failure to use a safety device, nor was I under the influence of alcohol or narcotics at the time of injury, nor did I willfully intend to bring about injury or death upon myself or another, and;

(d) Such medical examinations will be undergone by me as are requested by the Worker's Compensation Division of the Law Department and my agency, and when found fit for duty by said physicians, I shall return to my employment.

☐ OPTION 2: I elect to receive Worker's Compensation benefits in their entirety with no charge against sick and/or annual leave.

Injured employee's signature		Date
This shaded section should be completed only if the injured employee cannot sign and must designate an authorized person to sign in his behalf	Authorized designee's name (print)	Relationship to injured employee
	Authorized designee's address	
	Authorized designee's signature	Date
	Witness's name (print)	
	Witness's address	
	Witness's signature	Date

Employing Department should forward duplicate copy to Worker's Compensation Division of Law Department

10. Lt. Perry is reviewing a DP 2002 form (see above) that was prepared as a result of an agent's on-the-job injury. Which one of the following statements concerning this form is CORRECT? 10.____

A. If all of the agent's sick leave and annual leave have been used up, only *OPTION 1* may be selected.
B. The person who signs as a witness must have seen the accident and must be willing to swear that the agent was not at fault.
C. If the agent wishes to switch from Option 1 to Option 2 when sick leave and annual leave have been used up, both *OPTION 1* and *OPTION 2* should be checked.

D. An agent with sufficient sick leave and annual leave who wishes to continue receiving a regular pay check should choose *OPTION 1.*

11. Lt. Martin was conducting an inspection of agents' drivers licenses when she noticed a discrepancy on Traffic Enforcement Agent Van Dyck's license. Although this agent is listed in all department records as having a last name that begins with a *V,* the first letter of his license number begins with a capital *D* followed by a series of numbers. She also noticed that the license had expired at the end of the previous month. 11.____
Which one of the following would be the BEST action for Lt. Martin to take?

A. Advise the agent of the error and expiration date and have him take annual leave time to resolve the matter with the Department of Motor Vehicles.
B. Assign the agent to a dual motorized patrol and have the other agent drive the department vehicle.
C. Advise the agent that he cannot work a motorized patrol until he receives clearance from the TCD Office of Investigations.
D. Assign the agent to a foot patrol tour until his license is renewed.

12. While Lt. Howard is conducting Roll Call inspection of her squad, Traffic Enforcement Agent Browne, a member of the squad, comes into the muster room ten minutes late and punches his time card. The agent then goes into the locker room to change into his uniform. When Agent Browne returns, Lt. Howard is distributing TCD-210 sheets to the agents who are ready to go out to patrol. 12.____
When she gives Agent Browne his TCD-210, Lt. Howard should instruct him to

A. record his presence at the District Office as his first entry and indicate his lateness on the following line
B. note his lateness as his first entry and record his presence at the District Office on the following line
C. make an entry to correct his previously stamped *To Field* time
D. account for his lateness by subtracting the time lost from the total hours recorded on the top of his Field Patrol Sheet

13. Lt. Fox is instructing newly assigned agents concerning *No Hit* lists for their sectors. To help them understand the concept of *No Hit* lists, Lt. Fox gives some examples. Which one of the following would be the BEST example of the *No Hit* category? 13.____

A. Alternate Side Parking
B. Meter Feeding
C. 24-Hour Storage
D. Self-Enforced Areas

14. During Roll Call inspection, Lt. Hill questioned Traffic Enforcement Agent Jones about his unshaven appearance. Agent Jones informed Lt. Hill that he decided to start growing a beard when he woke up that morning. 14.____
Lt. Hill should inform Agent Jones that according to departmental procedures, he

A. should see the Captain about this matter before starting his tour of duty
B. must start a beard on the first day of four consecutive days off
C. may only grow a mustache, not a beard
D. must give notification prior to his regular day off that he intends to grow a beard

15. While conducting Roll Call inspection, Lt. Joseph notices that Traffic Enforcement Agent Ward has muddy, unpolished shoes. 15.____
Which one of the following actions should Lt. Joseph take?

A. Hold the agent behind and allow him to polish his shoes.
B. Send the agent home because he is unprepared for duty.
C. Tell the agent he must have the problem corrected by his next work day.
D. Have the agent get his shoes shined while in the field.

16. Lt. Howard, Supervisor #6 at the T202 Command in the South Bronx, is instructing several agents on the proper techniques for identifying themselves over the portable radio. As an example, he is about to convey the following information: *Lt. Howard of the South Bronx to Control.* Which one of the following is the APPROPRIATE radio designation? 16.____

A. *T-202,* then proceed with the message
B. *T-202 Supervisor 6 to Control K*
C. *South Bronx Supervisor 6 to Control K*
D. *T-202 Lt. Howard to Control K*

17. During Roll Call, Lt. Day reads a department notice that Alternate Side Parking is suspended because of a Snow Emergency. He explains to his squad which regulations fall into the Alternate Side Parking category and which do not.
The Lieutenant should also explain that, even though Alternate Side Parking is suspended, the agents could still issue summonses for violations of *No Parking* 17.____

A. 8 AM-11 AM Mon.-Wed.-Fri.
B. 8 AM-6 PM Mon. thru Fri.
C. 11 AM-2 PM Tue.-Thur.-Sat.
D. 8 AM-11 AM Mon.

18. Lt. Bear has received an updated departmental memorandum on documented and undocumented leave days. When he reads the memorandum at Roll Call, Traffic Enforcement Agent Cleaver asks him to explain the Department's policies on this topic in greater detail.
In addition to giving such an explanation, the Lieutenant should tell Agent Cleaver that she can get more information on this topic in the Rules and Regulations under the heading of 18.____

A. Emergency Overtime
B. Military Leave
C. Examination by a Physician
D. Absence Control

19. Lt. Green is making notations of summons returns on the Summons Distribution Form (TCD-301 and 302). She is approached by Officer Baker, who states that he lost his pink copy of summons number 78-601301-4.
In order to properly *sign in* this summons, the Lieutenant should 19.____

A. take another pink copy from the preceding summons and insert it in the proper place
B. sign the back of her 321 sheet (Lieutenant's Daily Field Patrol Sheet) to report the loss
C. report the loss to the local precinct by using a TCD-608 form (Lost Property)
D. substitute a *dummy summons* for the lost pink copy and insert it in numerical order

20. Before leaving for his tour, Traffic Enforcement Agent Smith signs out for a book of 25 summonses. He checks the summons pack and counts only 24 summonses. Agent Smith reports this information to Lt. Barrett, who confirms that the manufacturer had made an error in packaging the summonses. 20.____
The NEXT step Lt. Barrett should take is to record the missing summons number

A. on the agent's Field Patrol Sheet (TCD-210)
B. as a Non-Processed Summons (TCD-110)
C. on the Record of Summons Error (TCD-306)
D. on the Summons Distribution Records (TCD-301)

21. Traffic Enforcement Agent Benson approaches Lt. Lee after Roll Call. She is obviously very upset and seems ready to start weeping. She tells the Lieutenant, *I cannot perform my duties today because of severe personal problems. Is there anyone I can go to for help?* 21.____
In this situation, the Lieutenant should advise the agent to

A. report to the Department of Personnel
B. go to her assigned post and meet with Lt. Lee after her tour of duty
C. contact the Employees' Assistance Program
D. go home since she is unprepared for duty, and see her doctor or clergyman on her own time

22. Lt. Able has completed Roll Call and is giving TCD-210 sheets to agents who are ready to go out on patrol. Among the agents in Lt. Abie's squad are: 3.____
1. Traffic Enforcement Agent Hart, who has been assigned to perform clerical duties in the District Office
2. Traffic Enforcement Agent Glazer, who must deliver a vehicle to the Maspeth Garage for repairs
3. Traffic Enforcement Agent Flores, who must report directly to court after Roll Call to appear as a witness.

In this situation, Lt. Able should give TCD-210 sheets to Agents

A. Hart and Glazer, but not Flores
B. Hart and Flores, but not Glazer
C. Glazer and Flores, but not Hart
D. Hart, Glazer, and Flores

Questions 23-24.

DIRECTIONS: Questions 23 and 24 are to be answered on the basis of the drawings and information below.

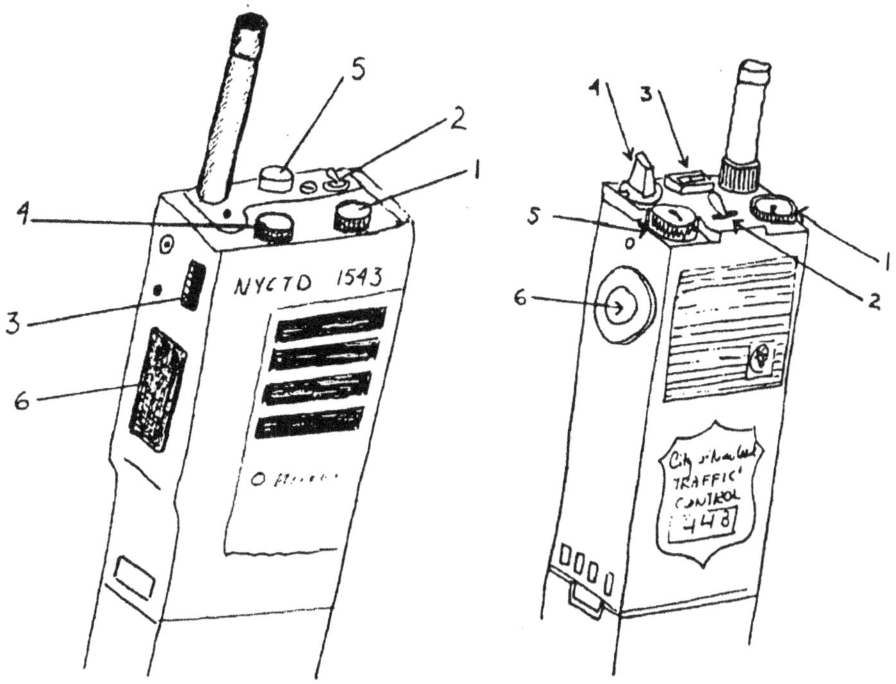

Assume that Lieutenant Wellington is checking the agents' radios for proper charge and functioning.

23. Which one of the following choices CORRECTLY identifies Parts 1, 2, and 3 of the radios shown in the drawings on the preceding page? 23.____

A. 1. Frequency selector switch
   2. Squelch control
   3. Microphone jack
B. 1. Volume on-off switch
   2. Channel guard
   3. Microphone jack
C. 1. Squelch control
   2. Volume on-off switch
   3. Channel guard
D. 1. Transmitter button
   2. Frequency selector switch
   3. Volume on-off switch

24. Which one of the following choices CORRECTLY identifies Parts 4, 5, and 6 of the radios shown in the drawings on the preceding page? 24.____

A. 4. Battery jack
   5. Volume on-off switch
   6. Transmitter button
B. 4. Transmitter button
   5. Battery lock
   6. Frequency selector switch
C. 4. Frequency selector switch
   5. Squelch control
   6. Transmitter button
D. 4. Volume on-off switch
   5. Battery lock
   6. Squelch control

25. Lt. Smith is assigned Vehicle #1520 and is preparing to drive some agents into the field. Upon entering the vehicle, they discover garbage on the floor. The agents say that this is a frequent problem.
Lt. Smith should tell the agents that, according to department policy, anyone who finds garbage left in a vehicle by the prior user should 25.____

A. refuse to take the vehicle into the field
B. ignore the condition of the vehicle and take it into the field
C. immediately report the condition to their supervisor and submit a written report
D. clean the vehicle and inform their supervisor later

KEY (CORRECT ANSWERS)

1. B
2. D
3. A
4. B
5. A

6. A
7. C
8. B
9. B
10. D

11. A
12. B
13. D
14. A/B
15. A

16. B
17. B
18. D
19. D
20. D

21. C
22. D
23. B
24. C
25. C

TEST 2

DIRECTIONS: Each question or incomplete statement is followed by several suggested answers or completions. Select the one that BEST answers the question or completes the statement. *PRINT THE LETTER OF THE CORRECT ANSWER IN THE SPACE AT THE RIGHT.*

1. After dismissing her squad into the field, Lt. Bloch notices that Radio #1106, signed out by Traffic Enforcement Agent Moore on the Equipment Distribution Log, is actually in the radio repair shop. Agent Norris, who is waiting to go on a special assignment with the Lieutenant, states that he saw Agent Moore take Radio #1107. 1.____
   Which of the following is the MOST appropriate action for Lt. Bloch to take?

   A. Have Agent Moore return to the District Office immediately to sign in the proper space for Radio #1107.
   B. Have Agent Norris make a notation on the Log that he witnessed Agent Moore take Radio #1107.
   C. Sign the radio out for the agent in the correct space.
   D. Have Agent Moore complete the entry for Radio #1106 when he completes his tour.

2. While driving her Traffic Enforcement Agents to their posts, Lt. Chu notices numerous vehicles parked in front of a school that is in session. She checks the vehicles and discovers that most of them display Board of Education permits. The posted regulations state *No Parking School Days* without a rider. 2.____
   Of the following, Lt. Chu should direct the agents on the post to

   A. issue summonses only to the vehicles without permits and request signs excusing the teachers
   B. advise the principal of the school concerning these violations
   C. hold off on issuing summonses until the situation has been investigated further
   D. issue summonses to all of the vehicles parked at these signs

3. Radio Control has notified Lt. Green that Traffic Enforcement Agent Jones has become ill in the field. Lt. Green must pick up Agent Jones in his assigned area and bring him back to the District Office. 3.____
   In this situation, Lt. Green should drive with the roof lights

   A. on, and proceed through any red traffic lights with caution
   B. on, using the P.A. system to clear traffic, and proceed as quickly as possible while obeying all traffic laws
   C. off, and obey all traffic laws
   D. off, and proceed through any red traffic lights with caution

4. While Traffic Enforcement Agent Hoyt was patrolling his assigned area, an irate motorist approached and began to physically assault him. Lt. Timms, who was standing nearby, saw the attack and ran over to restrain the motorist. 4.____
   Which one of the following forms should Lt. Timms complete to document the incident?

   A. Employer's Notice of Injury Form (WCD-23)
   B. Accident Report (Form 23)
   C. Workmen's Compensation Form (C-II)
   D. Witnesses' Statement Form (WCD-26)

5. At approximately 9:10 A.M., Lt. Garcia, T-101, and Lt. Diaz, T-101, are patrolling their individual sectors. Lt. Garcia receives a radio call to report back to her District Office to pick up an important package containing personnel folders to be delivered to Inspector Gray at T-606. When Lt. Garcia arrives at her District Office, she is told that the Inspector needs this package immediately in order to prepare for a 10:00 meeting. On her way to deliver the package, Lt. Garcia receives a request from one of her agents to 10-85 him because he is unsure of how to proceed in writing up a traffic violation. Lt. Garcia radios Lt. Diaz, informs him of the situation, and asks him to respond to the 10-85. 5.____
What should Lt. Garcia do NEXT?

A. Return the package to T-101 for someone else to deliver and then assist the agent.
B. Radio the Inspector that she will be late because she is needed by a subordinate.
C. Call the closest motorized agent to deliver the package and respond immediately to the 10-85.
D. Deliver the package to the Inspector and consult with Lt. Diaz as soon as possible regarding the 10-85.

6. Lt. Beam receives a report of an injury to an agent in the field. He responds to the scene and finds that the agent needs medical attention. 6.____
Of the following, the NEXT step the Lieutenant should take is to notify

A. Control and then accompany the agent to the hospital
B. Control, administer first aid, and direct the agent to report to the hospital
C. his Captain and bring the agent to the District Office
D. the hospital that he will be there shortly with the agent, giving all pertinent information

7. Lt. Susan West is with Traffic Enforcement Agent Holly at North General Hospital for treatment of an injury to the agent's hand. 7.____
Since it is near the end of the Lieutenant's tour of duty, she should

A. inform Agent Holly that she will have to leave at the end of her tour
B. call the District Office and ask for another Lieutenant to relieve her at the hospital
C. return promptly to the District Office after making appropriate notations on Agent Holly's TCD-210
D. call the District Office and ask for the Captain to come to the hospital

Question 8.

DIRECTIONS: Question 8 is to be answered on the basis of the following form.

SUMMONS REFUSAL REPORT — TCD-304

Parking Enforcement Agent	Shield #	District Office	Date
Holly, Albert	5869	T-117	4/10/09

Attached Summons Number	Location of Violation	Time of Issuance
69-181249-6	420 Elm Street	4:10 PM

The motorist drove off after you advised him that he was being served a summons.

Yes [X] No [ ]

The motorist physically prevented you from issuing the summons.

Yes [ ] No [X]

Other circumstances: ______________________

8. On April 10, 2009, Lt. Mack was observing and coaching Traffic Enforcement Agent Albert Holly. Agent Holly wrote Summons #69-181249-6 at 4:10 P.M. opposite 420 Elm Place. While reviewing the TCD-304 shown above, Lt. Mack should have noticed an error in the entry dealing with the 8.____

   A. Time of Issuance
   B. Location of Violation
   C. Attached Summons Number
   D. Date of Issuance

9. While Lt. Jones was patrolling Area 18, he observed Traffic Enforcement Agent Carson exiting Lacy's Department Store with three Lacy's bags under her arms. Upon checking the agent's Field Patrol Sheet, he noted that she was on a personal from 10:45 A.M. to 11:15 A.M. When Lt. Jones returned to the District Office, he found a written reprimand in Agent Carson's personnel folder regarding one other instance of shopping while on duty. According to Departmental regulations, what is the MOST appropriate action for Lt. Jones to take? 9.____

   A. Initiate disciplinary charges against the agent.
   B. Issue the agent a verbal reprimand and advise her to avoid large stores in the future.
   C. Make a recommendation to the Captain to suspend the agent immediately.
   D. Prepare a second written reprimand to be placed in the agent's personnel file.

Question 10.

DIRECTIONS: Question 10 is to be answered on the basis of the following form.

EMPLOYEE'S NOTICE OF INJURY

ANSWER ALL QUESTIONS FULLY. THIS IS YOUR NOTICE TO YOUR EMPLOYER OF INJURY ON THE JOB. PRINT OR WRITE LEGIBLY.

Full name of injured person MARY (First) M (Middle) DOE (Last)

Address 110 FINKEL ROAD

Employee's S.S. No. 172-00-1001 Date of Birth 10/20/80

Name of employer CITY OF NEW YORK—DEPARTMENT OF TRANSPORTATION

Date of accident 5/6/09 Hour 1015 (A.M.)

Exact location where accident happened 1ST AVE AND E. 57TH ST. NORTH WEST CORNER

How did accident happen? (describe fully) WHILE WALKING ON 1ST AVE AND E. 57TH ST. I STEPPED INTO A POT HOLE, FELL AND SPRAINED MY RIGHT ANKLE AND MY LEFT WRIST.

Nature and extent of injury SPRAINED LEFT ANKLE AND LEFT WRIST

Did you inform your superior of this accident? YES Date 5.6.09

Name such person LT. FUDD

Names and addresses of witnesses LT. FUDD 182 MULHOLLAND DR. N.Y. 11726

5.6 2009 (Sign here) Mary Doe

THIS IS NOT A CLAIM FORM. A CLAIM FORM MAY BE SECURED AT ANY OFFICE OF THE STATE WORKERS' COMPENSATION BOARD.

10. On May 6, 2009, Traffic Enforcement Agent Mary M. Doe, SS# 172-00-1001, had an accident at 10:15 A.M. while patrolling her sector. She was walking south on the east side of 1st Avenue and was about to cross East 57th Street when she tripped on a pothole and fell, spraining her right ankle and left wrist. Lt. Fudd was on the scene at the time and witnessed the accident. After the agent received medical treatment, Lt. Fudd reviews the Employee's Notice of Injury form shown above, including the reports of the: 10.___
    1. Description of the injury
    2. Date and time of the accident
    3. Location where the accident occurred
    4. Employee's Social Security number.

    Which of the above entries are correct and which are incorrect?
    _______ are correct, but _______ are incorrect.

    A. 1 and 2; 3 and 4
    B. 1 and 3; 2 and 4
    C. 2 and 4; 1 and 3
    D. 3 and 4; 1 and 2

11. While in the field, Lt. Barnes is approached by a civilian who tells her that an agent around the corner is accepting money for not issuing summonses. The Lieutenant goes around the corner and observes an agent writing a summons. The agent does not see the Lieutenant. A motorist approaches the agent and gives him some money. The agent stops writing the summons and walks away. The Lieutenant feels she has reasonable cause to suspect that this agent is accepting bribes and notifies the Captain. According to the Mayor's Executive Order #16, Lt. Barnes should also contact the 11.____

A. Agency Inspector General
B. District Attorney
C. Special Prosecutor's Office
D. Police Department

12. Lt. Cobero is on vehicle patrol and notices that traffic is backing up at a major intersection. She sees that the cause of the problem is an *All Out* condition. 12.____
Of the following, the MOST appropriate action for the Lieutenant to take would be to

A. personally check the traffic box for defects and repair it, if possible
B. pick up an agent to direct traffic and request a repair by landline when she returns to the District Office
C. immediately note the condition on a TCD-321 (Daily Activity Report) and radio an agent to cover the condition
D. immediately call Traffic Control to report the condition

13. Traffic Enforcement Smith has been assigned to patrol a busy commercial street. When Lt. Norris reviews his Daily Field Patrol Sheet (TCD-210), he notices that the agent has made no indications of commercial observations, although agents assigned to this post usually give many summonses to commercial vehicles. 13.____
Lt. Norris realizes that, of the following, the BEST way for Agent Smith to improve his patrol techniques and productivity would be to

A. note *first observations* on the back of his TCD-210
B. record the summons numbers of all tickets issued for commercial observations on the back of his TCD-210
C. note *first observations* in the space for *time issued*
D. record only the license plate numbers for commercial vehicles on the summons forms to serve as *first observations*

Question 14.

DIRECTIONS: Question 14 is to be answered on the basis of the following form.

TCD-124

TRAFFIC CONTROL BUREAU
MEDICAL RELEASE FORM

1 To: St. Clair HOSPITAL
2 Lt. Leroy Hurt hereby authorizes release of medical records regarding treatment for injuries
3 incurred on 5/13/09 .

SIGNED Jean Simpson

14. On Wednesday, May 13, 2009, Lt. Leroy Hurt and Traffic Enforcement Agent Jean Simpson returned to the District Office from the Emergency Room at St. George Hospital. Agent Simpson had tripped on the sidewalk earlier in the day and had sprained her ankle. Later, in reviewing the Workmen's Compensation forms, Lt. Hurt realizes that the Medical Release Form, shown above, was completed improperly. Which of the lines in the above form were filled out incorrectly? 14.____
Lines ______, but not ______.

A. 1 and 2; 3 or 4
B. 1 and 3; 2 or 4
C. 2 and 3; 1 or 4
D. 2 and 4; 1 or 3

Question 15.

DIRECTIONS: Question 15 is to be answered on the basis of the form which is shown on the next page.

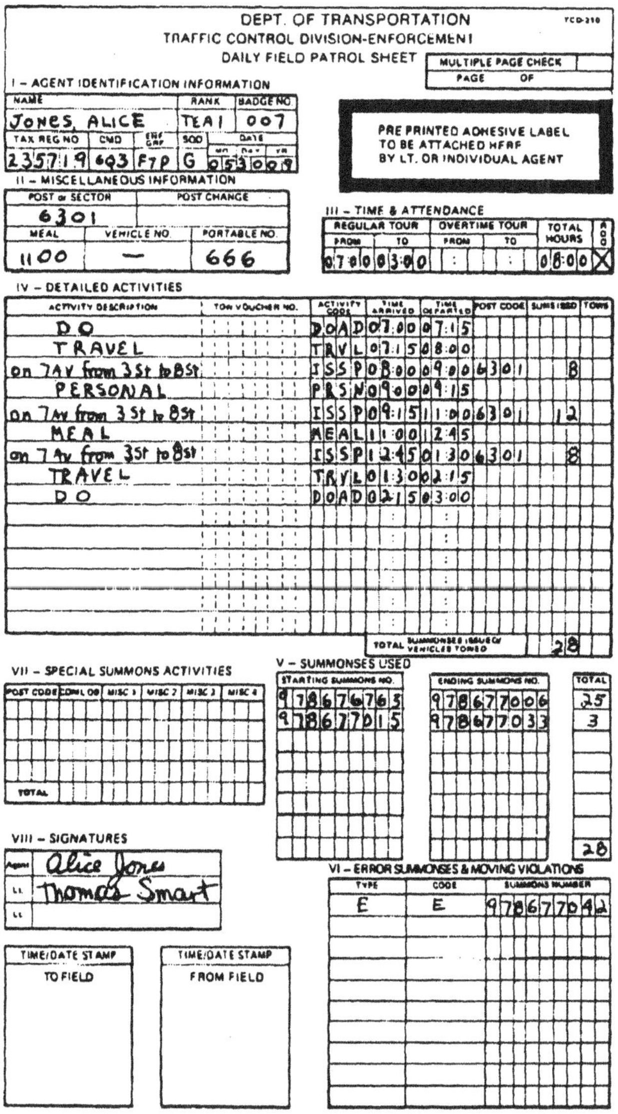
DEPT. OF TRANSPORTATION TCD-210
TRAFFIC CONTROL DIVISION-ENFORCEMENT
DAILY FIELD PATROL SHEET

MULTIPLE PAGE CHECK
PAGE OF

I – AGENT IDENTIFICATION INFORMATION

NAME	RANK	BADGE NO.
JONES, ALICE	TEA I	007

TAX REG NO	CMD	ENF GRP	SQD	DATE MO	DAY	YR
235719	603	F7P	G	05	13	09

PRE PRINTED ADHESIVE LABEL TO BE ATTACHED HERE BY LT. OR INDIVIDUAL AGENT

II – MISCELLANEOUS INFORMATION

POST or SECTOR	POST CHANGE	
6301		
MEAL	VEHICLE NO.	PORTABLE NO.
1100	—	666

III – TIME & ATTENDANCE

REGULAR TOUR FROM	REGULAR TOUR TO	OVERTIME TOUR FROM	OVERTIME TOUR TO	TOTAL HOURS	ROO
07:00	03:00	:	:	08:00	X

IV – DETAILED ACTIVITIES

ACTIVITY DESCRIPTION	TOW VOUCHER NO.	ACTIVITY CODE	TIME ARRIVED	TIME DEPARTED	POST CODE	SUMS ISSD	TOWS
DO		DOAD	07:00	07:15			
TRAVEL		TRVL	07:15	08:00			
on 7AV from 3St to 8St		ISSP	08:00	09:00	6301	8	
PERSONAL		PRSN	09:00	09:15			
on 7Av from 3 St to 8St		ISSP	09:15	11:00	6301	12	
MEAL		MEAL	11:00	12:45			
on 7 Av from 3St to 8St		ISSP	12:45	01:30	6301	8	
TRAVEL		TRVL	01:30	02:15			
DO		DOAD	02:15	03:00			

TOTAL SUMMONSES ISSUED OR VEHICLES TOWED: 28

V – SUMMONSES USED

STARTING SUMMONS NO.	ENDING SUMMONS NO.	TOTAL
978676765	978677006	25
978677015	978677033	3
		28

VI – ERROR SUMMONSES & MOVING VIOLATIONS

TYPE	CODE	SUMMONS NUMBER
E	E	978677042

VII – SPECIAL SUMMONS ACTIVITIES

POST CODE	COML OB	MISC 1	MISC 2	MISC 3	MISC 4
TOTAL					

VIII – SIGNATURES

Agent: Alice Jones
Lt.: Thomas Smart
Lt.:

TIME/DATE STAMP TO FIELD

TIME/DATE STAMP FROM FIELD

15. Lt. Howard is reviewing Traffic Enforcement Agent Jones' Daily Field Patrol Sheet (TCD-210), the front side of which is shown on the preceding page. 15.____
The Lieutenant checks the following entries:
1. Activity Codes
2. Summonses Used
3. Signatures
4. Post Codes 5. Time and Attendance

The Lieutenant should notice that there are errors in ______, but not ______.

A. 1 and 4; 2, 3, and 5
B. 2 and 3; 1, 4, and 5
C. 2 and 5; 1, 3, and 4
D. 1, 3, and 5; 2 and 4

16. While making a field inspection, Lt. Mackowitz notices a vehicle parked next to a fire hydrant with a summons affixed to the windshield. In reviewing the summons, Lt. Mackowitz finds that the Violation Box for Hydrant was not marked, and the number of feet from the hydrant was not entered. According to Departmental procedures, Lt. Mackowitz should 16.____

A. fill in the correct information on the summons and issue the agent a corrective memo
B. note all information from the summons on his Field Patrol Sheet (TCD-321) and write an advisory memo to the Captain for her appropriate action
C. write down the summons number and then review the error with the agent at the end of the tour
D. remove the summons from the vehicle, prepare a corrected summons, and issue the agent a memo

17. While on patrol, Lt. Edmund is approached by an angry young woman who says, *Why do taxpayers like me get parking tickets, while foreign diplomats never get tickets?* 17.____
The Lieutenant might appropriately respond that diplomats do, in fact, receive summonses for the more serious or *highly prohibitive* offenses, and that they are exempt only from summonses for minor offenses such as:

A. obstructing a fire hydrant or parking at a *No Standing* fire zone
B. parking at a meter without activating it, or parking at a *No Parking 11-2* sign at noon
C. parking in a bus stop or in a crosswalk
D. double parking or obstructing traffic

18. Lt. Mancuso arrives at the scene of an assault and is informed by the agent that the motorist yelled at her and then punched her on the arm when she served a summons to his vehicle. The motorist then screams at the Lieutenant, *I punched her because I was only parked here a few minutes and this witch shouldn't have given me a ticket.* Lt. Mancuso should IMMEDIATELY 18.____

A. radio her Captain and have him notify the Assault Investigation Squad
B. radio Control and instruct them to make the proper notifications
C. call 911 at the nearest telephone and have them send the police as soon as possible
D. transport the motorist and the agent to the nearest police station in her traffic vehicle

19. While on patrol, Lt. Gruen notices that an agent on intersection duty is engaged in a loud dispute with a motorist whose car is causing a gridlock problem. The agent is repeating, *Show me your license and registration,* and the motorist is calling the agent several very rude names. 19.____
In order to mediate this dispute, it would be MOST advisable for the Lieutenant to

A. walk around to the driver's door, ask for his license and registration, and reach into the car for them
B. say nothing, walk to the front of the vehicle, wait until the driver is looking, and then start to write a summons
C. motion the driver to move the vehicle to the nearest curb, and politely say, *Sir, may I see your license and registration?*
D. tell the driver to get out of the vehicle, admonish him for his behavior, and direct the agent to write a summons

20. While Lieutenant Oliver is on patrol, she notices Traffic Enforcement Agent O'Park talking to a woman at a commercial truck loading zone. The agent and the woman ask the Lieutenant how the traffic rules apply to her vehicle. 4.____
The woman says she knows she cannot use this vehicle for deliveries in the garment center, but she says she believes it is OK to deliver here since it is not the garment center. The woman's car is a sedan with NY commercial license plates and has large cardboard signs saying *Linda Knits, Inc., 270 East Broadway, NYC* in 3 1/2-inch high letters. The signs are taped to the side of the car. The back seat and passenger seat have bundles of sweaters stacked on them. The woman says she needs to park at the truck loading zone to deliver her sweaters and pick up more wool. Following are four reasons the Lieutenant might give the woman as to why she could not make her delivery in the truck loading zone: The vehicle:
1. does not have permanent signs
2. is not a truck or station wagon
3. has a rear seat
4. does not have signs with four-inch lettering

Which of the following CORRECTLY classifies the above reasons into those that are correct and thost that are not?
______ are correct, but ______ are not.

A. 1 and 2; 3 and 4
B. 1 and 3; 2 and 4
C. 2 and 4; 1 and 3
D. 3 and 4; 1 and 2

21. While on a late tour, Lt. Grey observes the following four situations involving agents on dual motorized patrol: 21.____

Vehicle 1: Operator Traffic Enforcement Agent Borris is issuing a summons in the middle of the block while his partner is issuing a summons around the corner.

Vehicle 2: Passenger Traffic Enforcement Agent Malone is preparing a summons inside the vehicle.

Vehicle 3: Operator Traffic Enforcement Agent Maldoon is talking with the agent on foot patrol while his partner issues a summons to a motorist for an expired meter.

Vehicle 4: Operator Traffic Enforcement Agent Jones is parking the vehicle next to an expired meter in order for his partner to issue a summons.

In which of the above situations should Lt. Grey advise the agents that their actions are in violation of the Department's Standard Operating Procedures?
Vehicles ______, but not ______.

A. 1 and 3; 2 or 4
B. 2 and 3; 1 or 4
C. 2 and 4; 1 or 3
D. 3 and 4; 1 or 2

22. While supervising her assigned agents in the field, Lt. Moses comes upon Vehicle #892 parked in violation of a *No Standing Anytime* sign at approximately 9:15 A.M. At 9:30 M., the agent returns to the vehicle, and Lt. Moses asks to see his Field Patrol Sheet. The sheet shows that the agent was on a personal during that time. 22.____
The Lieutenant should advise the agent that

A. personals are to be limited to ten minutes
B. roof lights should be left on when a Department vehicle is illegally parked
C. a Department vehicle should be parked legally, or at only a minor violation location
D. agents are required to obtain permission from a Lieutenant prior to taking a personal

Question 23.

DIRECTIONS: Question 23 is to be answered on the basis of the form shown on the following page.

10 (#2)

TCD - 305
Rev. 5/86
DOC. AUDIAL

D.O. 109

TO: Thomas B. Doyle, Asst. Commissioner — DATE: May 28, 2009

FROM: TEA John Boswell — SUBJECT: Summons Error

When I wrote summons # 97625671-6, I made an error in one of the following: (Please check where applicable)

(1)

---

(2)

- [X] Parking Meter Number
- [ ] Plate Number
- [ ] Make, Color, Type of Veh.
- [ ] Place of Occurrence
- [ ] Other ______
- [ ] Date or Time of Preparation
- [ ] Description of Violation
- [ ] Section, Sub-division, Code
- [ ] Plate Type

John Boswell
T.E.A. (Signature)

---

(3)

A. [ ] I concur that summons # ______ was issued to the same car. (in duplicate)

---

(4)

______ Lieutenant (Signature)

______ Captain (Signature)

______ Inspector (Signature)

B. [X] No additional summons served.
Comment : Valid SVI permit

(To be completed at Headquarters)

RECEIVED AT HEADQUARTERS (STAMP & BACK TO D.O.)

BY : ______ (Signature)

REVIEWED BY : ______ (Signature)

A/C ______ Thomas B. Doyle

INSTRUCTION: If summons Box A (turnover) is checked, only the Captain signs and forwards direct to Headquarters. If no additional summons served, Box B is checked, Captain and Inspector should investigate, endorse, and forward to Headquarters. Form shall be prepared and forwarded in duplicate. Second copy will be receipted and returned to Captain from the Headquarters.

23. After completing Summons #97625671-6 for an expired meter on May 28, 2009, Traffic Enforcement Agent John Boswell noticed that the vehicle had a valid SVI permit. The agent completed the TCD-305 shown above and submitted it along with the summons to Lt. Howard for his review. 23._
In checking the form, Lt. Howard should notice an error in the section that has been numbered Section

A. 1 B. 2 C. 3 D. 4

24. While on patrol, Lt. Mason notices an overturned dump truck which has spilled dirt and rocks over the roadway. The Lieutenant parks his vehicle, investigates the situation, and determines that special action is needed in order to remove this hazard. When he radios Control, Lieutenant Mason should ask that two other City Agencies respond to the scene. 24._
The two agencies whose assistance is needed are the

A. Environmental Protection Agency and Sanitation Department
B. Police Department and Board of Health
C. Fire Department and Board of Health
D. Police Department and Sanitation Department

Question 25.

DIRECTIONS: Question 25 is to be answered on the basis of the summons which is shown on the following page.

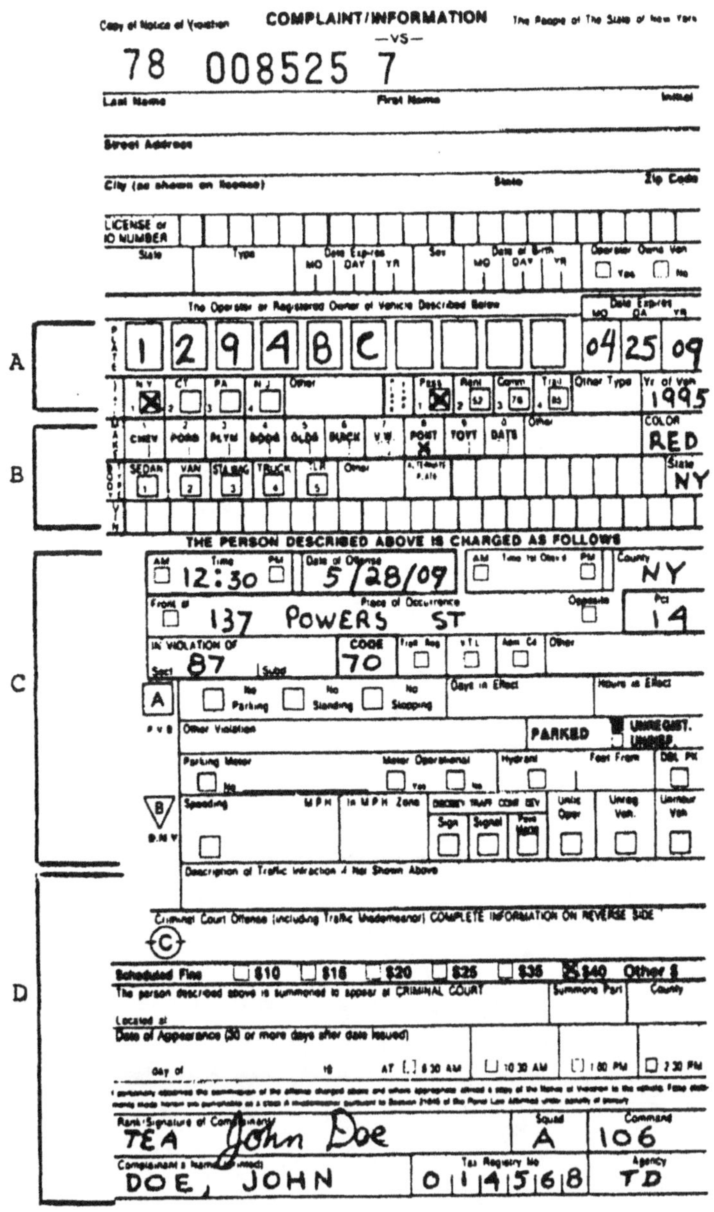
COMPLAINT/INFORMATION

—VS—

78 008525 7

Last Name / First Name / Initial

Street Address

City (as shown on license) / State / Zip Code

LICENSE or ID NUMBER

The Operator or Registered Owner of Vehicle Described Below

A — Plate: 1 2 9 4 B C — Date Expires: 04 25 09 — NY — Pass — Yr of Veh: 1995

B — Make: PONT — Color: RED — State: NY

THE PERSON DESCRIBED ABOVE IS CHARGED AS FOLLOWS

C — Time: 12:30 — Date of Offense: 5/28/09 — County: NY — Place of Occurrence: 137 POWERS ST — Pct: 14 — In Violation of Sect: 87 — Code: 70 — PARKED

Description of Traffic Infraction if Not Shown Above

D — Criminal Court Offense (including Traffic Misdemeanor) COMPLETE INFORMATION ON REVERSE SIDE

Scheduled Fine: $10 $15 $20 $25 $35 $40 Other $

Rank/Signature of Complainant: TEA John Doe — Squad: A — Command: 106

Complainant's Name (printed): DOE, JOHN — Tax Registry No: 0114568 — Agency: TD

25. While on field patrol, Lt. Lee reviews the summonses prepared by Traffic Enforcement Agent Doe on his tour. The Lieutenant notices that there are errors on Summons #78-008525-7, shown above. 25.____

Of the following, which sections of the summons are correct and which sections have errors?

Sections ______ are correct, but ______ have errors.

A. A and C; B and D
B. A and D; B and C
C. B and C; A and D
D. B and D; A and C

KEY (CORRECT ANSWERS)

1. A
2. D
3. C
4. D
5. D

6. A
7. B
8. B
9. A
10. C

11. A
12. D
13. A
14. A
15. C

16. D
17. B
18. B
19. C
20. B

21. A
22. C
23. B
24. D
25. B

EXAMINATION SECTION
TEST 1

DIRECTIONS: Each question or incomplete statement is followed by several suggested answers or completions. Select the one that BEST answers the question or completes the statement. *PRINT THE LETTER OF THE CORRECT ANSWER IN THE SPACE AT THE RIGHT.*

1. Lt. Barry receives a phone call from a local hospital concerning summonses issued to doctors by Traffic Enforcement Agent Phillips. The Lieutenant notices that Agent Phillips has issued several Error Summonses for parking adjacent to a local hospital. When she discusses this matter with the agent, she discovers that he does not understand which areas should be considered *adjacent* to a hospital, so she decides to instruct the agent. In which one of the following diagrams does the shaded area indicate the area that should be considered adjacent to the hospital? 1.____

A.

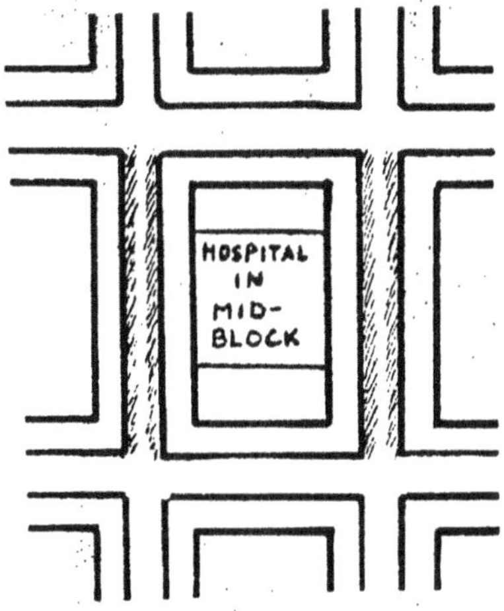

B.

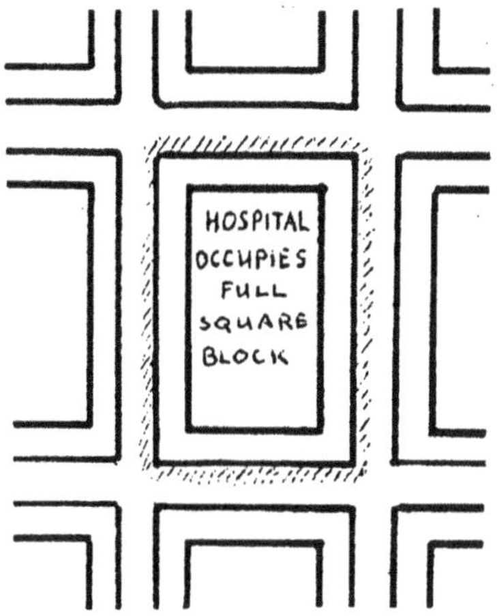

C.

D.

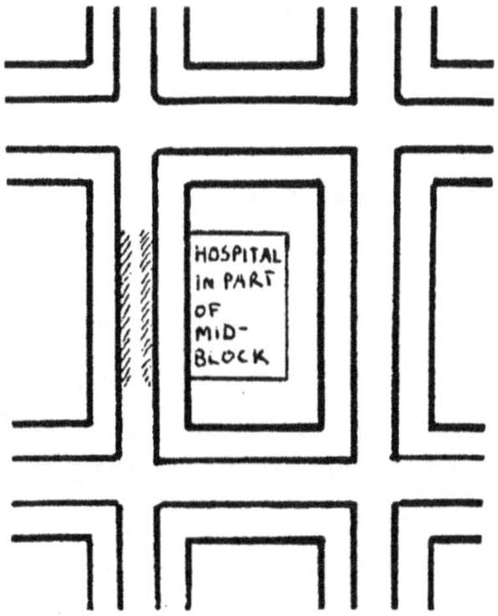

2. Lt. Manning was on field patrol when Traffic Enforcement Agent McCoy approached her regarding a broken handle on a parking meter. Agent McCoy had been patrolling an off-street metered parking lot when he noticed a meter with a time expired flag. Upon investigating, he found that the handle knob was missing. Unsure of how to proceed, he asked Lt. Manning for her advice. 2.____
According to Departmental guidelines, what should the Lieutenant tell Agent McCoy?

A. Inform him that agents are not to patrol off-street parking lots.
B. Recommend that he complete a TCD-339 and make a first observation on the vehicle.
C. Instruct the agent to record the information on his TCD-210, but not to ticket the vehicle.
D. Advise the agent to issue a summons and to record the information on his TCD-210.

3. Traffic Enforcement Agent Bolin, assigned to dual motorized patrol, approached Lt. O'Toole regarding a personal matter. She confided to the Lieutenant that her partner, Agent Stone, was very negligent concerning his personal hygiene, and she was having trouble riding in the car with him. Lt. O'Toole tells the agent that he will discuss personal hygiene habits at this afternoon's Rap Session. 3.____
Discussing this issue during a Rap Session should be considered

A. *proper* because appropriate grooming and personal hygiene are an important part of the job
B. *improper* because Agent Stone's personal hygiene is not Lt. O'Toole's business
C. *proper* because Agent Stone should be given a public reprimand to set an example
D. *improper* because Rap Session topics are to be decided by the Captain

Question 4.

DIRECTIONS: Question 4 is to be answered on the basis of the following information.

While on patrol, Lt. Custer arrives at the scene of a dispute between a civilian and an agent. The civilian has placed his hands on the agent's arms to stop her from issuing a summons.

Following are four actions that the Lieutenant might take in order to mediate this dispute:
1. Direct the civilian to take his hands off the agent, and tell both to step apart.
2. Speak in a loud voice and use strong language to show that he means business.
3. Physically separate the pair by pushing the civilian away, always being ready to defend himself.
4. Act calmly and speak politely and rationally to help calm the situation.

4. Which of the following CORRECTLY classifies the above actions into those that are correct and those that are not? 4.____
______ are correct, but not ______.

A. 1 and 2; 3 and 4
B. 1 and 4; 2 and 3
C. 2 and 3; 1 and 4
D. 1, 3, and 4; 2

5. Traffic Enforcement Agent Heather was driving Vehicle #1501 when it was rear-ended by a taxi carrying a passenger. Agent Long and Lt. Franz were passengers in Vehicle #1501. Agents Heather and Long were both injured in the accident. The Lieutenant fills out Workmen's Compensation papers and a Witness Statement of Accident form. In addition, the Lieutenant should obtain Witness Statement of Accident forms from Agent(s) 5.____

   A. Heather and Long
   B. Heather and Long and the passenger in the taxi
   C. Heather, the taxi driver, and the passenger in the taxi
   D. Long and the passenger in the taxi

Questions 6-9.

DIRECTIONS: Questions 6 through 9 are to be answered on the basis of the following form.

TCD 125 SUPERVISOR's ASSAULT REPORT REV: 2/85

LAST NAME____ FIRST____ INITIAL__ BADGE #____
OFFICE____ TOUR OF DUTY____ AGE____ DATE OF APPOINTMENT____
HOME ADDRESS____ HOME PHONE#____ EMERG.#____
DATE ASSAULTED____ TIME____ DAYTIME____ NIGHTTIME____
LOCATION____ BORO.____ POLICE PCT____
AGENT STATES:____
(Use Reverse side for Addition Information)

A

WAS TRAFFIC VEHICLE INVOLVED?__ VEH#____ DAMAGED: YES____ NO____
DESCRIBE____
RANK: TEA I__ TEA II__ TEA III__ OTHER____ TEA (M)__ (F)__ PERP (M)__ (F)__
TEA's ACTION AT TIME: FOOT PATROL____ MOTORIZE____ INTERSECTION____ TOWING____
DID THE TEA WISH TO PRESS CHARGES? YES____ NO____
WEAPON USED: YES____ NO____ TYPE__ DESCRIPTION____

B

DEFENDANT APPREHENDED: YES__ NO__ PERPETRATORS NAME____
ADDRESS____ VEHICLE#____ LICENSE #____
STATE____ DESCRIPTION OF PERPETRATOR AND VEHICLE____
WITNESSES NAMES____ ADDRESS____ PHONE____

C

HOW WAS POLICE ASSISTANCE CALLED: 911 DIALED____ RADIO TO CONTROL____
EXPLAIN____
WAS POLICE COOPERATIVE: YES__ NO__ EXPLAIN____
IF POLICE ISSUED UNIVERSAL SUMMONS: UNIVERSAL SUMMONSES#____
APPEARANCE DATE____ MUST BE THIRTY (30) DAYS OR MORE
POLICE OFFICER DECIDING DISPOSITION____ BADGE#____
RELEASED/NO ACTION____ EXPLAIN____
UF61 #____ AIDED #____ REFERRED TO COURT____
WAS A DETECTIVE ASSIGNED: YES__ NO__ (IF YES) NAME____ PHONE#____
DEFENDANT TAXI DRIVER: YES____ NO____ MEDALLION #____
MEDICAL CARE REQUIRED: YES__ NO__ HOSPITAL____
DEGREE OF INJURY: NONE____ MINOR,NOT VISIBLE____ VISIBLE____
HOSPITALIZED: YES____ NO____ DESCRIPTIONS OF INJURIES____

D

TIME LOST DUE TO INCIDENT____ STILL OUT____
CHIEF/INSPT/CAPT/LT RESPONDING NAME____
TO SCENE____ PCT____ HOSPITAL____
HAVE YOU SUBMITTED MEMOS FROM ALL TEA's INVOLVED? YES____ NO____
NAME OF SUPERVISOR WHO FILLED OUT THIS FORM____

E

6. In responding to the assault of an agent, Lt. O'Brien found Police Officer Salk, Badge Number 385, who was already on the scene, to be very helpful in investigating the incident. The Officer had already gathered most of the facts regarding the motorist, including his description and information pertaining to his vehicle. 6.____
Where should Lt. O'Brien enter this information on the Supervisor's Assault Report? Section(s)

A. B B. C C. A and B D. C and D

7. While issuing summonses, Traffic Enforcement Agent Miller is suddenly drenched with pink-colored liquid from water-filled balloons exploding around him. He looks up and sees and hears laughing children leaning over the roof of the building to his right. The angry agent radios a 10-50, and Lt. Perry responds to the scene. Once the agent calms down, he says that he is not hurt and does not want to *make a big thing out of this,* but he does want to be reimbursed for the cost of cleaning his uniform. 7.____
In this situation, should the Lieutenant complete a Supervisor's Assault Report?

A. Yes, because the agent's uniform has been damaged.
B. No, because the agent refused to press charges
C. Yes, because this incident qualifies as an assault.
D. No, because the incident is only a child's prank.

8. While performing his assigned foot patrol duties, a Traffic Enforcement Agent was assaulted by a motorist who pulled a baseball bat out of his van and struck the agent across the arm. The agent was accompanied to Columbus Hospital by Lt. Lee, where the arm was x-rayed and treated. 8.____
In completing the Supervisor's Assault Report, Lt. Lee should enter this information in Sections

A. A and D B. B and D
C. A, B, and C D. B, D, and E

9. Lt. Corry is preparing a Supervisor's Assault Report, a sample of which is shown on the previous page. 9.____
Which of the following should be entered in the space labeled *Time Lost Due to Incident?*
The

A. amount of time the agent lost from the start of the incident until his return to work
B. amount of time the agent lost from the start of the incident until the report was sent in
C. amount of time the agent lost on the day of the incident
D. combined time lost by the agent, the Lieutenant, and the Assault Squad due to the incident

10. Lt. White is on patrol at 12:30 P.M., Thursday, when she notices a summons affixed to the windshield of a vehicle in violation of a *No Parking 11 A.M. to 2 P.M. Monday and Thursday* regulation. While checking the summons, the Lieutenant finds that 10:50 A.M. is the time Traffic Enforcement Agent Benson entered on the summons. According to Departmental regulations, what is the MOST appropriate action for Lt. White to take? 10.____

A. Radio Agent Benson to report back to the location to issue a corrected summons.
B. Write the plate number of the vehicle in violation on her TCD-321 (Lieutenant's Daily Field Patrol) sheet and take the error summons back to the District Office.

C. Write a summons correcting the error and take the error summons back to the District Office.
D. Leave the error summons on the vehicle and report the facts to the Captain.

11. Lt. Bell is at the scene of an *All-Out* condition at a busy intersection. He has requested that two agents meet him at the intersection. Lt. Bell is wearing his reflective vest and is directing traffic until the agents arrive. 11.____
Which of the hand signals shown below should Lt. Bell use to stop traffic?

A.

B.

C.

D.

12. Lt. West accompanies Traffic Enforcement Agent Grant to the hospital to have a foreign object removed from the agent's left eye. 12.____
After the doctor has treated the eye, Lt. West should document this medical care by obtaining

A. a doctor's note with a notation of the diagnosis, prognosis, and specific time for convalescence
B. doctor's lines on the hospital letterhead and the doctor's signature
C. a doctor's note with a notation of the exact return to work date and the time of the next appointment
D. doctor's lines with an estimate of the length of disability and the probable return date

13. Lt. Green is on patrol at 9 A.M. when she comes upon a motorist parking his vehicle next to a fire hydrant. The driver turns on his emergency signals and exits the vehicle along with his passenger. When Lt. Green approaches them, the man explains that they have a prescription to fill and will only be a few minutes.
In this situation, Lt. Green should 13.____

A. direct the motorist to find a metered parking space
B. explain to the motorist that vehicles are never to be parked next to fire hydrants
C. issue the vehicle a summons for the fire hydrant violation
D. instruct the motorist to remain with the vehicle while his passenger goes into the pharmacy

14. While on patrol in a department vehicle, Lt. Bream receives a call from Traffic Enforcement Agent Morris. The agent cannot start his car and wants to get a *jump start* from the Lieutenant's battery.
Which of the following is the CORRECT way to attach the booster cables? 14.____

A. From the Lieutenant's positive to the agent's negative; from the Lieutenant's negative to the agent's negative

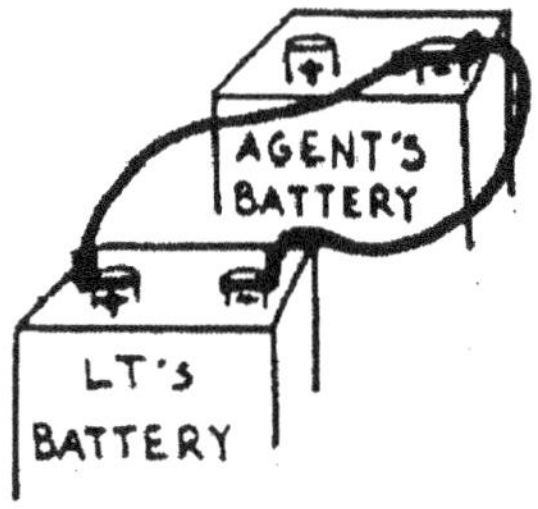

B. From the Lieutenant's positive to the agent's positive; from the Lieutenant's negative to a ground on the agent's chassis

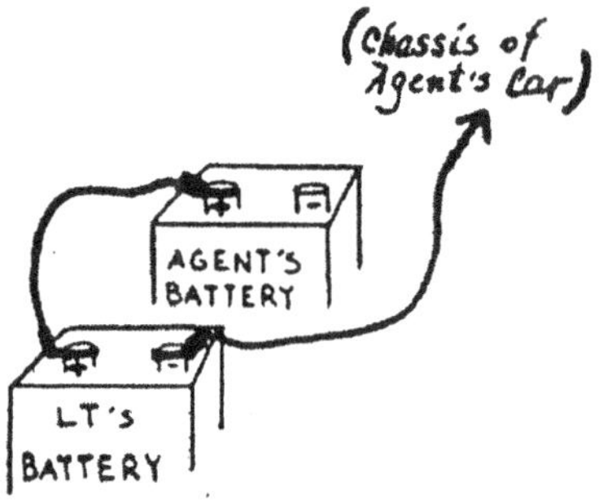

C. From the Lieutenant's positive to the agent's positive; from the Agent's negative to a battery charging machine

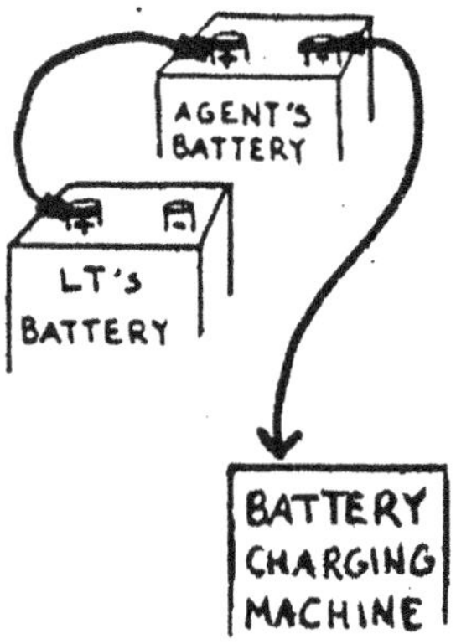

D. From the Lieutenant's positive to the agent's negative; from the Lieutenant's negative to the agent's positive

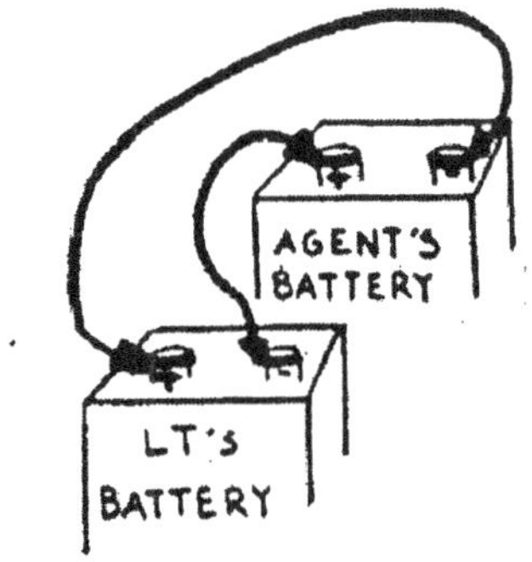

15. Lt. Smith is on patrol when she notices that a passenger van that is waiting in a *No Standing Anytime* zone is obstructing traffic. Lt. Smith approaches the van and is informed by the driver that he is waiting for commuters from a nearby office building to board his van in about fifteen minutes.
In this situation, Lt. Smith should 15.____

A. allow the driver to wait because livery vans are allowed to pick up and drop off passengers
B. explain to the driver that although passenger vans are allowed to wait in *No Standing* zones, they may do so only if they don't obstruct the flow of traffic
C. have the agent assigned to that sector check on the van in half an hour to see if he has moved
D. advise the driver to move his van or he will be issued a summons

16. Traffic Enforcement Agent Jones was on dual patrol with Agent Parisi when he slipped into a hole and sprained his ankle. Agent Parisi witnessed the accident. Agent Jones was treated at Mercy Hospital and sent home. Their Patrol Supervisor, Lt. Lee, is reviewing the Medical Release Form and notices that Agent Jones neglected to sign the form. Prior to submitting the Medical Release Form to the main office for processing, Lt. Lee should 16.____

A. sign the form because she is the Patrol Supervisor
B. ask the Staff Lieutenant who was on duty at the time to sign the form
C. direct Agent Jones to sign the form
D. tell Agent Parisi to sign the form since he witnessed the accident

17. On Monday, at 8:30 A.M., while on patrol in midtown Manhattan, Lt. Siegel passes Simpson Elementary School and notices that a school bus is unable to discharge its students because of the following traffic conditions: 17.____
1. A peddler whose van is parked at corner of the school
2. A parent double-parked watching her child in the playground
3. A livery van discharging passengers across the street from the school
4. A woman with a Board of Education placard parked in a *No Parking School Days* space

In this situation, which of the above motorists should Lt. Siegel instruct to move their vehicle?

A. 1 and 4, but not 2 or 3
B. 1, 2, and 3, but not 4
C. 1, 2, and 4, but not 3
D. 2, 3, and 4, but not 1

18. Lt. Willis is directing the activity of Traffic Enforcement Agents Allen and Burns on a sunny day in March. The agents are issuing summonses to approximately fifty vehicles parked at a construction site near a hospital. In this situation, Lt. Willis should direct 18.____

A. both agents to remain in the vehicle and slowly drive along the street, reaching out the window to place summonses in the doors or under the wipers of the vehicles
B. the agents to park their vehicle in a legal spot and issue summonses on foot while keeping each other in sight
C. one agent to remain in the vehicle as driver, while the other writes the summonses in the vehicle and then gets out to place them under the windshield wipers
D. one agent to drive and write the summonses in the car while the other gets out to place them under the windshield wipers

19. Lt. Sanchez is observing Traffic Enforcement Agent Andrews on the agent's first day of intersection duty. Lt. Sanchez hears an emergency vehicle approaching and observes that Agent Andrews has become confused and is unsure of what to do. 19.____
Which one of the following is the MOST appropriate action for the Lieutenant to take?

A. Step into the intersection and personally direct the emergency vehicle through the traffic.
B. Step into the intersection and personally direct the emergency vehicle onto the side street.
C. Direct the agent to stand on the sidewalk in order to clear the turning lane for use by the emergency vehicle.
D. Direct the agent to stop all traffic until the emergency vehicle comes into view.

20. While Lt. Bright is on patrol in Queens, she notices that all of the traffic lights at the corner of 82nd Avenue and Busy Street are burnt out. 20.____
Which of the following would be the CORRECT transmission to report this condition to Control?

A. Pedestrian lamps out; Queens Eighty-Second Avenue and Busy Street. K.
B. Queens; Eight-Two Avenue and Busy Street; All Out Condition. K
C. Steady signal condition at Eight-Two Avenue and Busy Street in Queens. K
D. Eighty-Second Avenue and Busy Street; Queens; Multiple signal lamps out. K

21. Lt. Haire, who is Supervisor #7 of the T117A Command, wishes to direct Traffic Enforcement Agent Plant to return to the District Office. Agent Plant is presently directing traffic at Park Road and Busy Street. 21.____
Of the following, the CORRECT radio transmission for Lt. Haire to use is

A. Lt. Haire to Park Road and Busy Street - return to D.O. K.
B. T117A Park Road and Busy Street. Return to the Office. K.
C. T117A Supervisor #7 to Park Road and Busy Street. Return to D.O. K.
D. Lt. #7 to Busy Street and Park Road. Return to D.O. K.

22. Lieutenant McMerry has noticed that Traffic Enforcement Agent Willis is not using appropriate radio codes and language. She decides that this agent needs some remedial training. 22.____
Which of the following would be a PROPER instruction?

A. All calls must be routed through Control, even those that are to someone on the same frequency.
B. When responding to a call, you should say *go* to acknowledge that you are ready to receive the message.
C. The signal *10-40* should be used to acknowledge that a transmission was received.
D. The word *Emergency* should be used only in true emergency situations.

23. Lt. Flag is at the intersection of First Street and Birch Avenue when she witnesses a two-car accident. The agent assigned to this post is on his meal. 23.____
Lt. Flag should use her radio to

A. direct the agent assigned to this post to return from meal immediately
B. notify Operations and log the agent *Off Post*
C. request that the agent on the nearest post report to the scene of the accident
D. call the District Office for a relief Agent to take over the intersection

24. While on patrol, Lt. Bright notices that traffic is backed up at an intersection. Upon investigation, she sees that a crowd has formed around an elderly woman who tripped in a pothole and may have broken her hip. Following are four actions the Lieutenant might take: 4.____

1. Direct the civilians to move the woman gently onto the sidewalk.
2. Direct traffic at the scene
3. Radio Communications to report the incident
4. Prepare an Unusual Occurrence card.

Which one of the following CORRECTLY classifies the above actions into those that are correct and those that are not?

A. 1 and 3 are correct, but 2 and 4 are not.
B. 2 and 4 are correct, but 1 and 3 are not.
C. 1, 2, and 3 are correct, but 4 is not.
D. 2, 3, and 4 are correct, but 1 is not.

Question 25.

DIRECTIONS: Question 25 is to be answered on the basis of the forms which appear on the following pages.

Page___of___Pages

HAVE YOU READ THE INSTRUCTIONS IN SECTION A ON THE BACK?

State of New York - Department of Motor Vehicles

REPORT OF MOTOR VEHICLE ACCIDENT

MV-104 (11/74)

Your Vehicle No. 1 | ACCIDENT DATE MO. / DAY / YEAR | DAY OF WEEK | TIME ☐ AM ☐ PM | NUMBER OF VEHICLES | LEFT SCENE ☐ | DID POLICE INVESTIGATE ACCIDENT AT SCENE? ☐ YES ☐ NO | NAME OF POLICE AGENCY | Other Vehicle No. 2

MOTORIST IDENTIFICATION NUMBER EXACTLY AS PRINTED ON LICENSE

LAST NAME OF DRIVER 1 | FIRST NAME | MIDDLE INITIAL

NUMBER AND STREET

CITY | STATE | ZIP CODE

DATE OF BIRTH MO. / DAY / YEAR | SEX | STATE OF LICENSE

DRIVER

MOTORIST IDENTIFICATION NUMBER EXACTLY AS PRINTED ON LICENSE

LAST NAME OF DRIVER 2 | FIRST NAME | MIDDLE INITIAL

NUMBER AND STREET

CITY | STATE | ZIP CODE

DATE OF BIRTH MO. / DAY / YEAR | SEX | STATE OF LICENSE

LAST NAME OF OWNER 1 | FIRST NAME | MIDDLE INITIAL

NUMBER AND STREET

CITY | STATE | ZIP CODE

OWNER

LAST NAME OF OWNER 2 | FIRST NAME | MIDDLE INITIAL

NUMBER AND STREET

CITY | STATE | ZIP CODE

NO. OF OCCUPANTS | PLATE NUMBER | VEHICLE TYPE | VEH. TOWED AWAY? ☐ YES ☐ NO

ESTIMATED COST OF REPAIRS ☐ $50 OR LESS ☐ $51-$200 ☐ $201-$250 ☐ $251-$300 ☐ $301-$750 ☐ OVER $750 | VEHICLE YEAR & MAKE | STATE OF REG.

VEH

NO. OF OCCUPANTS | PLATE NUMBER | VEHICLE TYPE | VEH. TOWED AWAY? ☐ YES ☐ NO

ESTIMATED COST OF REPAIRS ☐ $50 OR LESS ☐ $51-$200 ☐ $201-$250 ☐ $251-$300 ☐ $301-$750 ☐ OVER $750 | VEHICLE YEAR & MAKE | STATE OF REG.

DESCRIBE DAMAGE TO VEH. NO. 1

CHECK ONE OF THE 8 DIAGRAMS BELOW IF IT ADEQUATELY DESCRIBES THE ACCIDENT, OR DRAW YOUR OWN DIAGRAM IN THE SPACE TO THE RIGHT

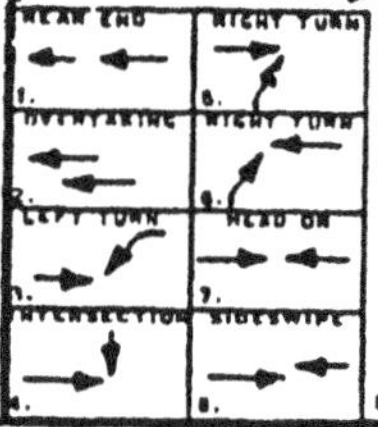

ACCIDENT DIAGRAM

NUMBER THE VEHICLES, YOUR VEHICLE IS NO. 1

DESCRIBE DAMAGE TO VEH. NO. 2

REFERENCE MARKER NEAREST TO SITE | COUNTY OF ACCIDENT | ☐ CITY ☐ TOWN OF ☐ VILLAGE | ADDRESS/LANDMARKS AT SCENE

ROUTE NO. OR STREET NAME | ON | ☐ MILES ☐ FEET ☐ AT INTERSECTION WITH | ☐ N ☐ S ☐ E ☐ W OF | ROUTE NO. OR STREET NAME

INJURY SECTION: FILL OUT SPACE BELOW FOR EVERY PERSON INJURED OR KILLED IN THE ACCIDENT.

NAME AND ADDRESS	8. IN VEH. NO.	12. AGE	13. SEX	DESCRIBE INJURIES	CHECK PROPER COLUMN(S) SEE INSTRUCTION B ON BACK 18. K	A	B	C	DATE OF DEATH

ACCIDENT DESCRIPTION

IDENTIFY DAMAGED PROPERTY OTHER THAN VEHICLE(S)

NAME OF INSURANCE COMPANY WHICH ISSUED POLICY | POLICY NUMBER

NAME AND ADDRESS OF POLICYHOLDER | POLICY PERIOD FROM TO

IF VEHICLE WAS OPERATED UNDER PERMIT OF ICC OR NYS DOT GIVE NO. | NAME AND ADDRESS OF PERMIT HOLDER

IS FORM SR-23 (FLEET COVERAGE) ON FILE WITH THE COMMISSIONER? | IF SELF-INSURED GIVE CERTIFICATE NO. | AND STATE

DATE FILED | SIGNATURE OF DRIVER OF VEHICLE NO. 1 | IF SIGNED BY PERSON OTHER THAN DRIVER, GIVE REASON.

SECTION A

An accident in New York State causing death, personal injury or damage over $200 to the property of any one person must be reported within 10 days. Failure to report within 10 days is a misdemeanor and subjects License and/or Registration to suspension until report is filed.

INSTRUCTIONS

PLEASE PRINT OR TYPE ALL INFORMATION
USE BLACK OR DARK BLUE INK

Begin by folding along this line and follow the instructions at the top of Section B.

1. If you were involved in an accident with a pedestrian, enter the pedestrian information in the DRIVER block of the space provided for other Vehicle No. 2, and print "PEDESTRIAN" in the OWNER block.

   If you were involved in an accident with a vehicle other than a motor vehicle, e.g., snowmobile, mini-bike, aircycle, all-terrain vehicle, trail bike or other non-motor vehicle, enter the driver, owner and vehicle information as you would normally for Other Vehicle No. 2.

   If a vehicle is unoccupied, enter all available information. Be sure to enter the correct vehicle plate number and vehicle type in the appropriate VEHICLE block.

2. Driver information must be entered exactly as it appears on each driver's license.

   Owner information must be entered exactly as it appears on the Registration of each vehicle involved in the accident.

3. If you were involved in an accident in which there were more than two vehicles, an additional one of these report forms must be filled out. On that form, place the information for the third vehicle in the space marked "Your Vehicle No. 1" and mark it No. 3. Use the space marked "Other Vehicle No. 2" for the fourth vehicle, and mark it No. 4 and so on.

4. The location of the accident is very important and you should describe it as accurately as possible in the space provided. In addition, if the accident occurred on a State highway, you will find a small green sign, called a Reference Marker, somewhere near the crash site. They are posted each 10th of a mile along the highway. The reference marker section should include the number exactly as it appears on the sign.

5. For each person injured in the accident, describe his injuries and check the injury code K, A, B, or C, that applies. When a Pedestrian is injured, place a "P" in the box labeled "In Vehicle Number". Injuries are defined as follows:

K	A
Any injury that results in death	Severe lacerations, broken or distorted limbs, skull fracture, crushed chest, internal injuries, unconscious when taken from the accident scene, unable to leave accident scene without assistance.

B	C
Lump on head, abrasions, minor lacerations	Momentary unconsciousness, limping, nausea, hysteria, complaint of pain (no visible injury).

   If there are more than three persons injured, another one of these report forms is needed. In the injury section of that report, record the required information for all additional injured persons.

6. Attach any additional report forms to page one. Each page of the report must be numbered in the upper left corner, dated and signed on the bottom line and submitted to:

   COMMISSIONER OF MOTOR VEHICLES
   EMPIRE STATE PLAZA
   ALBANY, NEW YORK 12228

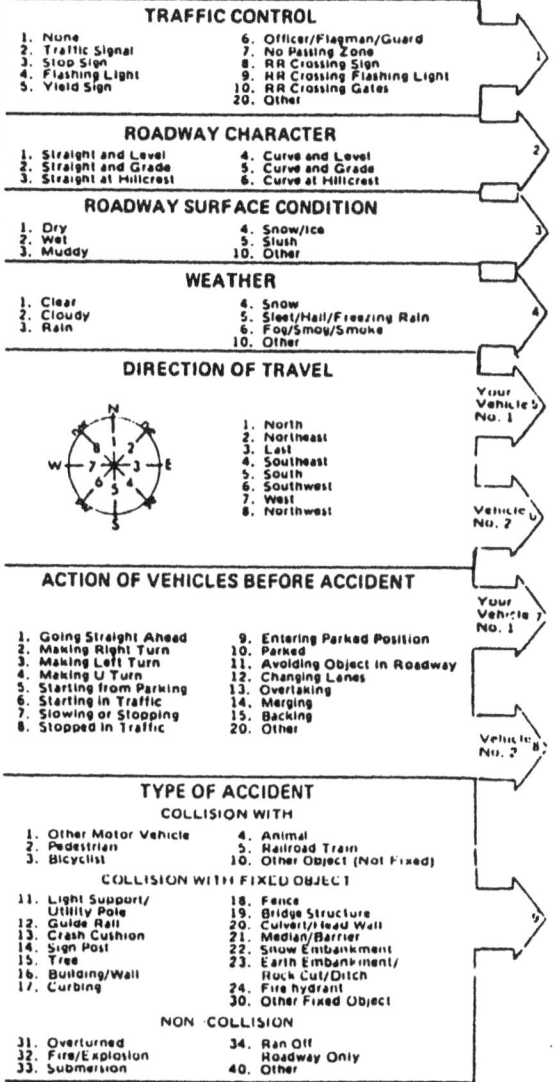

SECTION B

State of New York - Department of Motor Vehicles

MV-104 (11/74)

REPORT OF MOTOR VEHICLE ACCIDENT

BE SURE FORM IS FOLDED ALONG THIS LINE BEFORE ANSWERING THE QUESTIONS BELOW.

FILL IN THE 9 BOXES TO THE RIGHT BY ENTERING THE NUMBER OF THE ITEM WHICH BEST DESCRIBES THE CIRCUMSTANCES OF THE ACCIDENT.

IF A QUESTION DOES NOT APPLY ENTER A DASH (–)

IF AN ANSWER IS UNKNOWN ENTER AN "X"

TRAFFIC CONTROL (1)

1. None
2. Traffic Signal
3. Stop Sign
4. Flashing Light
5. Yield Sign
6. Officer/Flagman/Guard
7. No Passing Zone
8. RR Crossing Sign
9. RR Crossing Flashing Light
10. RR Crossing Gates
20. Other

ROADWAY CHARACTER (2)

1. Straight and Level
2. Straight and Grade
3. Straight at Hillcrest
4. Curve and Level
5. Curve and Grade
6. Curve at Hillcrest

ROADWAY SURFACE CONDITION (3)

1. Dry
2. Wet
3. Muddy
4. Snow/Ice
5. Slush
10. Other

WEATHER (4)

1. Clear
2. Cloudy
3. Rain
4. Snow
5. Sleet/Hail/Freezing Rain
6. Fog/Smog/Smoke
10. Other

DIRECTION OF TRAVEL

1. North
2. Northeast
3. East
4. Southeast
5. South
6. Southwest
7. West
8. Northwest

Your Vehicle No. 1 (5)
Vehicle No. 2 (6)

ACTION OF VEHICLES BEFORE ACCIDENT

1. Going Straight Ahead
2. Making Right Turn
3. Making Left Turn
4. Making U Turn
5. Starting from Parking
6. Starting in Traffic
7. Slowing or Stopping
8. Stopped in Traffic
9. Entering Parked Position
10. Parked
11. Avoiding Object in Roadway
12. Changing Lanes
13. Overtaking
14. Merging
15. Backing
20. Other

Your Vehicle No. 1 (7)
Vehicle No. 2 (8)

TYPE OF ACCIDENT (9)

COLLISION WITH

1. Other Motor Vehicle
2. Pedestrian
3. Bicyclist
4. Animal
5. Railroad Train
10. Other Object (Not Fixed)

COLLISION WITH FIXED OBJECT

11. Light Support/ Utility Pole
12. Guide Rail
13. Crash Cushion
14. Sign Post
15. Tree
16. Building/Wall
17. Curbing
18. Fence
19. Bridge Structure
20. Culvert/Head Wall
21. Median/Barrier
22. Snow Embankment
23. Earth Embankment/ Rock Cut/Ditch
24. Fire hydrant
30. Other Fixed Object

NON COLLISION

31. Overturned
32. Fire/Explosion
33. Submersion
34. Ran Off Roadway Only
40. Other

PLEASE READ INSTRUCTIONS 1 THROUGH 6 ON OTHER SIDE OF FOLD BEFORE COMPLETING THE INSIDE OF REPORT.

25. Lt. Berry is completing a Report of Motor Vehicle Accident (MV-104) form for an accident in which a Department vehicle slammed into a van, which in turn hit a parked truck. In order to record the information relating to this accident, Lt. Berry should 25.____

A. complete an additional MV-104, placing the information on the truck in the space marked *Your Vehicle No. 1* and mark it *No. 3*
B. use the *Accident Description* section of the report to record the information on the truck and label it *Vehicle No. 3*
C. attach a memo to the report to include the information on the truck
D. use the *Last Name of Owner 1* section of the MV-104 to record the information on the truck since this section does not apply to Department vehicles

KEY (CORRECT ANSWERS)

1.	A	11.	C
2.	B	12.	A
3.	A	13.	D
4.	B	14.	B
5.	D	15.	D
6.	D	16.	C
7.	C	17.	C
8.	D	18.	B
9.	C	19.	A
10.	C	20.	B

21. C
22. D
23. C
24. D
25. A

TEST 2

DIRECTIONS: Each question or incomplete statement is followed by several suggested answers or completions. Select the one that BEST answers the question or completes the statement. *PRINT THE LETTER OF THE CORRECT ANSWER IN THE SPACE AT THE RIGHT.*

1. One of Lt. Washington's many responsibilities is driving the agents to and from their assigned foot posts. She does this at the beginning and end of each tour and sometimes drives agents during the day. One rainy Tuesday, Lt. Washington receives the following requests by radio from three of her agents: 3.____
   1. Traffic Enforcement Agent Earth asks to be driven into another sector during his lunch so he can eat at Burger Barn
   2. Traffic Enforcement Agent Mary Eager asks to be driven into another sector in the District so she can write extra summonses at a shopping mall even though her area is productive
   3. Traffic Enforcement Agent Steve Milo asks to be driven back to the District Office because he thinks he is coming down with the flu and wants to go home.

   In this situation, Lt. Washington should

   A. comply with Agent Eager's request, but deny those of Agents Barth and Milo
   B. comply with the requests of Agents Barth, Eager, and Milo
   C. comply with Agent Mile's request, but deny those of Agents Barth and Eager
   D. deny the requests of Agents Barth, Eager, and Milo

2. While directing traffic at a busy intersection in his sector, Lt. Andrews is approached by a woman who is visibly upset. She explains that she was shopping in a store across the street. After talking to a clerk for a few moments, she looked back and her small child was gone. In this situation, it would be MOST appropriate for Lt. Andrews to 2.____

   A. give the woman directions to the nearest police precinct
   B. advise the woman to return to the store and contact the Manager
   C. radio Control and notify them of the situation
   D. apologize to the woman and explain that Traffic Control personnel cannot become involved in situations of this kind

3. Lt. #1 of T-117A is on a special assignment for the day, giving traffic reports to the Command Van for 8th Street to 20th Street. She wishes to take a personal. 3.____
   Of the following, which radio message should the Lieutenant transmit to go *out of service*? T117A Super 1 to

   A. Command Van, requesting a 10/85. K.
   B. Control, requesting a 10/60. K.
   C. Command Van, requesting a 10/61. K.
   D. Control, requesting a 10/61. K.

4. It is a cold, wet winter day. Lt. Wells has been asked to pick up the paychecks for her District at 40 Worth St. and deliver them back to the District Office. When she is on her way back with the checks, she sees Traffic Enforcement Agent Foster, who is in her squad. The agent signals her to stop. The Lieutenant stops her car and asks, *What's the matter?* The agent says, *I'm freezing. Could you please take over this intersection while I warm up?* The Lieutenant studies the intersection and sees that the traffic is very heavy. In this situation, the Lieutenant should 4.____

   A. take over the intersection, let the agent warm up in the car, and give him his check
   B. take over the intersection, let the agent warm up in the car, but say nothing about the paychecks
   C. direct the agent to drive to the District Office to deliver the checks while she covers the intersection
   D. radio the relief agent and have him give the agent a warm-up

5. Lt. Rivers comes upon a busy intersection and finds that there has been a serious three-car accident. While investigating, the Lieutenant finds that one of the passengers is bleeding heavily from a head wound. The Lieutenant radios Control to inform them of the location and nature of the accident. Which of the following should Lt. Rivers advise Control to notify? 5.____

   A. The Police Department and an ambulance
   B. The Assault Squad and the Police Department
   C. An ambulance and the Fire Department
   D. A tow truck, the Police Department, and an ambulance

Question 6.

DIRECTIONS: Question 6 is to be answered on the basis of the form which appears on the following page.

3 (#2)

CITY OF NEW YORK

EMPLOYEE'S NOTICE OF INJURY

(Pursuant to §18 of Workers' Compensation Law)

FORWARD TO: LAW DEPARTMENT, WORKERS' COMPENSATION DIVISION

100 Church Street, New York, N. Y. 10007

(TOGETHER WITH C2 WHEN POSSIBLE)

ANSWER ALL QUESTIONS FULLY. THIS IS YOUR NOTICE TO YOUR EMPLOYER OF INJURY ON THE JOB. PRINT OR WRITE LEGIBLY.

1. Full name of injured person Thomas (First) (Middle) BARTON (Last)
2. Address 16 Pine Grove Avenue, N.Y., 10313

   Employee's S.S. No. 111-11-1111 Date of Birth 9/6/75
3. Name of employer: CITY OF NEW YORK—DEPARTMENT OF TRANSPORTATION
4. Date of accident 5/7/07 Hour 9:15 AM (circled) PM
5. Exact location where accident happened corner of 11th avenue and 8th Street
6. How did accident happen? (describe fully) While I was standing on 8th Street, I was knocked over by a messenger and hurt my arm and leg
7. Nature and extent of injury fracture of right leg and dislocated shoulder
8. Did you inform your superior of this accident? Yes Date? 5/7/07

   Name such person Lt Smith
9. Names and addresses of witnesses Lt. Smith 316 Willow Lane, N.Y. 11919

Dated 5/8 2007

(Sign here) Thomas Barton

THIS IS NOT A CLAIM FORM. A CLAIM FORM MAY BE SECURED AT ANY OFFICE OF THE STATE WORKERS' COMPENSATION BOARD.

6. At 9:15 A.M. on May 7, 2007, while directing traffic at the intersection of 11th Avenue and 8th Street, Traffic Enforcement Agent Thomas Barton was knocked to the ground by a mail messenger on a bicycle. The agent was not seriously hurt, but felt a tingling in his left arm and a shooting pain in his right leg. Lt. Smith, who was across the street at the time, accompanied Agent Barton to Union Hospital. In the Emergency Room, the attending physician told Lt. Smith that Agent Barton had fractured his left elbow and dislocated his right leg when he hit the ground. 6.____

   The following day, while reviewing Agent Barton's Employee's Notice of Injury form (WCD-23), Lt. Smith should notice that there are errors in lines

A. 1, 4, and 9
B. 1, 8, and 9
C. 2, 5, and 8
D. 5, 6, and 7

7. Toward the end of his tour on motorized patrol, Lt. Smith notices that the gas gauge in his vehicle indicates less than half a tank. 7.____
According to department regulations, which of the following should the Lieutenant do?

A. Return the vehicle to the District Office so the supervisor on the next tour can fill the gas tank.
B. Fill the gas tank at the assigned department facility.
C. Call the Staff Lieutenant to report the situation.
D. Fill the gas tank at the nearest service station.

8. While returning to the District Office, Lt. Bavaro observes a down green Mercedes Benz on the Brooklyn-Queens Expressway, ten feet in front of the Brooklyn Bridge ramp. 8.____
According to departmental procedures, what is the MOST appropriate action for Lt. Bavaro to take?
Call

A. Control and give the location and description of the vehicle
B. the Pound and have a tow truck respond to the scene
C. the Bridge Car to respond to the location to assess the situation
D. the Highway Unit to have a car respond

9. Lt. Ambrose is conducting an informal Rap Session with his squad regarding confrontations between Traffic Enforcement Agents and civilians. During the session, two new agents begin arguing about the procedure to follow when a civilian puts his hand on an agent's hand in order to prevent the agent from writing a summons. 9.____
Which of the following is the MOST appropriate action for the Lieutenant to take in this situation?

A. Instruct the agents to go outside if they plan to continue arguing.
B. Take no action since new agents must eventually learn how to handle such incidents on the street.
C. Separate the agents so they won't disrupt the training and write them up after the session.
D. Tell both agents to calm down and ask an experienced squad member to explain how she would handle this situation.

10. Lt. Ortega is preparing a Workmen's Compensation Control form for Traffic Enforcement Agent Sparks, who was recently injured while trying to win a $20 bet. The bet required Agent Sparks to jump over a parking meter. In attempting the jump, the agent slipped and broke his ankle. In the past, Lt. Ortega had warned Agent Sparks several times about similar reckless behavior. In particular, the Lieutenant told him not to accept this bet after hearing about it from the other agents. 10.____
In this situation, Lt. Ortega should endorse the form as a ______ injury; agent ______ be considered for excused time under Workmen' s Compensation.

A. preventable; should not
B. preventable; should
C. non-preventable; should not
D. non-preventable; should

11. Lt. Hampton is reviewing the pink copies of several summonses issued by Traffic Enforcement Agent Grey. She notices that this agent has been repeating the same error when writing summonses for vehicles with out-of-state registrations, placing a line through the registration's *Date Expires* box. When the Lieutenant asks the agent why he crossed out this box, he explains that he did so because the vehicles did not have registration stickers on their windshields. 11.____
The Lieutenant should advise the agent that, for such vehicles, he should

A. issue a second summons for a missing registration
B. write *none* in the registration box
C. place the last day of the present month in the registration *Date Expires* box
D. draw a line through the registration box and write *No Registration Sticker* on top of the summons

12. Traffic Enforcement Agent Hall is unsure of when Leave Request Forms (TCD-105) are required and asks Lt. Caldor for clarification. 12.____
Lt. Caldor should instruct the agent that he is required to submit a TCD-105 when the agent reports back from

A. Criminal Court, along with documentation from the Assault Squad
B. Traffic Court regarding the issuance of a summons
C. Jury Duty, along with a certificate of service
D. Scheduled Leave which was posted on the Annual Vacation Schedule

Question 13.

DIRECTIONS: Question 13 is to be answered on the basis of the following form.

D.O. 101

TO: Thomas B. Doyle, Asst. Commissioner DATE: 5-29-07

FROM: TEA Francis Boyd SUBJECT: Summons Error

When I wrote summons # 67991685-2, I made an error in one of the following: (Please check where applicable)

SECTION I

- [ ] Parking Meter Number
- [ ] Plate Number
- [X] Make, Color, Type of Veh.
- [ ] Place of Occurrence
- [ ] Other ______
- [ ] Date or Time of Preparation
- [ ] Description of Violation
- [ ] Section, Sub-division, Code
- [ ] Plate Type

______ T.E.A. (Signature)

SECTION II

A. [X] I concur that summons # 6791686-1 was issued to the same car. (in duplicate)

______ Lieutenant (Signature)

______ Captain (Signature)

______ Inspector (Signature)

B. [X] No additional summons served.
Comment : conflicting signs

SECTION III

(To be completed at Headquarters)

RECEIVED AT HEADQUARTERS (STAMP & BACK TO D.O.)

BY : TEA Boyd (Signature)

REVIEWED BY : ______ (Signature)

A/C ______ Thomas B. Doyle

SECTION IV

INSTRUCTION: If summons Box A (turnover) is checked, only the Captain signs and forwards direct to Headquarters. If no additional summons served, Box B is checked, Captain and Inspector should investigate, endorse, and forward to Headquarters. Form shall bo prepared and forwarded in duplicate. Second copy will be receipted and returned to Captain from the Headquarters.

13. Traffic Enforcement Agent Boyd submits the form shown above. 13.____
In reviewing the form, Lt. Grey should notice that there are errors in Sections ______, but not ______.

A. I and II; III and IV
B. III and IV; I and II
C. I, II, and III; IV
D. II, III, and IV; I

14. Lt. Chong must report as a witness in a case involving an assault on Traffic Enforcement Agent Steele. Although Lt. Chong's normal tour of duty is from 1:30 P.M. to 9:30 P.M., Monday through Friday, he is informed that the court appearance is scheduled for Tuesday at 9:00 A.M. In this situation, Lt. Chong should 14.____

A. request that the Assault Squad reschedule the court time to coincide with his tour of duty
B. realize that his tour of duty will be changed to enable him *to* appear in court at the assigned time
C. contact the Assault Squad to inform them that he will be unable to appear due to the time of the hearing
D. report to court prior to his tour of duty

15. Captain Hooke asks Lt. Mack to help conduct the summer uniform inspection. Traffic Enforcement Agent Holly fails the inspection because his summer slacks are worn through at the crotch and back hems and, therefore, must be replaced. Agent Holly asks Lt. Mack what he should do to pass the inspection. 15.____
According to department rules and regulations, it would be MOST appropriate for Lt. Mack to direct the agent to

A. have the slacks repaired or bring in another pair of summer slacks or a receipt for their purchase within seven days
B. bring in another pair of summer slacks within ten days
C. bring in another pair of summer slacks or a receipt for their purchase within ten days after the next payday
D. have the slacks repaired temporarily and be sure to get new summer slacks before June 1, when the summer uniform must be worn

16. The Captain has directed Lt. Wilkins to assist in conducting the semi-annual uniform inspection. The Lieutenant notices that Traffic Enforcement Agent Alexander's reefer coat is ripped at the underarm seam. 16.____
According to department rules and regulations, Agent Alexander should be directed to repair the coat

A. by the first work day after payday
B. within ten days
C. within one week
D. immediately after the inspection

17. While reviewing the old listings of agents' drivers licenses, ID cards, and gas cards, Lt. Hall finds that some of the ID cards have expired and some of the drivers licenses would be expiring in a few weeks. 17.____
According to the Department code of conduct, what action should Lt. Hall take?

A. Conduct an unannounced inspection of drivers licenses, ID cards, and gas cards.
B. Schedule a monthly check of licenses, ID cards, and gas cards.
C. Inform the squad that there will be a license and card inspection at tomorrow's Roll Call.
D. Inspect licenses, gas cards, and ID cards at every Roll Call until the matter is resolved.

18. Lt. Howard is preparing a Workmen's Compensation Control form. To complete the form, she must obtain a case number. Between the hours of 8 A.M. - 4 P.M., Monday through Friday, Lt. Howard can get a case number by contacting 18.____

A. the Clerical Unit at headquarters
B. Radio Control
C. the Captain on duty
D. a Police Administrative Aide at the precinct in which the incident occurred

Questions 19-20.

DIRECTIONS: Questions 19 and 20 are to be answered on the basis of the form appearing on the following page..

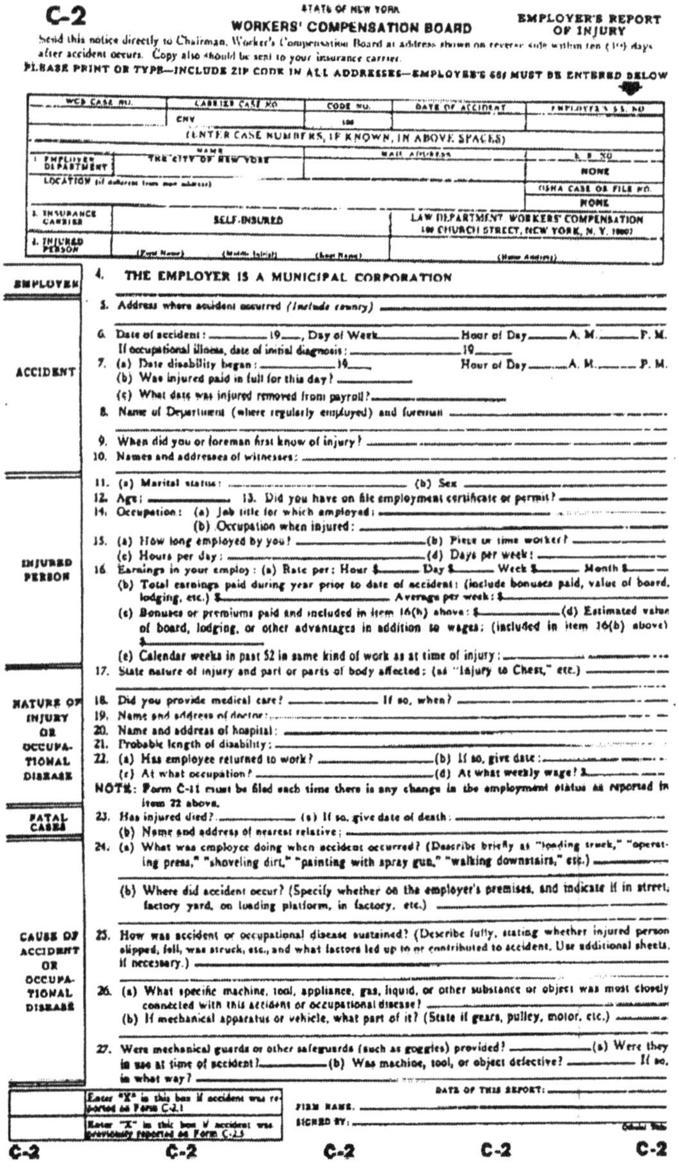

C-2

STATE OF NEW YORK
WORKERS' COMPENSATION BOARD

EMPLOYER'S REPORT OF INJURY

Send this notice directly to Chairman, Worker's Compensation Board at address shown on reverse side within ten (10) days after accident occurs. Copy also should be sent to your insurance carrier.

PLEASE PRINT OR TYPE—INCLUDE ZIP CODE IN ALL ADDRESSES—EMPLOYER'S 68# MUST BE ENTERED BELOW

WCB CASE NO.	CARRIER CASE NO	CODE NO.	DATE OF ACCIDENT	EMPLOYER'S S.S. NO
	CNY	100		

(ENTER CASE NUMBERS, IF KNOWN, IN ABOVE SPACES)

	NAME	MAIL ADDRESS	S. S. NO
1. EMPLOYER DEPARTMENT	THE CITY OF NEW YORK		NONE
LOCATION (if different from mail address)			OSHA CASE OR FILE NO.
			NONE
2. INSURANCE CARRIER	SELF-INSURED	LAW DEPARTMENT WORKERS' COMPENSATION 100 CHURCH STREET, NEW YORK, N. Y. 10007	
3. INJURED PERSON	(First Name) (Middle Initial) (Last Name)	(Home Address)	

EMPLOYER

4. THE EMPLOYER IS A MUNICIPAL CORPORATION

ACCIDENT

5. Address where accident occurred (*Include county*) ____
6. Date of accident: ____ 19__, Day of Week ____ Hour of Day ____ A. M. ____ P. M.
If occupational illness, date of initial diagnosis: ____ 19__
7. (a) Date disability began: ____ 19__ Hour of Day ____ A. M. ____ P. M.
(b) Was injured paid in full for this day? ____
(c) What date was injured removed from payroll? ____
8. Name of Department (where regularly employed) and foreman ____
9. When did you or foreman first know of injury? ____
10. Names and addresses of witnesses: ____

INJURED PERSON

11. (a) Marital status: ____ (b) Sex ____
12. Age: ____ 13. Did you have on file employment certificate or permit? ____
14. Occupation: (a) Job title for which employed: ____
(b) Occupation when injured: ____
15. (a) How long employed by you? ____ (b) Piece or time worker? ____
(c) Hours per day: ____ (d) Days per week: ____
16. Earnings in your employ: (a) Rate per: Hour $____ Day $____ Week $____ Month $____
(b) Total earnings paid during year prior to date of accident: (include bonuses paid, value of board, lodging, etc.) $____ Average per week: $____
(c) Bonuses or premiums paid and included in item 16(b) above: $____ (d) Estimated value of board, lodging, or other advantages in addition to wages: (included in item 16(b) above) $____
(e) Calendar weeks in past 52 in same kind of work as at time of injury: ____

NATURE OF INJURY OR OCCUPATIONAL DISEASE

17. State nature of injury and part or parts of body affected: (as "Injury to Chest," etc.) ____
18. Did you provide medical care? ____ If so, when? ____
19. Name and address of doctor: ____
20. Name and address of hospital: ____
21. Probable length of disability: ____
22. (a) Has employee returned to work? ____ (b) If so, give date: ____
(c) At what occupation? ____ (d) At what weekly wage? $____
NOTE: Form C-11 must be filed each time there is any change in the employment status as reported in item 22 above.

FATAL CASES

23. Has injured died? ____ (a) If so, give date of death: ____
(b) Name and address of nearest relative: ____

CAUSE OF ACCIDENT OR OCCUPATIONAL DISEASE

24. (a) What was employee doing when accident occurred? (Describe briefly as "loading truck," "operating press," "shoveling dirt," "painting with spray gun," "walking downstairs," etc.) ____
(b) Where did accident occur? (Specify whether on the employer's premises, and indicate if in street, factory yard, on loading platform, in factory, etc.) ____
25. How was accident or occupational disease sustained? (Describe fully, stating whether injured person slipped, fell, was struck, etc., and what factors led up to or contributed to accident. Use additional sheets, if necessary.) ____
26. (a) What specific machine, tool, appliance, gas, liquid, or other substance or object was most closely connected with this accident or occupational disease? ____
(b) If mechanical apparatus or vehicle, what part of it? (State if gears, pulley, motor, etc.) ____
27. Were mechanical guards or other safeguards (such as goggles) provided? ____ (a) Were they in use at time of accident? ____ (b) Was machine, tool, or object defective? ____ If so, in what way? ____

	Enter "X" in this box if accident was reported on Form C-2.1
	Enter "X" in this box if accident was previously reported on Form C-2.3

DATE OF THIS REPORT: ____
FIRM NAME. ____
SIGNED BY: ____ Official Title

C-2 C-2 C-2 C-2 C-2

19. Lt. Stabille is completing an Employer's Report of Injury form for Traffic Enforcement Agent Mills, who was injured on duty. A copy of this form is provided on the previous page.
When completing Line 15b, the Lieutenant should enter 19.____

A. salary B. piece C. time D. exempt

20. Lt. Billings is completing an Employer's Report of Injury form for Traffic Enforcement Agent Luna, a Level III Agent who used to write summonses and is newly assigned to tow duty. A copy of this form has been provided on the previous page. When she reaches Line 14a, the Lieutenant is not sure what to write, so she asks the Captain. The Captain replies, *You should put in the job title for which the agent was first hired.*
Therefore, the CORRECT entry at Line 14a would be 20.____

A. Traffic Enforcement Agent I
B. Traffic Enforcement Agent III
C. Tow Truck Operator
D. Probationary Agent Trainee

21. Lt. Howard is reviewing a Motor Vehicle Accident Report prepared by Traffic Enforcement Agent Benson, who was involved in a traffic accident earlier in the day. As Agent Benson was traveling southbound on Cherry Street, he was struck by a private vehicle which went through a stop sign while heading east on Ventura Place.
Which one of the following diagrams should be checked off as an ACCURATE description of the accident? 21.____

A. Rear End

B. Head On

C. Intersection

D. Intersection

Question 22.

DIRECTIONS: Question 22 is to be answered on the basis of the following form.

Election of Rate Of Charge Against Annual and/or Sick Leave Balances for Absence Due To Injury Sustained in the Performance of Official Duties

(Pursuant to Regulation 7.0 of the Leave Regulations for employees who are under the Career and Salary Plan)

> *INSTRUCTIONS: The injured employee, or an authorized person acting in his behalf, should submit this election notice (in duplicate) to the head of his department or agency within the first seven calendar days of absence due to injury sustained in the performance of official duties.*

I, JANE WILLIS (Print name of injured employee), employed in DEPT. OF TRANSPORTATION (Print name of city department or agency) in a position which is subject to the Leave Regulations for employees who are under the Career and Salary Plan, or my authorized agent, do hereby elect the option designated below, subject to the conditions attached thereto, as the one to be applied in determining the charge, if any, to be made against my annual and/or sick leave balances for absence due to injury sustained in the performance of my official duties.

(Check one option only)

☑ OPTION 1: I elect to receive the difference between the amount of my weekly salary and the compensation rate, subject to the following conditions:

(a) A pro-rated charge shall be made against my sick leave and/or annual leave balances equal to the number of working days of absence less the number of working days represented by the Worker's Compensation payments, and,

(b) My accrued sick leave and/or annual leave balances, or such leave credits advanced to me in accordance with the Career and Salary Plan Leave Regulations, are adequate to meet the charges made against them for supplementary pay, and;

(c) The injury sustained by me was not the result of my willful gross disobedience of safety rules or my willful failure to use a safety device, nor was I under the influence of alcohol or narcotics at the time of injury, nor did I willfully intend to bring about injury or death upon myself or another, and;

(d) Such medical examinations will be undergone by me as are requested by the Worker's Compensation Division of the Law Department and my agency, and when found fit for duty by said physicians, I shall return to my employment.

☐ OPTION 2: I elect to receive Worker's Compensation benefits in their entirety with no charge against sick and/or annual leave.

Employing Department should forward duplicate copy to Worker's Compensation Division of Law Department

Injured employee's signature	Jane Willis	Date: 9/3/07
This shaded section should be completed only if the injured employee cannot sign and must designate an authorized person to sign in his behalf	Authorized designee's name (print): WILLIAM WILLIS	Relationship to injured employee: SPOUSE
	Authorized designee's address: 123 GREBE STREET	
	BROOKLYN, N.Y.	
	Authorized designee's signature: William Willis	Date: 9/3/07
	Witness's name (print):	
	Witness's address:	
	Witness's signature:	Date:

22. Traffic Control Agent Jane Willis suffered a broken leg when she was hit by a bus while directing traffic. Lt. Bream is reviewing the Employee's Option form which was prepared in connection with this incident. Agent Willis has told the Lieutenant that she wishes to receive her paychecks by charging her absence against her sick leave and annual leave. In reviewing the form, Lt. Bream notices an error. Which of the following CORRECTLY describes this error? 22.___

A. Since the injury was not the result of an assault, Agent Willis should have chosen *Option 2.*
B. A witness's signature is required before the form can be processed.
C. The shaded section of the form should not have been completed.
D. In order to use sick and annual leaves, Agent Willis should have chosen *Option 2.*

Question 23.

DIRECTIONS: Question 23 is to be answered on the basis of the following forms.

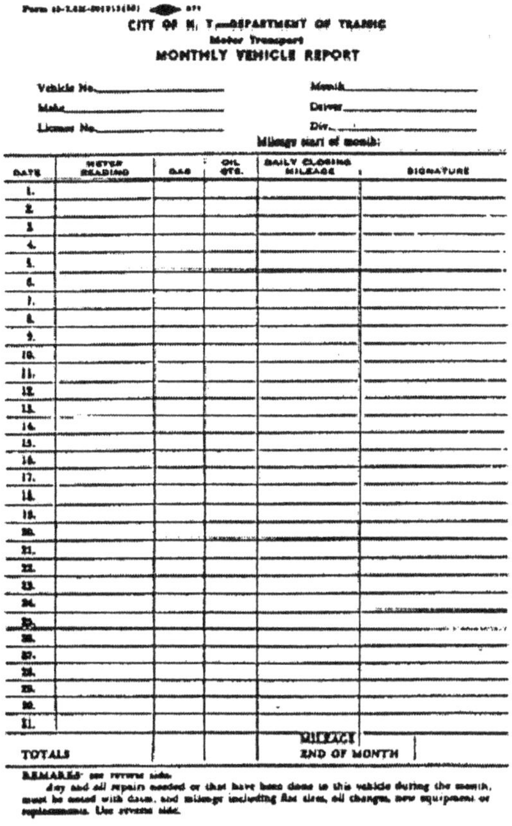

CITY OF N. Y.—DEPARTMENT OF TRAFFIC
Motor Transport
MONTHLY VEHICLE REPORT

Vehicle No. ______ Month ______
Make ______ Driver ______
License No. ______ Div. ______
Mileage start of month:

DATE	METER READING	GAS	OIL ETC.	DAILY CLOSING MILEAGE	SIGNATURE
1.					
2.					
3.					
4.					
5.					
6.					
7.					
8.					
9.					
10.					
11.					
12.					
13.					
14.					
15.					
16.					
17.					
18.					
19.					
20.					
21.					
22.					
23.					
24.					
25.					
26.					
27.					
28.					
29.					
30.					
31.					
TOTALS				MILEAGE END OF MONTH	

REMARKS: see reverse side.

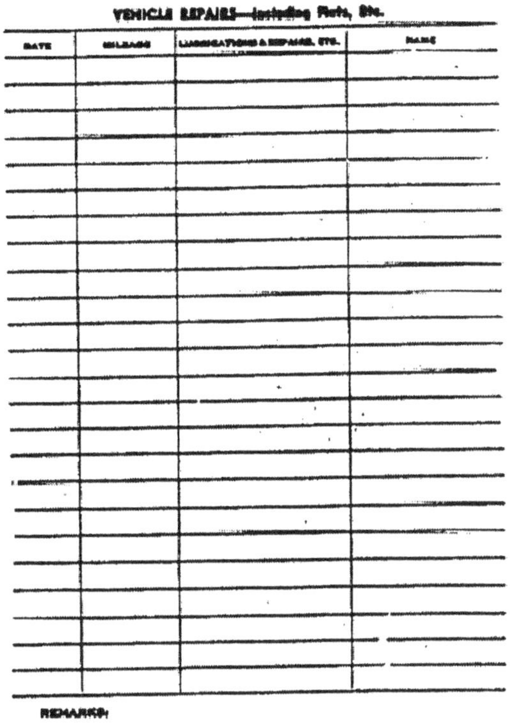

VEHICLE REPAIRS—including Flats, Etc.

DATE	MILEAGE	LUBRICATIONS & REPAIRS, ETC.	NAME

REMARKS:

23. Lt. Doris Early is preparing her Motor Transport Monthly Vehicle Report for a vehicle that is used by both herself and Lt. Ray Stefano, who works on a later tour. 23.____
Which of the following statements regarding the preparation of this form is TRUE?

A. Lt. Early and Lt. Stefano should maintain their own separate Monthly Vehicle Report cards.
B. Monthly totals for gas, oil, and mileage must be calculated and entered.
C. Daily average mileage must be calculated at the end of the month.
D. Lt. Early should make entries in the *Daily Closing Mileage* column, and Lt. Stefano should make entries in the *Meter Reading* column.

KEY (CORRECT ANSWERS)

1. C
2. C
3. C
4. D
5. A
6. D
7. B
8. A
9. D
10. A
11. B
12. C
13. D
14. B
15. C
16. D
17. A
18. A
19. C
20. A
21. D
22. C
23. B

EXAMINATION SECTION
TEST 1

DIRECTIONS: Each question or incomplete statement is followed by several suggested answers or completions. Select the one that BEST answers the question or completes the statement. *PRINT THE LETTER OF THE CORRECT ANSWER IN THE SPACE AT THE RIGHT.*

Questions 1-3.

DIRECTIONS: Questions 1 through 3 are to be answered SOLELY on the basis of the following map and information.

The flow of traffic is indicated by the arrows. If there is only one arrow shown, then traffic flows only in the direction indicated by the arrow. If there are two arrows, then traffic flows in both directions. You must follow the flow of traffic.

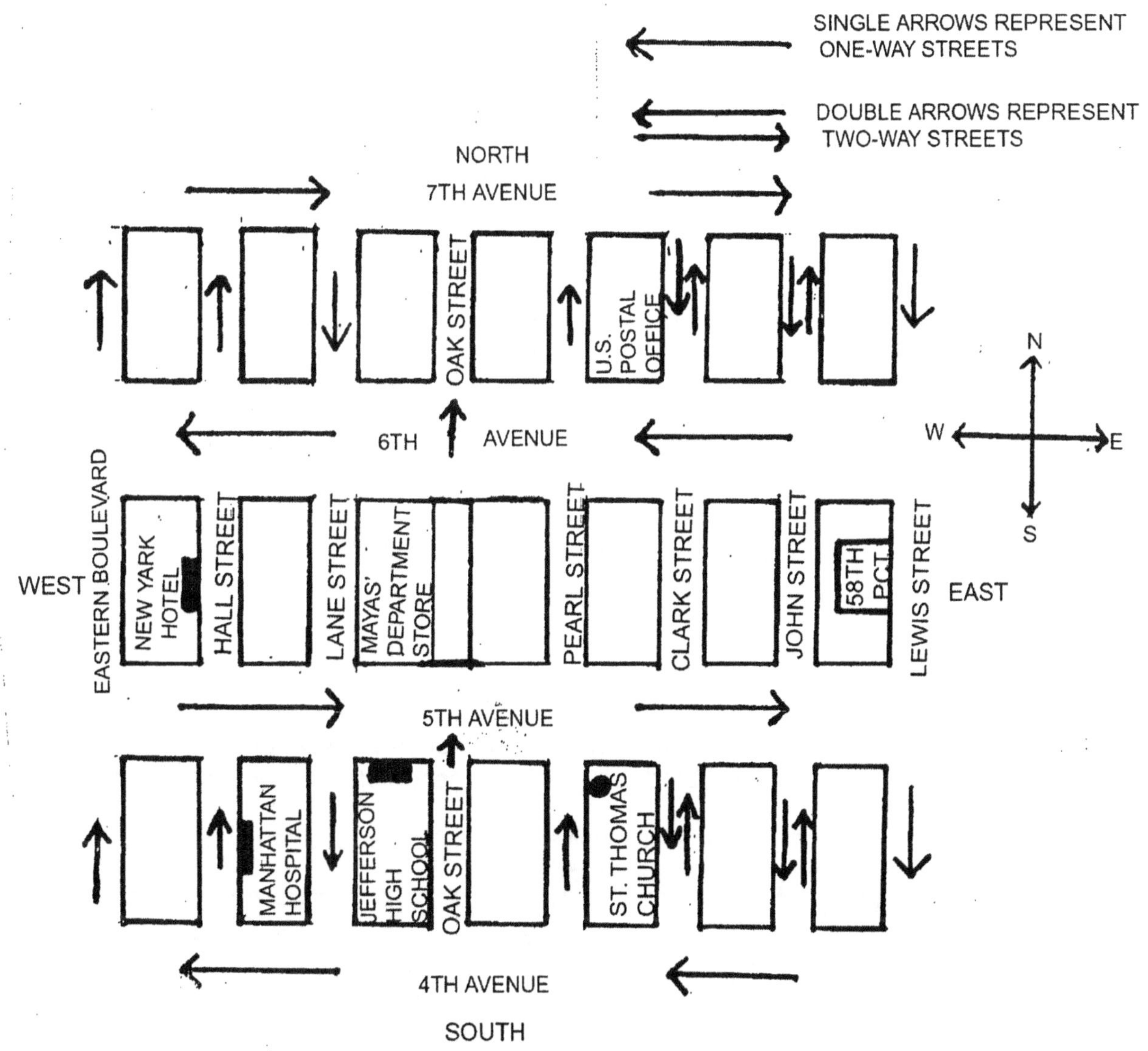

1. Traffic Enforcement Agent Fox was on foot patrol at John Street between 6th & 7th Avenues when a motorist driving southbound asked her for directions to the New York Hotel, which is located on Hall Street between 5th & 6th Avenues Which one of the following is the SHORTEST route for Agent Fox to direct the motorist to take, making sure to obey all traffic regulations? 1.____
Travel ______to the New York Hotel.

   A. north on John Street, then east on 7th Avenue, then north on Lewis Street, then west on 4th Avenue, then north on Eastern Boulevard, then east on 5th Avenue, then north on Hall Street
   B. south on John Street, then west on 6th Avenue, then south on Eastern Boulevard, then east on 5th Avenue, then north on Hall Street
   C. south on John Street, then west on 6th Avenue, then south on Clark Street, then east on 4th Avenue, then north on Eastern Boulevard, then east on 5th Avenue, then north on Hall Street
   D. south on John Street, then west on 4th Avenue, then north on Hall Street

2. Traffic Enforcement Agent Murphy is on motorized patrol on 7th Avenue between Oak Street and Pearl Street when Lt. Robertson radios him to go to Jefferson High School, located on 5th Avenue between Lane Street & Oak Street. Which one of the following is the SHORTEST route for Agent Murphy to take, making sure to obey all the traffic regulations? 2.____
Travel east on 7th Avenue, then south on ______, then east on 5th Avenue to Jefferson High School.

   A. Clark Street, then west on 4th Avenue, then north on Hall Street
   B. Pearl Street, then west on 4th Avenue, then north on Lane Street
   C. Lewis Street, then west on 6th Avenue, then south on Hall Street
   D. Lewis Street, then west on 4th Avenue, then north on Oak Street

3. Traffic Enforcement Agent Vasquez was on 4th Avenue and Eastern Boulevard when a motorist asked him for directions to the 58th Police Precinct, which is located on Lewis Street between 5th & 6th Avenues. 3.____
Which one of the following is the SHORTEST route for Agent Vasquez to direct the motorist to take, making sure to obey all traffic regulations?
Travel north on Eastern Boulevard, then east on ______ on Lewis Street to the 58th Police Precinct.

   A. 5th Avenue, then north
   B. 7th Avenue, then south
   C. 6th Avenue, then north on Pearl Street, then east on 7th Avenue, then south
   D. 5th Avenue, then north on Clark Street, then east on 6th Avenue, then south

4. Traffic Enforcement Agent Mason was involved in a vehicular accident while on patrol. The following information relates to this accident: 4.____

Date of Accident:	March 3
Time of Accident:	3:45 P.M.
Damage to Traffic Vehicle #344:	Dented front fender
Driver of Other Vehicle:	Cindy Wasserman
Other Vehicle:	Gray Honda

Agent Mason is preparing a report on the accident.
Which one of the following expresses the above information MOST clearly and accurately?

A. At 3:45 P.M., a gray Honda and traffic car #344 collided causing dents on the front fender. Cindy Wasserman drove a car on March 3.
B. The other vehicle was a gray Honda and on March 3 at 3:45 P.M. dents on the front fender were caused by a collision between traffic car #344 and Cindy Wasserman.
C. There were dents on the front fender because on March 3 Cindy Wasserman drove a gray Honda at 3:45 P.M.
D. It was March 3 at 3:45 P.M. when a collision occurred between a gray Honda, driven by Cindy Wasserman, and traffic car #344. Car #344 suffered dents on the front fender.

5. Traffic Enforcement Agent Tonelli is working at an intersection when he observes the following: 5.____

Condition:	Disabled Vehicle
Location:	41st Street exit of the Brooklyn-Queens Expressway
Lane Affected:	Southbound middle lane
Type of Vehicle:	Red Buick
License Plate Number:	689-BCZ
Assistance Needed:	Tow truck

Agent Tonelli is about to radio Traffic Control with this information.
Which one of the following expresses the above information MOST clearly and accurately?

A. A tow truck, license plate number 689-BCZ, is needed in the southbound middle lane of the Brooklyn-Queens Expressway at the 41st Street exit. A red Buick is disabled.
B. At the 41st Street exit of the Brooklyn-Queens Expressway, a red Buick, license plate number 689-BCZ, is disabled in the southbound middle lane and a tow truck is needed.
C. A disabled vehicle requires a tow truck in the southbound middle lane. A red Buick, license plate number 689-BCZ, is at the 41st Street exit of the Brooklyn-Queens Expressway.
D. The 41st Street exit of the Brooklyn-Queens Expressway requires a tow truck. In the southbound middle lane there is a red Buick. The disabled vehicle's license plate number is 689-BCZ.

Question 6.

DIRECTIONS: Question 6 is to be answered SOLELY on the basis of the following information.

When dealing with vehicles with Board of Education parking permits, Traffic Enforcement Agents should:

1. Issue a summons to all vehicles parked in areas covered by a *No Parking 7:00 A.M. - 5:00 P.M. School Days* sign, even if they display a Board of Education parking permit.
2. Allow vehicles with Board of Education permits to park in areas covered by a *No Parking 7:00 A.M. - 5:00 P.M. Except Board of Education* sign.

6. On Wednesday, October 10 at 5:15 P.M., Traffic Enforcement Agent Smith is on patrol in front of Public School 24 where a car is parked in a *No Parking 7:00 A.M. -5:00 P.M. School Days* zone. The car has a Board of Education parking permit in the front windshield. Agent Smith sees the permit and proceeds to issue a summons. In this situation, the action taken by Agent Smith was 6.____

A. *proper,* primarily because the car was parked in front of the school on a school day
B. *improper,* primarily because the car was legally parked
C. *proper,* primarily because the car was parked illegally
D. *improper,* primarily because there was a Board of Education permit displayed in the car window

7. Traffic Enforcement Agents begin their daily patrol by taking at least 75 new blank summonses out into the field with them. However, agents may issue more or less than 75 summonses per day. Below is a list of the number of summonses Agent Wilson took out into the field with him at the start of his patrol and the number of summonses he had issued by the end of his patrol. 7.____

Day	Blank Summonses At Start of Patrol	Summonses Issued by the end of Patrol
Monday	75	65
Tuesday	75	70
Wednesday	100	90

Agent Wilson needs to know the total number of summonses he has left, that is, the total number of summonses he has not issued, following his Monday-Wednesday patrol. Which one of the following formulas should he use?

A. (65+70+90) - (75+75+100)
B. (75+65) - (75+70) - (100+90)
C. (75+75+100) - (65+70+90)
D. (75-65) + (75-70) + (100+90)

8. Traffic Enforcement Agent Dunn was on patrol when he observed the following: 8.____

Violation: Parked by a fire hydrant
Location: 263 E. 54th Street
Vehicle Year and Model: 2008 Black Ford Taurus
License Plate Number: YYJ-134
Assistance Required: Tow truck

Agent Dunn is about to radio this information to Traffic Control. Which one of the following expresses the above information MOST clearly and accurately?

A. A tow truck is required by a fire hydrant at 263 E. 54th Street. A black Ford Taurus, license plate number YYJ-134 is parked.
B. A tow truck, license plate number YYJ-134, is required at 263 E. 54th Street. A black Ford Taurus is parked by a fire hydrant.
C. License plate number YYJ-134 is parked by a fire hydrant and a tow truck is required. A black Ford Taurus is at 263 E. 54th Street.
D. A black Ford Taurus, license plate number YYJ-134, is parked by a fire hydrant at 263 E. 54th Street. A tow truck is required.

Question 9.

DIRECTIONS: Question 9 is to be answered SOLELY on the basis of the following information.

If anyone offers an agent money or anything else of value to not write a summons or perform the agent's duty, the agent should do the following in the order given:

1. Ask for the person's drivers license.
2. Check the vehicle registration.
3. Call a supervisor.
4. Request the Police and the Assault Investigation Squad to respond.

9. On February 17, Traffic Enforcement Agent Soto was on foot patrol when he observed a vehicle parked in a bus stop. 9.____
As Agent Soto started to prepare a summons for this violation, the operator of the vehicle appeared on the scene. The operator offered to give Agent Soto ten dollars if the agent did not issue him a summons for this violation. In this situation, Agent Soto should NEXT

A. call for a supervisor to respond to the scene
B. ask the operator of the vehicle for his drivers license
C. request the Police and the Assault Investigation Squad to respond to the scene
D. check the registration of the vehicle

Questions 10-12.

DIRECTIONS: Questions 10 through 12 are to be answered SOLELY on the basis of the following passage.

Traffic Enforcement Agents Miner and LaBatt are assigned to direct traffic at the intersection of 181st Street and Broadway. While directing traffic, Agent LaBatt is informed by a motorist that there is a brown Ford Escort partially blocking the 181st Street exit of the Cross Bronx Expressway. While Agent LaBatt proceeds to investigate this report, Agent Miner radios Traffic Control and informs Traffic Lieutenant Wesley that Agent LaBatt has left the intersection in order to investigate the motorist's report.

When Agent LaBatt arrives at the scene, he sees the reported vehicle partially blocking the 181st Street exit ramp. Agent LaBatt inspects the vehicle and discovers that the right front fender is missing and the left rear fender is dented. Upon further inspection, he finds that the license plates are missing, as well as the car's registration sticker. Agent LaBatt, believing that the car is abandoned, follows the procedures for an abandoned vehicle by writing his District Office number and the date and time on both rear fenders. Agent LaBatt also believes that the vehicle creates a hazard to safe traffic flow. He radios Traffic Control with this information and informs Lt. Wesley that a tow truck will be necessary. Lt. Wesley instructs Agent LaBatt to remain with the vehicle and direct exiting traffic off the expressway until the tow truck arrives.

10. The vehicle blocking the exit was missing its 10.____

A. left rear fender, front license plate, and car registration sticker
B. right rear fender, left rear fender, and license plates
C. right front fender, license plates, and car registration sticker
D. left front fender, rear license plate, and car registration sticker

11. Agent LaBatt was directed to remain with the vehicle 11.____

A. to prevent the vehicle from being stripped
B. so the tow truck driver would know where to go
C. because traffic at 181st Street and Broadway was light
D. to direct traffic off the expressway

12. What are the procedures to be followed regarding an abandoned vehicle? 12.____
Write the date, time,

A. and the District Office number on the left and right rear fenders
B. District Office number and registration sticker number on both rear fenders
C. and the District Office number on both front fenders
D. the District Office number, and the license plate number on both front fenders

13. Traffic Enforcement Agent Jackson begins his patrol with 3 packages of summonses. 13.____
Each package contains 25 summonses. At the end of the work day, Agent Jackson returns with 1 package of summonses.
How many summonses did he issue?

A. 25 B. 35 C. 50 D. 75

Question 14.

DIRECTIONS: Question 14 is to be answered SOLELY on the basis of the following information.

When driving a Department of Transportation vehicle, a Traffic Enforcement Agent is strictly prohibited from committing any of the following violations, regardless of the circumstances:

1. Driving in the opposite direction of traffic
2. Backing their vehicle into an intersection
3. Passing through stop signs or signal lights
4. Making illegal turns
5. Speeding
6. Making unsafe lane changes
7. Entering the flow of traffic from the curb lane safely
8. Interfering with traffic by driving slowly

14. Traffic Enforcement Agent Sloan has just reviewed the above regulations. Before going out on patrol, Agent Sloan is instructed by Lieutenant Smith to immediately issue a summons for any double parking violation he observes. While on patrol, Agent Sloan notices a double-parked car on a westbound one-way street. Agent Sloan decides to walk up the block to the car and issue a summons. However, before he reaches the car, he sees the driver enter the vehicle. Fearing that the motorist will leave the scene before a summons can be issued for the violation, Agent Sloan gets back in his car and drives eastbound on the street in order to block the vehicle's path. 14.____
In this situation, the actions taken by the agent were

   A. *proper,* primarily because Lt. Smith instructed the agent to issue summonses to double-parked vehicles
   B. *improper,* primarily because the motorist moved his vehicle before the agent began to prepare a summons
   C. *proper,* primarily because the double-parked vehicle was interfering with the flow of traffic
   D. *improper,* primarily because the agent committed a violation of a traffic regulation

15. Traffic Enforcement Agent Phillips began his day with 5 packages of unused summonses. Each package contains 25 summonses. At the end of the day, Agent Phillips has 9 unused summonses. Agent Phillips has to tell his supervisor how many summonses he used that day. 15.____
Which one of the following formulas should Agent Phillips use to calculate how many summonses he issued?

   A. (25-9) x 5
   B. (5x25) - 9
   C. (25-9)/5
   D. (5x25) + 9

16. Traffic Enforcement Agent Williams is about to testify in court. The following information was recorded: 16.____

Date of Occurrence:	January 18
Time of Occurrence:	4:20 P.M.
Place of Occurrence:	Madison Avenue & 48th Street
Motorist's Name:	Joan Armstrong
Vehicle:	2007 Chevrolet
Violation:	Driving in a bus lane
Action Taken:	Summons issued

Agent Williams needs to be clear and accurate when testifying.
Which one of the following expresses the above information MOST clearly and accurately?

   A. On January 18, I issued a summons to Joan Armstrong for driving a 2007 Chevrolet in a bus lane on Madison Avenue and 48th Street at 4:20 P.M.
   B. On January 18, I issued Joan Armstrong a summons while driving in a bus lane on Madison Avenue and 48th Street, it was 4:20 P.M. and she was driving a 2007 Chevrolet.
   C. In a bus lane on Madison Avenue and 48th Street, I issued Joan Armstrong a summons for driving a 2007 Chevrolet on January 18 at 4:20 P.M.
   D. It was 4:20 P.M. when a 2007 Chevrolet drove in a bus lane on Madison Avenue and 48th Street. Joan Armstrong was issued a summons on January 18.

17. Traffic Enforcement Agents Cuff and O'Mara were directing traffic when Agent O'Mara was struck by a vehicle that then left the scene. The following information relates to this incident: 17.____

Incident:	Hit and run of Agent O'Mara
Place of Occurrence:	Intersection of Isham Street and Broadway
Time of Occurrence:	3:45 P.M.
Date of Occurrence:	July 9th
Description of Motorist:	Hispanic female; blonde hair
Description of Vehicle:	BMW sedan

Agent Cuff is testifying in Criminal Court about this incident.
Which one of the following expresses the above information MOST clearly and accurately?

A. On July 9th, Agent O'Mara was struck by an Hispanic female with blonde hair. She drove a BMW sedan at 3:45 P.M. at the intersection of Isham Street and Broadway.
B. On July 9th at 3:45 P.M., Agent O'Mara was struck by a BMW sedan at the intersection of Isham Street and Broadway. The driver of the vehicle was a Hispanic female with blonde hair.
C. At the intersection of Broadway and Isham Street, Agent O'Mara was struck at 3:45 P.M. A Hispanic female with blonde hair drove a BMW sedan on July 9th.
D. A BMW sedan was driven by a blonde haired Hispanic female at 3:45 P.M. On July 9th, Agent O'Mara was struck at the intersection of Isham Street and Broadway.

Questions 18-20.

DIRECTIONS: Questions 18 through 20 are to be answered SOLELY on the basis of the following passage.

Traffic Lieutenant Seaver informs Traffic Enforcement Agent Roberts that his assignment for the day is to direct traffic at the intersection of 72nd Street and Madison Avenue. At 11:30 A.M., Agent Roberts observes that the westbound lane at the corner of 120 E. 72nd Street is crumbling and water is pouring out of a huge crack in the street. Mrs. Perry, a resident at 140 E. 72nd Street is looking out her window at the time and immediately dials 911 to report the incident. Agent Roberts radios Traffic Control and informs them of the situation. He requests additional agents to respond to the scene. Traffic Control informs Agent Roberts that they will contact the appropriate utilities and city agencies. However, Agent Roberts is told that, until additional agents arrive, he should handle the situation. Fortunately for Agent Roberts, Mrs. Perry's call to 911 brought Police Officers Monroe and Lanier to the scene at 11:35 A.M. Since the crack is located in the westbound lane at 72nd Street and Madison Avenue, Police Officer Monroe proceeds to 72nd Street and 5th Avenue in order to divert westbound traffic before it reaches Madison Avenue. Police Officer Lanier proceeds to 71st Street and Madison Avenue to divert northbound traffic, while Agent Roberts diverts eastbound traffic at the 72nd Street and Madison Avenue intersection.

18. Police Officers Monroe and Lanier arrived at the scene at 18.____

A. 11:00 P.M.
B. 11:15 A.M.
C. 11:30 P.M.
D. 11:35 A.M.

19. Who diverted traffic at 71st Street and Madison Avenue? 19.____

A. Traffic Agent Roberts
B. Police Officer Lanier
C. Lieutenant Seaver
D. Police Officer Monroe

20. The water is pouring out of the street at the corner of 20.____

A. 120 W. 72nd
B. 140 E. 72nd
C. 120 E. 72nd
D. 140 W. 72nd

KEY (CORRECT ANSWERS)

1.	D	11.	D
2.	A	12.	A
3.	B	13.	C
4.	D	14.	D
5.	B	15.	B
6.	B	16.	A
7.	C	17.	B
8.	D	18.	D
9.	B	19.	B
10.	C	20.	C

TEST 2

DIRECTIONS: Each question or incomplete statement is followed by several suggested answers or completions. Select the one that BEST answers the question or completes the statement. *PRINT THE LETTER OF THE CORRECT ANSWER IN THE SPACE AT THE RIGHT.*

Question 1.

DIRECTIONS: Question 1 is to be answered SOLELY on the basis of the following information.

According to the Department of Transportation's Rules and Regulations, a *sitter* is a motorist who parks a vehicle in violation of a parking regulation and then remains or has a passenger remain in the vehicle. A summons may be issued without warning for a parking violation even if someone is sitting in the vehicle at the time of the violation.

1. Traffic Enforcement Agent Overton is on patrol when he sees a double-parked car. Agent Overton approaches the car and informs Ms. Ruiz, the occupant, that she must move the car or he will have to issue a summons for the violation. Ms. Ruiz informs Agent Overton that she is not the driver of the car. However, she assures Agent Overton that the driver will be back shortly. Agent Overton proceeds to issue a summons. In this situation, the actions taken by the agent were 1.____

   A. *proper,* primarily because he warned Ms. Ruiz before issuing a summons
   B. *improper,* primarily because Ms. Ruiz informed the agent she was not the driver of the vehicle
   C. *proper,* primarily because the vehicle was parked illegally
   D. *improper,* primarily because the agent did not wait for the driver to return and move the car

Question 2.

DIRECTIONS: Question 2 is to be answered SOLELY on the basis of the following information.

When a Traffic Enforcement Agent issues a summons for a moving violation (which is an offense that occurs when the vehicle is in motion), the agent should do the following in the order given:

1. Request the motorist's license and registration.
2. Advise the motorist of the type of violation committed.
3. Issue the summons.
4. Return the license and registration to the motorist.
5. Inform the motorist of the court date.
6. Return to assigned post.

2. Traffic Enforcement Agent Butler is directing traffic at an intersection when Bill Lee drives through the intersection ignoring the agent's hand signal directing the motorist to stop. Agent Butler blows his whistle in order to get Mr. Lee's attention and directs him to pull his car over to the side of the street. Agent Butler asks Mr. Lee for his license and registration and then informs Mr. Lee that he committed a moving violation by continuing to drive past the agent after he signaled him to stop. Agent Butler then issues Mr. Lee a summons. 2.____
The NEXT step Agent Butler should take is to

A. give back Mr. Lee's registration and license
B. return to the intersection
C. request Mr. Lee's license and registration
D. inform Mr. Lee of when he is to appear in court

3. Traffic Enforcement Agents are often asked by members of the public to radio for the police. It is up to the agent to determine if a situation actually requires police assistance. In which one of the following situations would it be MOST appropriate for an agent to notify the police? 3.____

A. Mr. Nicks tells Agent Jerrian he was just robbed.
B. Ms. Clay tells Agent Zelig that she saw another Traffic Enforcement Agent leave a liquor store.
C. Mr. Yee informs Agent Stewart that his car will not start.
D. Agent Castellano sees a suspicious looking man walking out of a bank.

4. Traffic Enforcement Agent Michaels is assigned to an intersection where workmen are repairing the street. He obtains the following information: 4.____

Name of Utility:	Consolidated Union
Location:	Intersection of 207th Street and Miles Avenue
Lanes Closed by Utility:	Westbound lane of 207th Street
Traffic Condition:	Slow moving traffic
Permit Number:	P576201

Agent Michaels is about to radio Traffic Control for a check of the permit number and to report the traffic condition.
Which one of the following expresses the above information MOST clearly and accurately?

A. Slow moving traffic has caused the closing of the westbound lane of 207th Street. Consolidated Union is working at the intersection of 207th Street and Miles Avenue. I request a check of permit number P576201.
B. P576201 is the permit number I request to be checked. At the intersection of 207th Street and Miles Avenue, there is slow moving traffic in the closed westbound lane of 207th Street. Consolidated Union closed it down.
C. Consolidated Union is working at the intersection of 207th Street and Miles Avenue. They have closed the westbound lane of 207th Street, and this has caused a slow moving traffic condition. I request that you check their permit number which is P576201.
D. Consolidated Union's permit number is P576201. At the intersection of 207th Street and Miles Avenue, there is a slow moving traffic condition because the westbound lane of 207th Street is closed. I request you check their permit number.

5. Traffic Enforcement Agent James' patrol vehicle was damaged while he was on patrol in the vehicle. The following facts are related to this incident: 5.____

Car Number:	829
Damage:	Broken rear axle
Cause of Damage:	Drove over a pothole
Date of Occurrence:	February 1
Place of Occurrence:	49th Street and 11th Avenue
Time of Occurrence:	4:20 P.M.

Agent James is preparing a report on the incident. Which one of the following expresses the above information MOST clearly and accurately?

A. The car broke its rear axle on a pothole at 49th Street and 11th Avenue. I drove car 829 on February 1 at 4:20 P.M.
B. It was 4:20 P.M. when on a pothole a broken rear axle occurred. On February 1 on 49th Street and 11th Avenue I drove car 829.
C. On February 1, I drove car 829 over a pothole breaking the car's rear axle. This occurred on 49th Street and 11th Avenue.
D. It was 4:20 P.M. when car 829 broke its rear axle. On 49th Street and 11th Avenue there was a pothole on February 1.

Question 6.

DIRECTIONS: Question 6 is to be answered SOLELY on the basis of the following information.

Before issuing a summons for a double-parked vehicle, a Traffic Enforcement Agent should do the following in the order given:

1. Check if a summons was already issued.
2. Check the license plate number.
3. Determine the vehicle type.
4. Check for the time of offense.
5. Determine the code number for the violation.

6. Agent Jefferson is on patrol when he notices a double-parked van in front of 14 E. 52nd Street. After observing that there were no summonses already issued to the vehicle, Agent Jefferson checks the license plate number. 6.____
The NEXT step Agent Jefferson should take is to

A. check the dashboard for summonses
B. determine the proper code number of the violation
C. look at his watch for the time
D. check what type of vehicle it is

7. Traffic Enforcement Agent Carter observes the following incident: 7.____

Obstruction:	Stalled bus
Location:	Intersection of Kent Avenue and 5th Street
Traffic Condition:	Slow moving traffic on 5th Street due to stalled bus
Assistance Needed:	Tow truck

Agent Carter is about to radio Traffic Control regarding this incident.
Which one of the following expresses the above information MOST clearly and accurately?

A. There is slow moving traffic on 5th Street and at the intersection of Kent Avenue and 5th Street a stalled bus needs a tow truck.
B. A tow truck is needed to remove slow moving traffic on 5th Street. There is a stalled bus at the intersection of Kent Avenue and 5th Street.
C. At the intersection of Kent Avenue and 5th Street, a bus is stalled. A tow truck is needed because of slow moving traffic on 5th Street.
D. A stalled bus at the intersection of Kent Avenue and 5th Street is causing slow moving traffic on 5th Street and a tow truck is needed.

Question 8.

DIRECTIONS: Question 8 is to be answered SOLELY on the basis of the following information.

When arriving at Traffic Court, a Traffic Enforcement Agent should do the following in the order given:

1. Sign his name in the log book.
2. Write the time he arrived in the log book.
3. Locate the court room where the hearing is to take place.
4. Notify the clerk in the court room that he is present.
5. Give testimony regarding the summons he issued.
6. Sign the log book stating what time he departed.

8. Agent Ginsberg arrives at Traffic Court to testify about a summons he wrote. After recording his name and the time of his arrival in the log book, Agent Ginsberg tries to find out what court room the hearing will be in. What should Agent Ginsberg do once he finds the court room? 8.____

A. Testify as to why the summons was issued.
B. Find the court clerk and inform him that he has arrived.
C. Record the time he arrived.
D. Sign out in the log book.

Questions 9-10.

DIRECTIONS: Questions 9 and 10 are to be answered SOLELY on the basis of the following passage.

Traffic Enforcement Agent Murray was on patrol in his vehicle at the corner of Chambers and Church Streets when he noticed an accident between a white van and a green station wagon at the intersection of Church and Duane Streets. The two drivers were involved in a heated argument when Agent Murray approached them. He advised them to move their vehicles out of the intersection and over to the curb. Once at the curb, Ms. Ambrose, the driver of the station wagon, informed Agent Murray that the van had cut her off. The driver of the van, Mr. Hope, informed Agent Murray that he was simply trying to change lanes when the station wagon hit his van. Agent Murray asked both drivers for their drivers licenses and registrations. He informed them that since no one was injured and the damage to the vehicles was minor, they should have driven their cars from the intersection before arguing as to who was at fault. Since they failed to do so, he was going to issue both drivers a summons for obstructing traffic. At this point, Mr. Hope jumped into his van and raced up Reade Street. Agent Murray completed two summonses, one for Ms. Ambrose and the other for Mr. Hope. He issued Ms. Ambrose her summons and at the end of the day returned to his District Office and prepared a Summons Refusal Form. He then attached Mr. Hope's summons to the Summons Refusal Form so that the summons could be mailed to Mr. Hope.

9. At what intersection did the accident occur? 9.____

   A. Chambers Street and Church Street
   B. Church Street and Duane Street
   C. Chambers Street and Reade Street
   D. Reade Street and Duane Street

10. When Agent Murray arrived at the scene, the drivers involved in the accident were 10.____

   A. moving their vehicles to a side street
   B. exchanging insurance information
   C. involved in an argument
   D. waiting for an ambulance

11. Traffic Enforcement Agent Clark observes the following incident: 11.____

Date of Occurrence:	November 27
Time of Occurrence:	5:00 P.M.
Place of Occurrence:	38th Street and Madison Avenue
Driver:	Laura Benton
Type of Vehicle:	2005 Mazda
Violation:	Illegal right turn
Action Taken:	Summons issued

Agent Clark is required to testify in court about this incident.
Which one of the following expresses the above information MOST clearly and accurately?

   A. Laura Benton made an illegal right turn at 38th Street and Madison Avenue. At 5:00 P.M. on November 22, she drove a 2005 Mazda and I issued her a summons.
   B. Making an illegal right turn, I issued Laura Benton a summons. A 2005 Mazda was on 38th Street and Madison Avenue on November 22.
   C. An illegal right turn was made on 38th Street and Madison Avenue and I issued a summons. On November 22 at 5:00 P.M. Laura Benton was driving a 2005 Mazda.

D. On November 22 at 5:00 P.M., Laura Benton, while driving a 2005 Mazda, made an illegal right turn at the corner of Madison Avenue and 38th Street. I issued her a summons.

12. Traffic Enforcement Agent Rivera was offered $10.00 from a motorist if he did not issue a summons for a parking violation. The following facts relate to this incident: 12.____

Date of Incident:	December 12
Time of Incident:	2:35 P.M.
Location of Incident:	148 Sherman Avenue
Name of Motorist:	Arnold Pratt
Amount Offered to Not Issue Summons:	$10.00
Action Taken:	Notified Traffic Control

Agent Rivera is preparing a memo on this incident.
Which one of the following expresses the above information MOST clearly and accurately?

A. Arnold Pratt of 148 Sherman Avenue offered me $10.00 not to issue a summons. I notified Traffic Control on December 12 at 2:35 P.M.
B. Arnold Pratt notified Traffic Control that $10.00 was offered at 2:35 P.M. on December 12. It was at 148 Sherman Avenue.
C. On December 12 at 2:35 P.M., Arnold Pratt offered me $10.00 not to issue him a summons. This took place in front of 148 Sherman Avenue, and I notified Traffic Control.
D. At 148 Sherman Avenue, $10.00 was offered to not issue a summons on December 12 at 2:35 P.M. Traffic Control was notified that Arnold Pratt is the name of a motorist.

Question 13.

DIRECTIONS: Question 13 is to be answered SOLELY on the basis of the following information.

Before issuing a summons for a parking meter violation, a Traffic Enforcement Agent must do the following in the order given:

1. Read the traffic signs in the area.
2. Check to see if there is a special parking permit on the dashboard of the vehicle.
3. Check the meter to see if it is working properly.
4. Check for the number of the meter.
5. Check the time of day.
6. Check the violation code card to determine the code number for the violation.

13. Traffic Enforcement Agent Hernandez is on patrol when he notices a car parked at an expired meter. After checking the traffic signs, the agent looks at the dashboard for a parking permit and finds none. He then turns the meter knob to make sure it is working properly. 13.____
The NEXT step Agent Hernandez should take is to

A. look at his watch to see what time it is
B. check his code card for the violation number
C. check the meter for its number
D. read all the traffic signs

Question 14.

DIRECTIONS: Question 14 is to be answered SOLELY on the basis of the following information.

Code	Violation
70	Inspection Sticker Expired or Missing
71	Front or Back License Plate Missing
72	No Match between License Plate and
73	Registration Sticker

14. Traffic Enforcement Agent Pezzo has come across a parked vehicle with a flat right rear tire, an expired registration sticker, and an expired parking permit. In addition, the vehicle's license plate and inspection sticker do not match. According to the information above, Agent Pezzo should issue a summons to the vehicle for a violation of code(s) 14.____

A. 70, but not 71, 72, or 73
B. 71 and 72, but not 70 or 73
C. 73, but not 70, 71, or 72
D. 70 and 73, but not 71 or 72

15. Traffic Enforcement Agent Barfield was directing traffic when he observed a robbery. The following facts relate to this incident: 15.____

Time of Robbery:	3:50 P.M.
Location of Robbery:	Corner of Ludlow and Clasp Streets
Victim:	Edna Walton
Suspect:	Black male wearing a red sweatsuit
Action Taken:	Requested Traffic Control to contact Police

Agent Barfield is writing a memo on the above incident. Which one of the following expresses the above information MOST clearly and accurately?

A. Edna Walton was the victim of a robbery at the corner of Ludlow and Clasp Streets. I requested that Traffic Control contact the police. At 3:50 P.M., a black male wore a red sweatsuit.
B. The corner of Ludlow and Clasp Streets was the location of a black male wearing a red sweatsuit and the robbery of Edna Walton at 3:50 P.M. I requested Traffic Control to contact the police.
C. I requested that Traffic Control contact the police at the corner of Ludlow and Clasp Streets. A black male wore a red sweatsuit while Edna Walton was robbed at 3:50 P.M.
D. At 3:50 P.M. on the corner of Ludlow and Clasp Streets, Edna Walton was robbed by a black male wearing a red sweatsuit. I requested Traffic Control to contact the police.

16. Traffic Enforcement Agent Burns witnessed an accident and recorded the following facts: 16.____

Place of Accident:	Intersection of 23rd Street and Park Avenue
Time of Accident:	6:00 A.M.
Drivers Involved:	Curtis Aldan, Jack Forbes
Violation:	Speeding
Action Taken:	Summons issued to Curtis Aldan

Agent Burns is informing his Lieutenant about the facts of the accident.
Which one of the following expresses the above information MOST clearly and accurately?

A. Curtis Aldan and Jack Forbes were involved in an accident at the intersection of 23rd Street and Park Avenue at 6:00 A.M. Mr. Aldan was issued a summons for speeding.
B. It was 6:00 A.M. when a summons was issued to Curtis Aldan for speeding. At the intersection of 23rd Street and Park Avenue, Curtis Aldan and Jack Forbes were involved in an accident.
C. Curtis Aldan and Jack Forbes were the drivers involved in an accident at 6:00 M. At the intersection of 23rd Street and Park Avenue, a summons was issued to Mr. Aldan for speeding.
D. A summons was issued to Curtis Aldan while speeding. It was at the intersection of 23rd Street and Park Avenue at 6:00 A.M. that Mr. Aldan and Jack Forbes were involved in an accident.

Questions 17-18.

DIRECTIONS: Questions 17 and 18 are to be answered SOLELY on the basis of the following passage.

At 2:00 P.M., Traffic Enforcement Agent Black was on foot patrol on Hack Avenue when Mrs. Herbet approached him about a faulty parking meter. She complained that for the two quarters she deposited, she is supposed to get two hours of parking time and not just the forty minutes that the meter shows. Agent Black accompanied Mrs. Herbet to her car which was parked at 243 Chief Street. He tested the meter by turning the knob and found that the meter was broken because any amount of money deposited in the meter would register forty minutes of parking time. He searched for the serial number of the meter which was P26601 and recorded it along with the location of the meter on his Daily Field Patrol Sheet. Agent Black informed Mrs. Herbet that she would have two hours of parking time, the maximum amount of time she would have received if the meter were working properly. He also informed her that he was starting this two hour limit as of 2:05 P.M. and recorded this time and her license plate number (DRE-927) on his Daily Field Patrol Sheet. The agent told Mrs. Herbet that if her car was parked at the meter past the two hour limit, he would have to issue her a summons. Mrs. Herbet thanked the agent and said she would be gone long before the limit was up.

At 4:15 P.M., Agent Black was again on Chief Street when he saw that Mrs. Herbet's car was still parked at the meter. He issued her a summons for a meter violation and continued on his patrol.

17. Which of the following is recorded on Agent Black's Daily Field Patrol Sheet? 17.____

A. 243 Hack Avenue, P26611, 2:05 P.M., DRE-927
B. 243 Chief Street, P26601, 2:05 P.M., DRE-927
C. 243 Hack Street, P26661, 2:00 P.M., DRE-927
D. 243 Chief Avenue, P26601, 2:05 P.M., DRF-927

18. Agent Black allowed Mrs. Herbet to park at the meter for two hours because 18.____

A. it is the maximum amount of parking time allowed if the meter-were working properly
B. he felt bad that she lost her money
C. she was complaining to him
D. she assured him she would be gone before the two hour limit was up

19. Traffic Enforcement Agent Edwards was directing traffic when he witnessed a vehicle accident. Agent Edwards recorded the following information: 19.____

Accident:	Hit and Run
Vehicle Hit:	Blue Saab
Hit and Run Vehicle:	Black Volvo
Description of Hit and Run Driver:	Male, White, blonde hair
Time of Occurrence:	11:15 A.M.
Place of Occurrence:	3rd Avenue and 33rd Street

Agent Edwards is testifying in court regarding this incident.
Which one of the following expresses the above information MOST clearly and accurately?

A. At 11:15 A.M., a white male with blonde hair was driving a blue Saab on 3rd Avenue & 33rd Street. A black Volvo was hit.
B. On 3rd Avenue and 33rd Street, a white male hit a blue Saab. He had blonde hair at 11:15 A.M. when he drove a black Volvo.
C. At 11:15 A.M., a white male with blonde hair, driving a black Volvo, hit a blue Saab on 3rd Avenue and 33rd Street.
D. It was a white male with blonde hair on 3rd Avenue and 33rd Street at 11:15 M. A blue Saab was struck by a black Volvo.

20. A Traffic Enforcement Agent is required to radio a supervisor if they become aware of a serious problem outside the agent's assigned patrol area. 20.____
In which one of the following situations would it be MOST appropriate for an agent to radio a supervisor of a serious problem that occurs outside the agent's assigned area?

A. A woman reports that her neighbors are constantly blocking her driveway with their car.
B. A motorist reports that a school bus is on fire near Exit 5 of the expressway.
C. A store owner reports that an abandoned vehicle has been parked in front of his store for 2 weeks.
D. A woman reports that her car is stalled in the Grand Safe Shopping Center.

KEY (CORRECT ANSWERS)

1. C
2. A
3. A
4. C
5. C
6. D
7. D
8. B
9. B
10. C
11. D
12. C
13. C
14. A
15. D
16. A
17. B
18. A
19. C
20. B

EXAMINATION SECTION
TEST 1

DIRECTIONS: Each question or incomplete statement is followed by several suggested answers or completions. Select the one that BEST answers the question or completes the statement. *PRINT THE LETTER OF THE CORRECT ANSWER IN THE SPACE AT THE RIGHT.*

1. A BASIC method of operation that a good supervisor should follow is to 1.____

   A. check the work of subordinates constantly to make sure they are not making exceptions to the rules
   B. train subordinates so they can handle problems that come up regularly themselves and come to him only with special cases
   C. delegate to subordinates only those duties which he cannot do himself
   D. issue directions to subordinates only on special matters

2. To do a good job of performance evaluation, it is BEST for a supervisor to 2.____

   A. compare the employees performance to that of another employee doing similar work
   B. give greatest weight to instances of unusually good or unusually poor performance
   C. leave out any consideration of the employees personal traits
   D. measure the employees performance against standard performance requirements

3. Of the following, the MOST important reason for a supervisor to have private face-to-face discussions with subordinates about their performance is to 3.____

   A. help employees improve their work
   B. give special praise to employees who perform well
   C. encourage the employees to compete for higher performance ratings
   D. discipline employees who perform poorly

4. Of the following, the CHIEF purpose of a probationary period for a new employee is to allow time for 4.____

   A. finding out whether the selection processes are satisfactory
   B. the employee to make adjustments in his home circumstances made necessary by the job
   C. the employee to decide whether he wants a permanent appointment
   D. determining the fitness of the employee to continue in the job

5. When an enforcement agent resigns his job, it is MOST important to conduct an *exit interview* in order to 5.____

   A. try to get the employee to remain on the job
   B. learn the true reasons for the employees resignation
   C. see that the employee leaves with a good opinion of the agency
   D. ask the agent if he would consider a transfer

6. Chronic lateness of employees is generally LEAST likely to be due to 6.____

   A. distance of job location from home
   B. poor personnel administration

C. unexpressed employee grievances
D. low morale

7. Of the following, the LEAST effective stimulus for motivating employees toward improved performance over a long-range period is 7.____

A. their sense of achievement
B. their feeling of recognition
C. opportunity for their self-development
D. an increase in salary

8. Suppose that not one of a group of employees has turned in an idea to the employees suggestion system during the past year. 8.____
The MOST probable reason for this situation is that the

A. money awards given for suggestions used are not high enough to make employees interested
B. employees in this group are not able to develop any good ideas
C. supervisor of these employees is not doing enough to encourage them to take part in the program
D. methods and procedures of operation do not need improvement

9. A subordinate tells you that he is having trouble concentrating on his work due to a personal problem at home. 9.____
Of the following, it would be BEST for you to

A. refer him to a community service agency
B. listen quietly to the story because he may just need a sympathetic ear
C. tell him that you cannot help him because the problem is not job related
D. ask him some questions about the nature of the problem and tell him how you would handle it

10. For you as a supervisor to give each of your subordinates EXACTLY the same type of supervision is 10.____

A. *advisable,* because doing this insures fair and impartial treatment of each individual
B. *not advisable*, because individuals like to think that they are receiving better treatment than others
C. *advisable,* because once a supervisor learns how to deal with a subordinate who brings a problem to him, he can handle another subordinate with this problem in the same way
D. *not advisable,* because each person is different, and there is no one supervisory procedure for dealing with individuals that applies in every case

11. A senior enforcement agent under your supervision tells you that he is reluctant to speak to one of the agents about his poor work habits, because this agent is *strong-willed* and he does not want to antagonize him. 11.____
For you to offer to speak to the agent about this matter yourself would be

A. *advisable,* since you are in a position of greater authority
B. *inadvisable,* since handling this problem is a basic supervisory responsibility of the senior agent

C. *advisable,* since the senior agent must work more closely with the agent than you do
D. *inadvisable,* since you should not risk antagonizing the agent yourself

12. Some of your subordinates have been coming to you with complaints you feel are unimportant. For you to hear their stories out is 12.____

A. *poor* practice; you should spend your time on more important matters
B. *good* practice; this will increase your popularity with your subordinates
C. *poor* practice; subordinates should learn to come to you only with major grievances
D. *good* practice; it may prevent minor complaints from developing into major grievances

13. Assume that an agency has an established procedure for handling employee grievances. An employee in this agency comes to his immediate supervisor with a grievance. The supervisor investigates the matter and makes a decision. However, the employee is not satisfied with the decision made by the supervisor.
The BEST action for the supervisor to take is to 13.____

A. tell the employee he will review the matter further
B. remind the employee that he is the supervisor and the employee must act in accordance with his decision
C. explain to the employee how he can carry his complaint forward to the next step in the grievance procedure
D. tell the employee he will consult with his own superiors on the matter

14. Enforcement agents and senior enforcement agents often must make quick decisions while in the field. The district commander can BEST help subordinates meet such situations by 14.____

A. training them in the appropriate action to take for every problem that may come up
B. limiting the areas in which they are permitted to make decisions
C. making certain they understand clearly the basic policies of the bureau and the department
D. delegating authority to make such decisions to only a few subordinates on each level

15. Studies have shown that the CHIEF cause of failure to achieve success as a supervisor is 15.____

A. an unwillingness to delegate authority to subordinates
B. the establishment of high performance standards for subordinates
C. the use of discipline that is too strict
D. showing too much leniency to poor workers

16. When a supervisor delegates to a subordinate certain work that he normally does himself, it is MOST important that he give the subordinate 16.____

A. responsibility for also setting the standards for the work to be done
B. sufficient authority to be able to carry out the assignment
C. written, step-by-step instructions for doing the work
D. an explanation of one part of the task at a time

17. It is particularly important that disciplinary actions be equitable as between individuals. This statement implies that 17.____

A. punishment applied in disciplinary actions should be lenient
B. proposed disciplinary actions should be reviewed by higher authority
C. subordinates should have an opportunity to present their stories before penalties are applied
D. penalties for violations of the rules should be standardized and consistently applied

18. You discover that from time to time a number of false rumors circulate among your subordinates.
Of the following, the BEST way for you to handle this situation is to 18.____

A. ignore the rumors since rumors circulate in every office and can never be eliminated
B. attempt to find those responsible for the rumors and reprimand them
C. make sure that your employees are informed as soon as possible about all matters that affect them
D. inform your superior about the rumors and let him deal with the matter

19. Supervisors who allow the *halo effect* to influence their evaluations of subordinates are MOST likely to 19.____

A. give more lenient ratings to older employees who have longer service
B. let one highly favorable or unfavorable trait unduly affect their judgment of an employee
C. evaluate all employees on one trait before considering a second
D. give high evaluations in order to avoid antagonizing their subordinates

20. For a supervisor to keep records of reprimands to subordinates about infractions of the rules is 20.____

A. *good* practice, because these records are valuable to support disciplinary actions recommended or taken
B. *poor* practice, because such records are evidence of the supervisors inability to maintain discipline
C. *good* practice, because such records indicate that the supervisor is doing a good job
D. *poor* practice, because the best way to correct subordinates is to give them more training

21. When a new departmental policy has been established, it would be MOST advisable for you, as a supervising agent, to 21.____

A. distribute a memo which states the new policy and instruct your subordinates to read it
B. explain specifically to your subordinates how the policy is going to affect them
C. make sure your subordinates understand that you are not responsible for setting the policy
D. tell your subordinates whether you agree or disagree with the policy

22. As a district commander, you receive several complaints about the rude conduct of an enforcement agent. The FIRST action you should take is to 22.____

A. request his transfer to another office
B. prepare a charge sheet for disciplinary action
C. assign a senior agent to walk patrol with him for a week
D. interview the agent to determine possible reason, and warn that correction is necessary

23. A supervising enforcement agent is MOST likely to get subordinates to work cooperatively toward accomplishing bureau goals if he 23.____

A. creates an atmosphere that contributes to their feeling of security
B. backs up subordinates even when they occasionally disobey regulations
C. shows interest in subordinates by helping them solve their personal problems
D. uses an authoritarian or *bossy* approach to supervision

24. A supervising agent is holding a staff meeting with his senior agents to try to find an acceptable solution to a problem that has come up.
Of the following, the CHIEF role of the supervising agent at this meeting should be to 24.____

A. see that every member of the group contributes at least one suggestion
B. act as chairman of the meeting, but take no other active part to avoid influencing the senior agents
C. keep the participants from wandering off into discussions of irrelevant matters
D. make certain the participants hear his views on the matter at the beginning of the meeting

25. An enforcement agent shows you a certificate that he has just received for completing two years of study in conversational Spanish. As his supervisor, it would be BEST for you to 25.____

A. put a note about this accomplishment in his personnel folder
B. assign him to areas in which people of Spanish origin live
C. congratulate him on this accomplishment, but tell him frankly that you doubt this is likely to have any direct bearing on his work
D. encourage him to continue his studies and become thoroughly fluent in speaking the language

KEY (CORRECT ANSWERS)

1. B
2. D
3. A
4. D
5. B

6. A
7. D
8. C
9. B
10. D

11. B
12. D
13. C
14. C
15. A

16. B
17. D
18. C
19. B
20. A

21. B
22. D
23. A
24. C
25. A

TEST 2

DIRECTIONS: Each question or incomplete statement is followed by several suggested answers or completions. Select the one that BEST answers the question or completes the statement. *PRINT THE LETTER OF THE CORRECT ANSWER IN THE SPACE AT THE RIGHT.*

1. A supervising enforcement agent is considering making a recommendation to install additional parking meters in a certain area. For this supervising agent to ask the opinion of his subordinates about the recommendation before sending it through would be 1.____

   A. *undesirable;* subordinates may lose respect for a supervisor who requests their opinions in such matters
   B. *desirable;* if additional meters are installed, it would mean more work for the subordinates, and they should have a right to help decide the matter
   C. *undesirable;* since only the supervisor would get credit for the recommendation, it would hurt the morale of the subordinates
   D. *desirable;* the subordinates may have some worthwhile suggestions concerning the recommendation

2. You have just been appointed district commander of an enforcement office new to you and overhear two of the senior enforcement agents discussing that you have a reputation for being overly strict. 2.____
   The BEST action for you to take in this situation is to

   A. call the two senior agents into your office and tell them that what they heard is not true
   B. say nothing and disregard the comments since, in your position, you should be above listening to such gossip
   C. call the two senior agents into your office and caution them against spreading rumors
   D. say nothing, but use the comments you overheard for self-evaluation

3. In instructing your clerical staff on proper maintenance of the office files, you should explain that the MOST important purpose of the files is to 3.____

   A. arrange filed material so that it may be quickly found when needed
   B. prevent material from being thrown out by mistake
   C. keep written proof of actions taken so that responsibility can be assigned
   D. reduce office workload

4. Some people work safely in dangerous surroundings, whereas others have accidents on jobs that seem quite safe. 4.____
   Of the following, the MOST valuable conclusion you, as a supervisor, can draw from this statement is that

   A. accident prevention depends, among other factors, upon the motivation of employees to work safely
   B. some employees are accident prone and there is nothing that can be done about it
   C. maintaining interest in safety is unnecessary if the work place and equipment are engineered for safety
   D. safety training is necessary only for certain types of employees

5. Suppose that, as a supervising enforcement agent, you have been responsible for setting up a special training program for your subordinates. 5.____
In measuring the effectiveness of this program after it is over, it would be MOST important for you to find out

   A. whether those attending the program liked the instructor
   B. whether the objectives of the program were met and to what degree they were met
   C. whether the time involved in this training was excessive
   D. the cost to the agency for giving this training

6. Which one of the following is the most RECENT development in methods of training supervisors that involves the human relations approach? 6.____

   A. Conference training
   B. Lecture method
   C. Case method
   D. Sensitivity training

7. During a discussion at a staff meeting, one of your senior agents makes a statement which you know to be factually incorrect. 7.____
If none of the other members of the group attempts to correct the statement or question it, it would be BEST for you to

   A. allow the discussion to continue without commenting
   B. correct the statement that has been made
   C. emphasize that statements made at the meeting by members of the group are not to be accepted as fact
   D. urge the group to decide for themselves whether or not to accept the statement that was made

8. For a supervisor to give his subordinates oral as well as written instructions on work that is detailed or complex is 8.____

   A. *desirable,* because it would give subordinates an overall view of the particular job and its relation to the agencys goals
   B. *undesirable,* because this would discourage initiative on the part of subordinates
   C. *desirable,* because the supervisor can find out if subordinates understand the written instructions and answer any questions they have
   D. *undesirable,* because subordinates should be able to work efficiently from the written instructions if they are complete

9. The lecture-demonstration method would be LEAST desirable in a training program set up for 9.____

   A. breaking in new employees
   B. changing the attitudes of older employees
   C. explaining how a new piece of equipment works
   D. informing subordinates about new agency procedures

10. The MAIN reason for having the department of traffic give out publicity about the work of the bureau of enforcement is to 10.____

   A. justify increased money for the department in future city budgets
   B. show the public the need for better salaries for employees of this very important bureau

C. free the top officials of the department from the pressures of special interest groups
D. inform the public about the work and problems of this bureau so that they will better understand and comply with its regulations

11. Suppose one of your agents was in an accident while on patrol. Two days later a man who says he is a newspaper reporter wants to interview you about what happened. It would be MOST advisable for you to tell him that 11.____

A. he must speak to the senior agent who saw the accident
B. you cannot give him any information because he may misquote you
C. he must contact the main office of the department of traffic for official information
D. the accident was not serious and is not worth reporting in the newspaper

12. While you are checking an area, a motorist in a private car complains to you that an agent issued a summons to him for double parking but that a passenger car parked right behind him did not get a summons. The BEST action for you to take is to tell him 12.____

A. to give you all the information and you will investigate the matter
B. to call the main office
C. that it was probably just an oversight and you will speak to the agent
D. that whether or not the other driver got a summons is not his business

13. Suppose you receive a letter from a man who complains that he was treated rudely by one of your enforcement agents. Of the following, the FIRST action you should take is to 13.____

A. write a letter of apology to the man for the enforcement agents discourtesy
B. disregard the complaint because this agent is known to be courteous at all times
C. obtain all details of the incident from the enforcement agent
D. forward the letter to the director of the bureau of enforcement

14. When a supervising agent speaks over the phone to members of the public who have questions or complaints, it is MOST important that what he says should 14.____

A. please the caller
B. give a good impression of the speaker
C. be as brief as possible
D. conform to bureau policies

15. When you are training new enforcement agents, you should instruct them that if a motorist is loud and rude to then they should 15.____

A. shout right back in the same manner
B. call a policeman and have the motorist arrested
C. say nothing and continue on patrol
D. hide their badge and refuse to give their number

16. Of the following, the LEAST important reason for having a department handbook and a bureau standard operating procedure is to 16.____

A. help in training new employees
B. provide a source of reference for department and bureau rules and procedures

C. prevent errors in work by providing clear guidelines
D. make the supervisors job easy

17. A Form 15 must be submitted by an employee of the bureau of enforcement for any absence EXCEPT 17.____

A. a civil service job interview
B. vacation days listed on the approved annual leave schedule
C. emergency leave
D. time off for overtime

18. Suppose you get a flat tire at 3:00 P.M. while on tour in a department vehicle. The CORRECT action you should take is to 18.____

A. ask the communications center to send the A.A.A.
B. leave the car at the curb and phone the district office
C. use a local garage to fix the flat and get a bill in duplicate
D. use the car radio to call the department shop for assistance

19. One of your enforcement agents is reporting a high number of summons refusals.
Of the following, the MOST effective way for you to handle the situation is to 19.____

A. give the agent an unsatisfactory performance evaluation
B. provide for retraining of the agent
C. arrange to have the agent reassigned to another district office
D. refer the matter to the principal enforcement agent

20. A supervisor is giving instructions to the agents under his supervision on the proper procedures to follow if assaulted while on patrol. Which one of the following statements should NOT be made by the supervisor to his subordinates? 20.____

A. Make a citizen's arrest of the assailant.
B. Obtain police assistance, if required.
C. Notify the district commander.
D. Obtain medical care if necessary.

21. When a supervising agent has been informed of summonses lost before being served, he should IMMEDIATELY notify the 21.____

A. traffic summons control bureau
B. parking violations bureau
C. police department
D. criminal court

22. A parking enforcement agent has been late 8 times in January, 2 times in February, and 6 times in March.
As the supervising agent, the CORRECT action for you to take is to 22.____

A. refer the matter to the deputy commissioner for administration
B. speak to the agent, emphasizing the need for promptness
C. direct the senior enforcement agent to issue a below-standard performance evaluation for this agent
D. arrange an appointment for the agent to speak with the bureau chief

23. A senior enforcement agent reports to the district commander that, on inspecting his squad prior to patrol, he has noted an agent improperly and unacceptably uniformed, and correction cannot be made immediately. 23.____
The district commander should properly

A. send the agent home and authorize no pay for the day
B. permit the agent to proceed on patrol, but warn him not to let this happen again
C. assign the agent to clerical work for the day
D. notify the principal enforcement agent right away

24. Of the following, the factor MOST likely to cause lowered morale among enforcement agents is 24.____

A. lack of higher salaries
B. necessity for working rotating shifts
C. abuse from citizens whom they have summoned
D. working in *paired* areas

25. In determining whether an agent is issuing a satisfactory number of summonses while on patrol, the supervisor should 25.____

A. set a daily summons quota and compare the agents record against this figure
B. take into consideration previous records of summonses issued in the areas patrolled by the agent
C. consider that the agent is doing satisfactory work if there are no complaints about him
D. consider the attitudes and personality of the agent rather than the number of summonses he issues

---

KEY (CORRECT ANSWERS)

1. D
2. D
3. A
4. A
5. B
6. D
7. B
8. C
9. B
10. D
11. C
12. A
13. C
14. D
15. C
16. D
17. B
18. C
19. B
20. A
21. C
22. D
23. A
24. C
25. B

EXAMINATION SECTION
TEST 1

DIRECTIONS: Each question or incomplete statement is followed by several suggested answers or completions. Select the one that Best answers the question or completes the statement. *PRINT THE LETTER OF THE CORRECT ANSWER IN THE SPACE AT THE RIGHT.*

Questions 1-4.

DIRECTIONS: Answer Questions 1 to 4 based on the information given in the traffic volume table below.

TRAFFIC VOLUME COUNTS

	Main Street		Cross Street	
Time (A.M.)	Northbound	Southbound	Eastbound	Westbound
7:00- 7:15	100	100	70	60
7:15- 7:30	110	100	80	70
7:30- 7:45	150	140	110	100
7:45- 8:00	170	160	140	130
8:00- 8:15	210	190	120	110
8:15- 8:30	180	170	90	80
8:30- 8:45	160	140	70	60
8:45-9:00	150	160	70	50
9:00- 9:15	140	150	50	50
9:15- 9:30	130	120	40	20
9:30- 9:45	120	110	30	30
9:45-10:00	120	100	30	30

1. The hour during which traffic, moving in both directions on Main Street, reached its *peak* was 1.____

   A. 7:30 - 8:30
   B. 7:45 - 8:45
   C. 8:00 - 9:00
   D. 8:15 - 9:15

2. The hour during which traffic volume, moving in both directions on Cross Street, reached its *peak* was 2.____

   A. 7:30 - 8:30
   B. 7:45 - 8:45
   C. 8:00 - 9:00
   D. 8:15 - 9:15

3. The HIGHEST average hourly volume over the three-hour period 7:00 to 10:00 was recorded for 3.____

   A. Main Street northbound
   B. Main Street southbound
   C. Cross Street eastbound
   D. Cross Street westbound

4. The *peak* 15-minute traffic volume for all directions of travel occurred between 4.____

   A. 7:30 - 7:45
   B. 7:45 - 8:00
   C. 8:00 - 8:15
   D. 8:15 - 8:30

5. Which of the following statements relating to one-way streets is CORRECT? 5.____
   One-way streets

A. increase turning movement conflicts between vehicles
B. decrease street capacity
C. decrease accident hazards for pedestrians
D. make it impossible to time traffic signals to control speeds

Questions 6-11.

DIRECTIONS: Answer Questions 6 to 11 based on the information given in Figure 1 below.

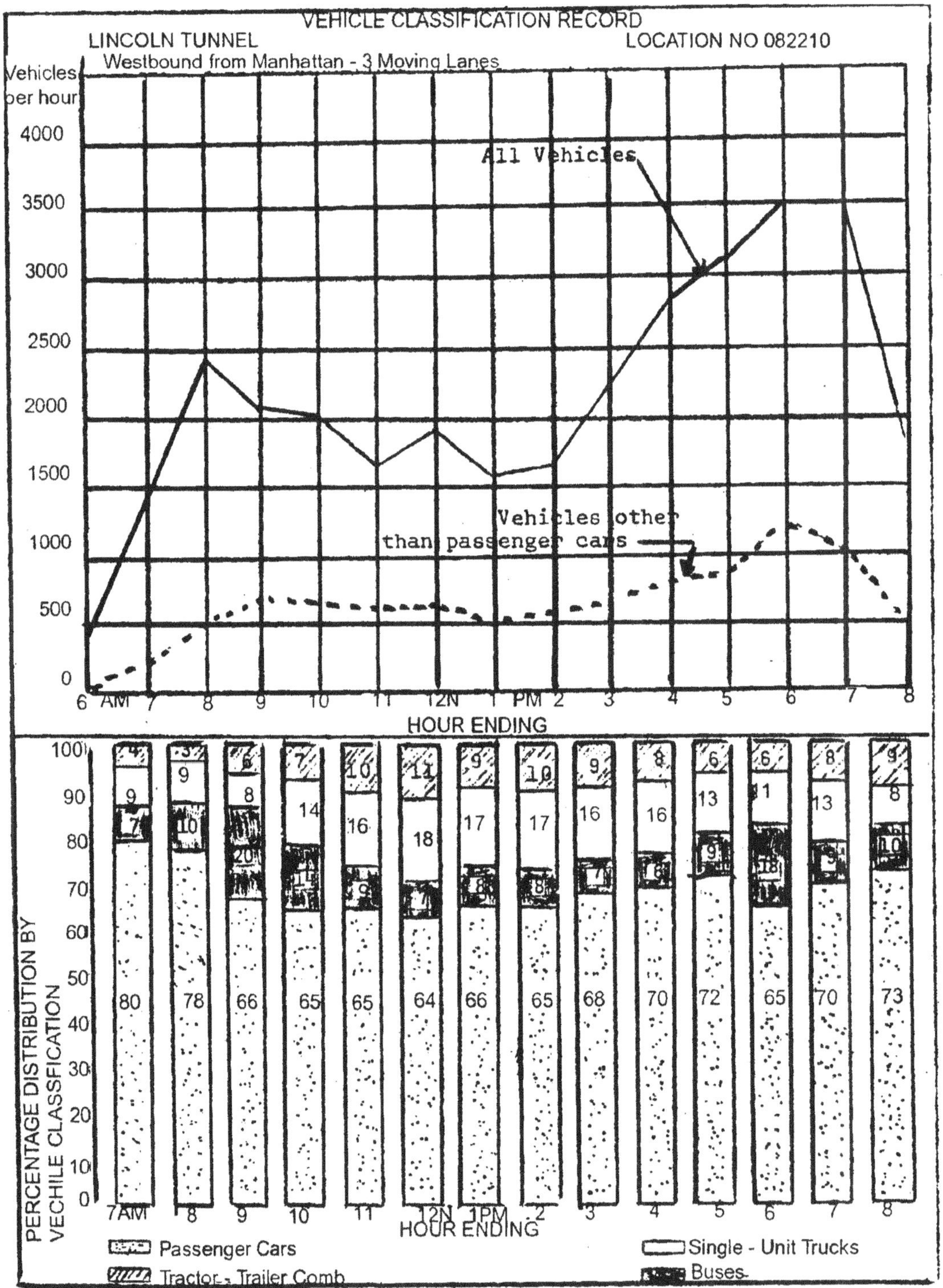

FIGURE 1

6. The total number of all vehicles traveling through the Lincoln Tunnel westbound from Manhattan between the hours of 6 A.M. and 12 Noon is *most nearly* 6.____

A. 5,500 B. 7,500 C. 9,500 D. 11,500

7. The number of passenger cars recorded during the hour ending at 7 P.M. was *most nearly* 7.____

A. 235 B. 1160 C. 2450 D. 3500

8. Excluding passenger cars, the AVERAGE number of vehicles per moving lane recorded during the peak hour was *most nearly* 8.____

A. 420 B. 1180 C. 1250 D. 3550

9. The percentage of buses recorded between 6 A.M. and 8 P.M. ranged between 9.____

A. 3% and 11%
B. 8% and 18%
C. 6% and 20%
D. 64% and 80%

10. During the study period, the percentage of single unit trucks *exceeded* the percentage of buses for _______ hours. 10.____

A. 4 B. 5 C. 9 D. 10

11. For all vehicles recorded, the recorded traffic volume during the morning peak hour was *most nearly* _______ of the volume during the evening peak hour. 11.____

A. 40% B. 50% C. 60% D. 70%

12. In urban areas, traffic volume is usually LOWEST during the month of 12.____

A. January B. March C. August D. October

13. In urban shopping areas, the *peak* traffic activity USUALLY occurs during 13.____

A. Monday afternoon and Friday night
B. Friday night and Saturday afternoon
C. Thursday night and Saturday afternoon
D. Monday night and Friday night

14. In the metric system, the unit that is closest to a mile is a 14.____

A. centimeter
B. liter
C. millimeter
D. kilometer

Questions 15-16.

DIRECTIONS: Questions 15 and 16 refer to the diagram at the top of the following Page 4.

15. Vehicle X in the diagram is heading in which direction? 15.____

A. Southeast
B. Southwest
C. Northeast
D. Northwest

16. If Vehicle X in the diagram makes a right turn at the intersection, it will be headed 16.____

A. southeast
B. southwest
C. northeast
D. northwest

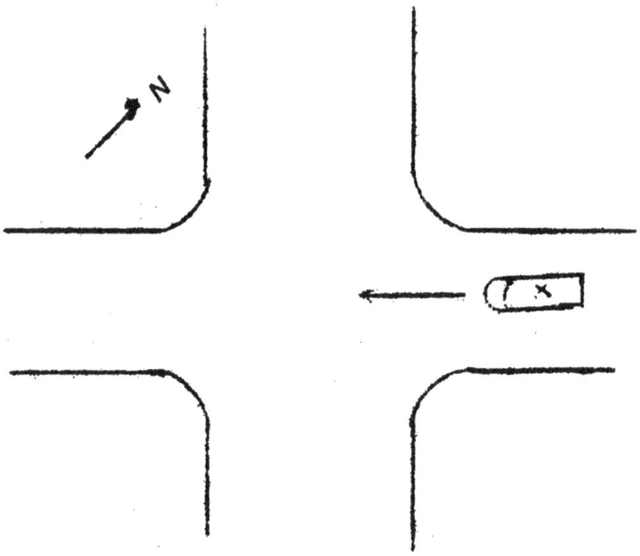

17. The one of the following that is NOT a function of channelization is 17.____

    A. control the angle of conflict
    B. favor certain turning movements
    C. protect pedestrians
    D. increase the pavement area within an intersection

18. The time of display of the yellow signal indication following the green signal indication is called the 18.____

    A. clearance interval
    B. time cycle
    C. traffic phase
    D. interval sequence

19. A lane constructed for the purpose of allowing vehicles entering a highway to increase speed to a rate that is safe for merging with through traffic is called a(n) ______ lane. 19.____

    A. auxiliary
    B. through
    C. acceleration
    D. deceleration

20. A traffic volume count which records the number and types of vehicles passing a given point is called a ______ count. 20.____

    A. rate-of-flow
    B. capacity
    C. classification
    D. roadway

21. On highways, the MAIN purpose served by barriers between traffic going in opposite directions is to 21.____

    A. stop cars if they get out of lane
    B. minimize the glare from oncoming cars
    C. prevent cars from overturning if they have blowouts
    D. prevent head-on accidents

22. Control count stations are USUALLY used to 22.____

    A. establish seasonal and daily traffic volume characteristics
    B. make short manual traffic counts
    C. classify traffic
    D. count traffic on weekends only

23. The MAIN purpose of off-center traffic lanes is to 23.____

    A. protect slow-moving traffic from the hazards of fast-moving traffic
    B. permit the use of special traffic control
    C. provide additional capacity in one direction of travel
    D. provide a slow-down area for disabled vehicles

24. Reserved transit lanes are used to 24.____

    A. make sure buses stop at the curb
    B. reduce bus and passenger car accidents
    C. decrease transit travel times by reducing friction between buses and other vehicles
    D. make it easier for people to get on and off buses

25. The slope or grade between points X and Y shown in the diagram below is 25.____

    A. 4% B. 10% C. 25% D. 50%

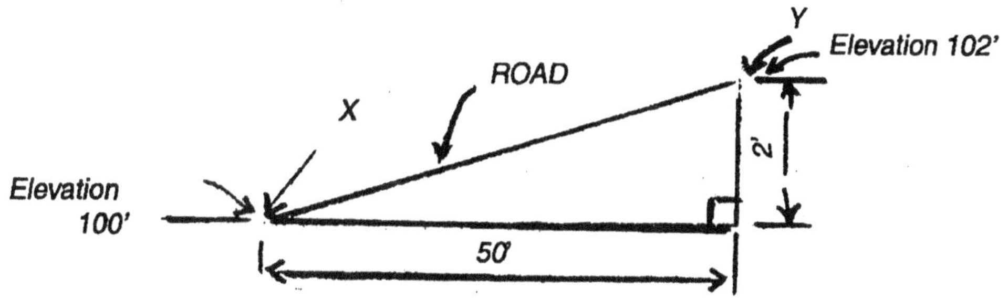

KEY (CORRECT ANSWERS)

1. B
2. A
3. A
4. C
5. C

6. D
7. C
8. A
9. C
10. C

11. D
12. A
13. B
14. D
15. B

16. D
17. D
18. A
19. C
20. C

21. D
22. A
23. C
24. C
25. A

TEST 2

DIRECTIONS: Each question or incomplete statement is followed by several suggested answers or completions. Select the one that BEST answers the question or completes the statement. *PRINT THE LETTER OF THE CORRECT ANSWER IN THE SPACE AT THE RIGHT.*

1. In the city, when parking is not otherwise restricted, commercial vehicles can park 1.____

   A. up to a maximum of one hour
   B. up to a maximum of three hours
   C. up to a maximum of eight hours
   D. without a time limitation

2. In the city, with respect to loading an parking, commercial vehicles are allowed to 2.____

   A. load or unload merchandise expeditiously in a no-standing zone
   B. park for one hour in a no-parking zone
   C. load or unload merchandise expeditiously in a no-parking zone
   D. park for one hour in a no-standing zone

3. On the Federal national highway system, highways ending in an even number run 3.____

   A. in the east-west direction
   B. both east-west or north-south
   C. in the north-south direction
   D. around cities and not through them

4. The *current* maximum allowed speed limit on Federal interstate highways is _______miles per hour. 4.____

   A. 50 B. 55 C. 60 D. 65

5. In the city, when a vehicle is too long for a single parking meter space, the vehicle may 5.____

   A. not be parked in the parking meter area
   B. be parked using more than one space but a coin must be deposited in the meter designated for each space occupied
   C. be parked using more than one space and a coin must be deposited only in the forward parking meter
   D. be parked using more than one space and a coin must be deposited only in the rear parking meter

6. In the city, some signs indicate that stopping, standing, or parking regulations are in effect every day except Sundays. Where this sign is used, stopping, standing, or parking regulations would apply on 6.____

   A. Washington's Birthday B. Brooklyn Day
   C. Columbus Day D. Election Day

7. In the city, unless signs are posted indicating specific hours during which play street regulations are in effect, such regulations are in effect on designated streets FROM 7.____

   A. 7 A.M. until 4 P.M.
   B. 8 A.M. until 1/2 hour before sunset

C. 8 A.M. to 1/2 hour after sunset
D. 8 A.M. to 8 P.M.

8. When preparing to make a turn while driving a vehicle on a roadway, a driver should signal his intention to turn AT LEAST ______ feet in advance of the turn. 8.____

A. 50 B. 100 C. 150 D. 200

9. Unless otherwise permitted or prohibited by posted signs, the MAXIMUM continuous period during which a vehicle may be parked on any roadway in the city is hours. 9.____

A. 8 B. 12 C. 24 D. 48

10. In the city, commercial vehicles may angle stand or angle park in 10.____

A. any area where no parking signs are installed, provided the street is wide enough to allow the vehicle to park at an angle
B. on any one-way street where standing is not prohibited, provided the street is wide enough to allow the vehicle to park at an angle
C. on a two-way street in areas authorized by signs, provided that the vehicle shall not occupy more than a parking lane plus one moving lane
D. on a two-way street in areas authorized by signs, provided that the vehicles shall not extend more than 10 feet from the curb

11. Which of the following is MOST restrictive to drivers of passenger cars? 11.____

A. Regulations relating to parking in front of fire hydrants
B. No parking regulations
C. No standing regulations
D. No stopping regulations

12. The MAXIMUM permitted speed limit in the city, unless signs indicate otherwise, is ______ mph. 12.____

A. 25 B. 30 C. 35 D. 40

13. With regard to right-of-way at an intersection that is NOT controlled by a traffic control device, the one of the following statements that is CORRECT is 13.____

A. the car on your right has the right-of-way
B. the car on your left has the right-of-way
C. a car preparing to enter the intersection has the right-of-way over a car in the intersection
D. a car turning left has the right-of-way over a vehicle going straight ahead

14. At an intersection controlled by traffic signals, a red arrow pointing to the right means that a right turn may 14.____

A. be made after coming to a full stop
B. be made providing the driver yields the right-of-way to all other vehicles and pedestrians
C. not be made during the period that the red arrow is illuminated
D. be made only if there is another indication showing a round green signal light

15. A flashing red traffic signal has the SAME meaning as a 15.____

A. stop sign
B. yield sign
C. flashing yellow traffic signal
D. hazardous intersection warning sign

16. Traffic signals are MOST frequently installed to reduce ______ collision accidents. 16.____

A. right-angle
B. rear-end
C. side-swipe
D. head-on

17. The CORRECT color combination for warning signs is 17.____

A. yellow lettering or symbols on a black background
B. white lettering or symbols on a red background
C. black lettering or symbols on a yellow background
D. black lettering or symbols on a white background

18. A PROGRESSIVELY timed traffic signal system will 18.____

A. turn all the signals red or green at the same time
B. usually increase the number of rear-end accidents but reduce the number of right-angle accidents
C. make it more hazardous for pedestrians to cross at the signalized intersections
D. decrease the number of stops traffic is required to make

19. The EFFECT of traffic signals on accidents is that traffic signals 19.____

A. always decrease accidents
B. sometimes increase accidents
C. never increase accidents
D. have no real effect on accidents

20. With respect to traffic devices, which of the following situations should receive the LOWEST priority in terms of repair or replacement? 20.____

A. Inoperative or malfunctioning traffic signals at an intersection
B. Missing "No Standing - Rush Hour" regulation signs
C. Missing "Yield" signs controlling the intersection of a minor street with a major street
D. Inoperative parking meters along one block in a retail shopping area

21. Of the following, the BEST reason why a stop sign would be used instead of a yield sign to control traffic at an intersection is 21.____

A. there are a larger number of rear-end accidents on the street being controlled
B. the street being controlled is less than 36 feet wide
C. visibility is limited at the intersection
D. the approaches to the intersection are offset to each other

22. The USUAL color combination used on interstate signs is ______ lettering and symbols on a ______ background. 22.____

A. white; green
B. green; white
C. white; black
D. black; white

23. The geometrical shape of a railroad crossing sign is that of a(n) 23.____

A. octagon B. circle C. rectangle D. triangle

24. The STANDARD pedestrian walking speed used in timing pedestrian signals is ______ per second. 24.____

A. 1 foot B. 4 feet C. 8 feet D. 12 feet

25. A driver approaching an intersection where a sign authorizes a right turn on a red traffic signal indication may make such a turn AND 25.____

A. has the right-of-way over all vehicles in the intersection
B. must yield right-of-way to all vehicles and pedestrians within the intersection
C. must yield right-of-way only to vehicles and pedestrians on the cross street
D. has the right-of-way over other turning vehicles

KEY (CORRECT ANSWERS)

1. B
2. C
3. A
4. D
5. C
6. B
7. C
8. B
9. C
10. C
11. D
12. B
13. A
14. C
15. A
16. A
17. C
18. D
19. B
20. D
21. C
22. A
23. B
24. B
25. B

EXAMINATION SECTION
TEST 1

DIRECTIONS: Each question or incomplete statement is followed by several suggested answers or completions. Select the one that BEST answers the question or completes the statement. *PRINT THE LETTER OF THE CORRECT ANSWER IN THE SPACE AT THE RIGHT.*

1. When a vehicle is so large that it must use two metered parking spaces, it should be parked 1.____

   A. with its front end alongside the forward meter and a coin deposited only in the forward meter
   B. with its front end alongside the forward meter and coins deposited in the meters for each, of the spaces filled by the vehicle
   C. with its tail end alongside the rear meter and a coin deposited in the meter closest to the rear of the vehicle
   D. in the approximate middle of the two spaces and a coin deposited in either of the meters alongside the vehicle

2. A senior enforcement agent finds the following cars parked at expired meters at a time when meter regulations are in effect: 2.____
   I. A vehicle with FC plates
   II. A vehicle with a Patrolman's Benevolent Association card on the sun visor
   III. An unmarked vehicle displaying a blue metal shield identifying it as a City Police Department car

   Which of the above vehicles should be given summonses?

   A. I, but not II and III
   B. II, but not I and III
   C. I and II, but not III
   D. II and III, but not I

3. An enforcement agent mistakenly issues a summons to an unoccupied automobile parked at a meter at a time when parking is not restricted. The agent realizes his error before the driver of the automobile returns. 3.____
   In this situation, the agent should

   A. destroy the summons but make a note of the circumstnces under which it was issued on the back of the agency copy
   B. leave a note on the automobile to the motorist telling him to disregard the summons since it was issued in error
   C. allow the motorist to receive the summons since the error can be corrected later
   D. return the summons to the district commander with a written memo describing the circumstances under which it was issued

4. Following are three practices a senior enforcement agent observes while on patrol: 4.____
   I. A person reserving a parking space in front of a fruit store by placing a crate in the roadway
   II. A motorcycle five feet long parked at an angle to the curb with one wheel touching the curb
   III. A food vendor parked at a metered parking space selling sodas and ice cream to passing pedestrians

Which one of the following correctly classifies the above practices into those which are LAWFUL and those which are NOT?

A. I is lawful, but II and III are not
B. II is lawful, but I and III are not
C. II and III are lawful, but I is not
D. I, II and III are not lawful

5. The MAIN purpose of instructing department enforcement personnel to disregard fraternal, labor, social, religious, and political identifications on vehicles is to 5.____

A. provide for impartial enforcement of regulations
B. simplify the work of Parking Enforcement Agents
C. make sure that no one group gets more summonses than any other group
D. increase the number of summonses issued

6. During the absence of the district commander, one of the senior enforcement agents from that district may be assigned to perform the duties of the district commander. If no one has been specifically named to take over this job, the senior who takes over for the district commander is the one 6.____

A. with the most seniority
B. who reports to work first
C. scheduled for a regular day off
D. who has not previously substituted for the district commander

7. While you are checking an area, a motorist in a private car complains to you that an agent issued a summons to him for double parking but that a passenger car parked right behind him did not get a summons. 7.____
The BEST action for you to take is to tell him

A. to give you all the information and you will investigate the matter
B. to call the main office
C. that it was probably just an oversight and you will speak to the agent
D. that whether or not the other driver got a summons is not his business

8. Special Vehicle Identification permits issued to handicapped drivers permit the holders to park 8.____

A. in areas regulated by "No Parking" signs
B. in areas regulated by "No Stopping" signs
C. at fire hydrants
D. at taxi stands

9. The one of the following items which does NOT have to be entered on an enforcement agent's field patrol sheet is the 9.____

A. report of an abandoned car which does not have a Sanitation Department sticker
B. completion of Univac (computer) cards to report missing, defective or vandalized meters
C. listing of the locations of the agent's personal and meal breaks
D. notation that the agent observed collectors from a Finance Department truck collecting money from parking meters

10. Assume that standing is prohibited in a certain area. According to the traffic regulations, the driver of a passenger vehicle in that area would be permitted to 10.____

A. stand in front of a private driveway
B. stop to discharge passengers
C. park temporarily in order to unload merchandise
D. stand for a period of no more than ten minutes provided he remains in the car

11. According to the traffic regulations, the MINIMUM period of time a vehicle may be parked before it is considered to be parked for the principal purpose of storing the vehicle is 11.____

A. 12 hours B. 24 hours C. 36 hours D. 48 hours

12. An enforcement agent finds each of the following three vehicles parked on a street with no posted parking restrictions: 12.____

I. A van with commercial plates which has been parked in front of a store for six hours
II. A car parked at the curb while the owner is changing a flat tire
III. A car parked in front of a private home while the owner is washing the car

According to the traffic regulations, *which one* of the following CORRECTLY classifies the above vehicles into those which should receive summonses and those which should not?

A. I and II should receive summonses, but III should not
B. II and III should receive summonses, but I should not
C. I and III should receive summonses, but II should not
D. I, II, and III should receive summonses

13. A senior enforcement agent should inspect the uniform and equipment of each member of his squad at least once a 13.____

A. day B. week C. pay-period D. month

14. When a senior enforcement agent cannot locate the parking enforcement agent assigned to a patrol area, she notes this fact and the time on her field patrol sheet. According to bureau procedures the FIRST action the senior should take when she sees the missing agent is to 14.____

A. order the agent to report to the district commander
B. ask the agent for an explanation of the absence
C. check the agent's field patrol sheet to see if there was a reason for the absence
D. submit a report on the incident to the district commander

15. In addition to their daily enforcement duties, senior enforcement agents are generally required to 15.____

A. accompany agents to a hospital when agents are injured or assaulted
B. make out probationary reports on clerical personnel
C. deliver completed summonses to the parking violations bureau
D. deliver notices of special assignments to agents who are off duty

16. An enforcement agent should be instructed to issue a summons to a car 16.____

A. that forms part of a funeral procession, double-parked in front of a funeral parlor
B. with DPL plates parked in a "No Standing" zone
C. with MD plates parked for two hours in front of a hospital
D. that displays an SVI card parked in a "No Parking" zone

17. An enforcement agent observes the driver of a passenger vehicle discharging passengers at a bus stop. 17.____
Of the following, the MOST appropriate action for the agent to take is to

A. continue on patrol
B. issue a summons
C. warn the driver that what he is doing is illegal
D. politely ask the driver to move

18. The *one* of the following who usually assigns enforcement agents to their daily patrol areas and rotates the agents from one patrol area to another is the 18.____

A. senior enforcement agent
B. district commander
C. regional commander
D. chief of the traffic control bureau

19. An enforcement agent on patrol discovers a traffic signal out of order. 19.____
The FIRST of the following actions the agent should take is to

A. regulate traffic at the intersection himself until repair service arrives
B. inform the Police Department of the problem
C. notify Control 800 on his portable radio
D. note the problem on the back of his field patrol sheet

20. Following are three statements concerning the uniforms and personal appearance of enforcement agents: 20.____

I. Dangling earrings and numerous rings are not to be worn on duty.
II. Uniforms may be worn to and from work.
III. A neat beard and trimmed mustache may be worn.

Which of the following classifies the above statements into those which are CORRECT and those which are NOT?

A. I is correct, but II and III are not
B. II is correct, but I and III are not
C. II and III are correct, but I is not
D. I and III are correct, but II is not

21. Of the following, a senior enforcement agent is responsible for 21.____

A. setting-up the weekly roll call
B. taking portable radios for necessary repairs
C. approving transfer requests
D. investigating reports of lost summonses

22. Assume that a private vehicle has stopped at an unmarked crosswalk to permit a pedestrian to cross the roadway. According to the traffic regulations concerning passing, the driver of another private vehicle approaching from the rear may 22.____

A. pass the stopped vehicle
B. not pass the stopped vehicle
C. pass the stopped vehicle only if weather conditions make it possible to do so safely
D. not pass the stopped vehicle unless he does so from the left

23. A senior enforcement agent notices that some of the agents in his squad have written their rank and signature in ink on several books of summonses before they go out into the field. 23.____
According to traffic control bureau policy, this practice is

A. *advisable,* PRIMARILY because it saves the agents time in the field
B. *advisable,* PRIMARILY because those summonses cannot be taken and used by other agents
C. *inadvisable,* PRIMARILY because an agent may resign or be transferred, leaving the district office with several pre-signed summonses
D. *inadvisable,* PRIMARILY because it wastes time in the district office

24. A senior enforcement agent notices that the uniform of one of the agents under his supervision is in such poor condition that the senior believes it should be replaced. According to traffic control bureau procedures, the NEXT step the senior should take is to 24.____

A. order the agent to purchase a new uniform
B. check to see that the agent purchases a new uniform within 10 days
C. make a note that the agent needs a new uniform and report this fact to the district commander at the next uniform inspection
D. ask the district commander to inspect the agent's uniform as soon as possible

25. A senior enforcement agent on patrol hears the following messages exchanged between an enforcement agent and the radio dispatcher: 25.____

ENFORCEMENT AGENT: 10-15, New York Plate IDA MARY PETER 1 - 2 - 3 - 4, K
DISPATCHER: 10-4, 10-6, K

This is followed by :

DISPATCHER: New York Plate IDA MARY PETER 1-2-3-4,10-17, K
ENFORCEMENT AGENT: 10-4, K

Which one of the following BEST describes this exchange of messages?

A. The agent is calling for a tow truck for a vehicle with New York license plate number IMP 1234, and the Dispatcher verifies that a tow truck is on the way
B. The agent is requesting information on a vehicle that may be stolen and the Dispatcher responds that the vehicle is not listed as stolen
C. The agent is requesting information on a vehicle that may be stolen and the Dispatcher responds that the vehicle is listed as stolen
D. The agent is reporting an accident involving a vehicle with New York license plate IMP 1234, and the Dispatcher verifies that the message has been received

26. *Which one* of the following is the PROPER way for an agent to correct a summons on which the agent entered an incorrect license plate number? 26.____

   A. Draw a line through the incorrect number and write the correction immediately above it
   B. Issue a new, correct summons and submit the original summons with a memo reporting the mistake to the district commander
   C. Discard the summons and the stub and renumber the next summons
   D. Erase the mistake, enter the correct information, initial the correction, and complete the summons

27. *When* should luminous safety vests and white glbves be worn by traffic control agents who are directing traffic? Luminous safety vests 27.____

   A. should be worn only during hours of darkness, and white gloves as weather conditions dictate
   B. should be worn at all times, and white gloves only during hours of daylight
   C. should be worn only during hours of darkness, and white gloves at all times
   D. and white gloves should be worn at all times

28. According to traffic control bureau procedures, *how frequently* should performance evaluation reports on probationary enforcement agents be prepared by senior enforcement agents? 28.____

   A. Every sixty days during the first year of employment
   B. Once a month during the first six months of employment
   C. Twice a month during the first year of employment
   D. Every week during the first six months of employment

29. Following are three statements concerning the use of time and leave in the traffic control bureau: 29.____

   I. An employee with more than twelve latenesses in any vacation year shall be charged double time for the latenesses.
   II. Sick leave is accrued at, the rate of 1 1/2 days a month.
   III. A request tp take time off for personal business must be submitted at least five days in advance.

   Which one of the following correctly classifies the above statements into those which are CORRECT and those which are NOT?

   A. I and II are correct, but III is not
   B. II and III are correct, but I is not
   C. II is correct, but I and III are not
   D. III is correct, but I and II are not

30. Traffic signs on certain streets indicate that stopping, standing or parking regulations do NOT apply on Sundays. These regulations are also suspended on certain holidays. *Which* of the following is NOT one of these "Sunday" holidays? 30.____

   A. Election Day
   B. Labor Day
   C. Independence Day
   D. Memorial Day

31. When the traffic commissioner declares a state of snow emergency, NO person may operate a 31.____

A. commercial vehicle on any street unless the vehicle is equipped with snow tires or chains
B. vehicle in Manhattan on any cross street between 59th Street and the Battery unless the vehicle is equipped with snow tires or chains
C. vehicle on the Brooklyn-Queens Expressway unless the vehicle is equipped with snow tires or chains
D. taxicab on any street in the city unless the vehicle is equipped with chains

32. A traffic control agent should NOT issue a summons when a vehicle makes an illegal left turn if the vehicle is 32.____

A. a car with MD license plates
B. a Sanitation Department sweeper engaged in cleaning the street
C. an official State government vehicle
D. a limousine with diplomatic license plates

33. An enforcement agent who has been assaulted and injured calls 911 for police assistance. When the police arrive, it would be INCORRECT for the agent to 33.____

A. let the police know he is injured and needs immediate medical attention
B. give both his office and home address to the police
C. notify the district office of his location and tell the office that the police have been summoned
D. take down the name, shield number and precinct of each police officer who participates in the incident

34. The duties of a senior parking enforcement agent include all of the following EXCEPT 34.____

A. distributing carfare to agents
B. filing charges against agents
C. assisting in the training of newly assigned agents
D. sending memos directly to the assistant director of the traffic control bureau

35. A senior parking enforcement agent should advise a traffic control agent that, while on duty at an intersection, it is generally proper to do all of the following EXCEPT 35.____

A. give brief directions to motorists stopped for a light
B. leave the intersection to report a fire by pulling a fire alarm box
C. monitor all calls on his radio to learn of conditions which might cause delays in his area
D. leave the intersection for a rest break between 7:00 a.m. and 9:00 a.m.

36. The one of the following duties which is NOT normally assigned to a senior parking enforcement agent is 36.____

A. going on car patrol
B. approving vacation requests
C. observing the on-the-job performance of traffic control agents
D. dropping off and picking up parking enforcement agents at distant field assignments

37. A senior parking enforcement agent has a tire "blowout" while driving an official department motor vehicle. 37.____
All of the following are generally correct actions to take in this situation EXCEPT

A. steering straight ahead
B. keeping a firm grip on the steering wheel
C. braking quickly to stop the car
D. releasing the gas pedal

38. While driving a department motor vehicle along the highway, you feel the car pull to the right. This is LEAST likely to be a sign of possible trouble with the 38.____

A. steering mechanism
B. wheel alignment
C. transmission
D. tires

39. It has been suggested that a driver should expect other drivers to do the wrong thing and be ready with a plan of action to counter the other driver's errors. Following this practice can BEST be described as 39.____

A. *advisable,* CHIEFLY because it develops a driver's skill in handling his vehicle
B. *advisable,* CHIEFLY because it helps to avoid accidents
C. *inadvisable,* CHIEFLY because most other drivers follow the rules of the road
D. *inadvisable,* CHIEFLY because it takes the driver's attention away from immediate conditions

40. A senior parking enforcement agent is driving an official department motor vehicle on patrol. She notices that the red emergency light is on, indicating that the engine is overheated. She sees steam coming out from under the engine hood. 40.____
Of the following, the MOST appropriate action for the senior to take in this situation is to

A. stop the car, open the engine hood, get a pail of cold water, and pour it over the engine
B. stop the car, open the engine hood, remove the radiator cap, and relieve the steam pressure in the radiator
C. stop the car, open the engine hood, wait until the car cools down, then drive it to the nearest service station
D. continue driving the car, but take it ti the repair shops instead of continuing on patrol

KEY (CORRECT ANSWERS)

1.	A	11.	B	21.	B	31.	C
2.	C	12.	C	22.	B	32.	B
3.	D	13.	A	23.	C	33.	B
4.	B	14.	C	24.	D	34.	D
5.	A	15.	A	25.	B	35.	D
6.	A	16.	B	26.	B	36.	B
7.	A	17.	A	27.	D	37.	C
8.	A	18.	B	28.	B	38.	C
9.	D	19.	C	29.	D	39.	B
10.	B	20.	A	30.	A	40.	C

TEST 2

DIRECTIONS: Each question or incomplete statement is followed by several suggested answers or completions. Select the one that BEST answers the question or completes the statement. *PRINT THE LETTER OF THE CORRECT ANSWER IN THE SPACE AT THE RIGHT.*

1. Department procedures permit operation of a department motor vehicle even when there is 1.____

   A. white exhaust vapor
   B. no transmission oil
   C. overheating
   D. low oil pressure

2. Following are three statements concerning safe following distances in highway driving: 2.____
   I. When traveling at 40 miles per hour on dry pavement, allow about 80 feet between your car and the car in front of you
   II. When driving at night at any speed, you will be able to stop within the distance lighted by your car's headlights
   III. When traveling at 30 miles per hour on wet pavement, allow about 60 feet of space between your car and the car in front of you

   Which one of the following *correctly* classifies the above statements into those which are CORRECT and those which are NOT?

   A. I is correct, but II and III are not
   B. II is correct, but I and III are not
   C. I and II are correct, but III is not
   D. I and III are correct, but II is not

3. Following are three statements concerning driving practices at intersections: 3.____
   I. When making a right turn, place your vehicle so as to block any vehicle that might try to squeeze between you and the curb
   II. When making a left turn, have your wheels turned while waiting for traffic to clear
   III. When driving through an intersection, have you foot off the accelerator and on the brake pedal as you approach the intersection

   Which one of the following *correctly* classifies the above statements into those that are PROPER and those that are NOT?

   A. I and II are proper, but III is not
   B. I and III are proper, but II is not
   C. II and III are proper, but I is not
   D. I, II and III are proper

4. Following are three statements concerning pedestrians in the city: 4.____
   I. Pedestrians are permitted to stand in the road to sell merchandise to passing motorists
   II. Pedestrians under 14 years of age typically have quick reaction time, good judgment, and are seldom involved in accidents
   III. Pedestrians may not always have the legal right of way but cars must always yield the right of way to a pedestrian

   Which one of the following *correctly* classifies the above statements into those which are CORRECT and those which are NOT?

   A. I and II are correct, but III is not
   B. II and III are correct, but I is not
   C. II is correct, but I and III are not
   D. III is correct, but I and II are not

QUESTIONS 5 and 6.

Questions 5 and 6 are based on the information given on the report forms pictured below and on the following page.

Chart I and Chart II are parts of the Field Patrol Sheets of two Parking Enforcement Agents. They show the numbers of violations issued on a particular day. Chart III is the Tally Sheet for that day prepared by the Senior Parking Enforcement Agent from the Field Patrol Sheets of the entire squad.

Chart I

Area or Post	TYPE OF VIOLATION										
	Mtrs	B/S	D/P	Hyd	N/S	N/Sp	Taxi	Curb	N/P	Alt	Other	Total
19	2	3	2	2	3	3	0	1	1	5	1	23
21	4	0	2	0	1	2	2	0	5	9	1	26
Totals	6	3	4	2	4	5	2	1	6	14	2	49

2/4/ — Date; 100 — Badge; PEA Browne — Signature

TCB-61 Checked by ____________ Date ______

Chart II

Area or Post	TYPE OF VIOLATION										
	Mtrs	B/S	D/P	Hyd	N/S	N/Sp	Taxi	Curb	N/P	Alt	Other	Total
31	8	2	0	0	3	2	2	0	4	5	0	26
33	7	0	1	2	3	1	2	0	6	3	0	25
Totals	15	2	1	2	6	3	4	0	10	8	0	51

2/4/ — Date; 101 — Badge; PEA Grey — Signature

TCB-61 Checked by ____________ Date ______

Chart III

TRAFFIC CONTROL BUREAU SENIORS TALLY SHEET													Enf. 23A
Name	Mtrs Ptld	Mtrs	Bus Stop	Dble Park	Hyd	No Stand	No Stop	Taxi Stand	Curb	No Park	Alt Park	Other	Total
Green		18	2	3	1	6	0	0	0	4	10	1	45
Browne		6	3	4	2	4	5	2	1	6	14	2	49
White		12	0	0	0	2	1	1	0	8	8	1	33
Black		20	5	2	3	8	7	5	1	5	4	0	60
Grey		15	2	1	2	9	3	4	0	10	8	0	51
Redding		17	0	1	3	7	5	3	0	8	6	0	50
TOTAL		88	12	11	11	36	21	15	2	41	50	4	288

5. The Senior Parking Enforcement Agent who prepared Chart III made an error in transferring the violation totals from the Field Patrol Sheets to the Seniors Tally Sheet. Which one of the following properly describes the Tally Sheet entry if this error were corrected? 5.____

   A. Parking Enforcement Agent Browne's overall total of summonses issued would be 50
   B. Parking Enforcement Agent Browne's total of summonses issued for Double-Parking violations would be 3
   C. Parking Enforcement Agent Grey's total number of summonses issued for meter violations would be 6
   D. Parking Enforcement Agent Grey's total number of summonses issued for No Standing violations would be 6

6. The parking enforcement agent who issued the MOST summonses for bus stop and taxi stand violations is 6.____

   A. Black B. Redding C. White D. Browne

7. A senior parking enforcement agent is shown a copy of an "Employee's Notice of Injury" form from an Agent who has been injured while on duty. Following is part of that report: 7.____

5. Exact location where accident happened One-half block West of the Northwest corner of Seventh Avenue and 34th Street (in front of 225 West 34th Street.)

6. How did accident happen? (describe fully) I slipped in the street because I didn't look where I was going.

7. Nature and extent of injury Broken foot

8. Did you inform your superior of this accident? Yes Date? Thursday

Which of the following lists ALL of the item numbers which the senior should point out to the agent as missing necessary information?

A. 5 and 6
B. 5, 6 and 7
C. 5, 6 and 8
D. 6, 7 and 8

8. For which of the following is the information recorded on the parking enforcement agent's field patrol sheets LEAST likely to be useful to a Senior Parking Enforcement Agent? 8.____

A. Gathering evidence for use in a disciplinary action against an agent
B. Determining whether agents have been enforcing regulations
C. Learning which agents have the most problems dealing with the public
D. Investigating a complaint that an agent has been absent from his post for several hours

9. Just as a parking enforcement agent has put a summons on an illegally parked car, the driver of the car comes out of a luncheonette and begins calling her names. 9.____
Of the following, the FIRST action the agent should take in this situation is to

A. ask the driver to apologize
B. call for police assistance
C. call the supervisor for assistance
D. walk away and say nothing

10. A senior parking enforcement agent is assigned to instruct the staff of a district office on the use of a new one-page form which will be put into use next month. 10.____
Of the following, the BEST way to teach the staff about this new form is to

A. call a staff meeting to explain the use of the new form and find out if the agents have any questions about its use
B. post the new form and the instructions for completing it on a bulletin board in the District Office
C. explain the use of the new form at morning roll call just before the agents go into the field
D. issue a written instruction booklet to each staff member

11. A person asks a traffic control agent for the address of a neighborhood restaurant and directions to it. 11.____
If the agent is unfamiliar with the restaurant, it would generally be BEST for him to tell the person

A. that he is sorry, but he has not heard of the restaurant and is unable to direct him
B. to look up the restaurant's address in a telephone book and come back to the agent for exact directions
C. to find a policeman who should be able to direct him
D. to look up the restaurant in a telephone book and phone them for directions

12. A senior parking enforcement agent on patrol observes an agent and a motorist shouting loudly and angrily at each other. It appears that a fight might start at any moment. Of the following, it would be MOST appropriate for the senior to 12.____

A. continue on patrol and ask the agent about the incident at the end of the tour
B. observe the incident from a distance and allow the agent to handle this situation alone
C. tell the agent that he will try to handle the situation himself
D. calm the motorist by scolding the agent in front of the motorist

13. An enforcement agent reports that one of the merchants in his patrol area with whom he is quite friendly has offered him a gift as a token of thanks for keeping people from misusing the parking spaces in front of his store. The agent explains that he would probably offend the merchant by rejecting the merchandise offered. 13.____
The senior should advise this agent

A. *not to accept* the gift, CHIEFLY because other agents do not receive such gifts
B. *not to accept* the gift, CHIEFLY because acceptance would violate the department code of conduct
C. *to accept* the gift, CHIEFLY because the Department prides itself on maintaining a good relationship with neighborhood merchants
D. *to accept* the gift, CHIEFLY because a gift is a personal matter between two friends and has nothing to do with the job

14. An enforcement agent whose performance has been generally good tells his senior that he would like to discuss some personal problems that have been interfering with his work. In this situation, it would generally be MOST appropriate for the senior to 14.____

A. tell the agent he has not noticed any change in his work lately and that his problems cannot be too serious
B. listen while the agent discusses his problems, but refer him for professional counseling if his problems seem serious
C. tell the agent that it is his responsibility to solve his own personal problems
D. ask one of the agent's close friends on the job to have a talk with him and find out the nature of the problem

15. An enforcement agent has just completed a summons for a meter violation when the driver approaches. The driver is annoyed and demands that the summons be destroyed. Of the following, *which* is the MOST appropriate response for. the agent to make? 15.____

A. "I'm extremely sorry, sir, but I'm only doing my job."
B. "I'm supposed to enforce the regulations strictly and without exception."
C. "Leave me alone, mister, we're not allowed to tear up tickets."
D. "Don't you know enough to put a dime in the meter, like everyone else parked on this block?"

16. A senior enforcement agent on foot patrol is checking summbnses on parked cars. He finds a summons on which the "scheduled fine" box is not filled in. The agent who issued the summons has already left the area. 16.____
In this situation, it would be MOST appropriate for the senior to

A. leave the summons as it is, since the motorist can find out the amount of the fine himself
B. find the agent and tell him to return to the car, fill in the missing information, and make a notation of the error in the district office at the end of the tour
C. fill in the correct amount of fine on the summons and make a note on the field patrol sheet to mention the error to the agent at the end of the tour
D. have the agent write a memorandum describing the error

17. Praise by a supervisor can be an important element in motivating subordinates. Following are three statements concerning a supervisor's praise of subordinates: 17.____
I. In order to be effective, praise must be lavish and constantly restated.
II. Praise should be given in a manner which meets the needs of the individual subordinate.
III. The subordinate whose work is praised should believe that the praise is earned.

Which of the following correctly classifies the above statements into those that are CORRECT and those that are NOT?

A. I is correct, but II and III are not
B. II and III are correct, but I is not
C. III is correct, but I and II are not
D. I and II are correct, but III is not

18. Assume that you are a senior enforcement agent and that several of the recently appointed agents on your squad have not been adequately enforcing alternate side of the street parking regulations. 18.____
Of the following, the MOST appropriate way for you to correct this situation is to

A. begin disciplinary proceedings against the individuals involved
B. call a brief meeting of your squad to review the regulations and emphasize the need for strict enforcement
C. spend more of your own patrol time issuing summonses for violations of alternate side of the street parking regulations
D. reprimand the entire squad during Roll Call for not enforcing alternate side of the street regulations

19. A senior enforcement agent notices that although there have been several defective meters in a recently appointed agent's patrol area, the agent has not turned in any of the Univac cards used to report broken parking meters. 19.____
Of the following, it would be MOST appropriate for the senior to assume that the

A. district office has run out of these cards
B. agent has spent too much time loafing to locate any broken meters
C. agent should be disciplined for not turning in these cards
D. agent may need more training in detecting broken meters and filling out the Univac cards

20. A senior enforcement agent, upon arriving in the district office for the 7:30AM-3:30PM tour, finds that the agent assigned to cover a priority patrol area has called in sick. Of the following, it would generally be MOST appropriate for the senior to 20.____

A. notify the district commander that there is no coverage for the priority patrol area
B. call in an agent who is scheduled for a regular day off to cover the priority patrol area
C. shift the patrol assignment of another agent to the priority patrol area
D. cover the priority area personally while out on patrol

21. Following are three statements concerning various ways of giving orders to enforcement agents: 21.____

I. An implied order or suggestion is usually appropriate for the inexperienced agent.
II. A polite request is less likely to upset a sensitive agent than a direct order.
III. A direct order is usually appropriate in an emergency situation.

Which of the following correctly classifies the above statements into those that are CORRECT and those that are NOT?

A. I is correct, but II and III are not
B. II and III are correct, but I is not
C. III is correct, but I and II .are not
D. I and II are correct, but III is not

22. A senior enforcement agent on patrol observes two agents entering a bar and ordering beer when they should be on patrol. Of the following, the *correct* procedure for the senior to follow is to 22.____

A. note how long they remain in the bar, say nothing to them at the time, but speak to the agents when they return to the district office
B. make no note of the incident and quietly tell the agents to leave the bar and continue their patrol duties
C. call the District Commander immediately to report the incident, and tell the agents to proceed directly to the district office
D. tell the agents to return to duty, enter the incident on his field patrol sheet and on theirs, and submit a memo to the District Commander at the end of the tour

23. A senior enforcement agent feels that he is about to lose his temper while reprimanding a subordinate. Of the following, the BEST action for the senior to take is to 23.____

A. postpone the reprimand for a short time until his self-control is assured
B. continue the reprimand because a loss of temper by the senior will show the subordinate the seriousness of the error he made
C. continue the reprimand because failure to do so will show that the senior does not have complete self-control
D. postpone the reprimand until the subordinate is capable of understanding the reason for the supervisor's loss of temper

24. Daily inspections by senior enforcement agents of their subordinates' uniforms are useful *chiefly* because 24.____

    A. they show the department that the seniors are performing their duties
    B. subordinates learn to expect the inspections and follow the rules automatically
    C. they help to insure the proper appearance of the agents before the public
    D. subordinates appreciate the attention they receive form their superiors

25. While in the field, an enforcement agent asks a senior a question about how to request maternity leave from the Department of Traffic. The senior does not know the answer. Of the following, it would be BEST for the senior to tell the agent 25.____

    A. to wait until she is ready to leave before inquiring about maternity leave
    B. that he does not know the answer but will get the information for her as soon as possible
    C. to call the District Commander from the field
    D. to write to her union representative

26. Enforcement agent Jones tells a senior enforcement agent that agent Smith has been taking lunch breaks of up to two hours.
Of the following, the FIRST thing for the senior to do in this situation is to 26.____

    A. tell agent Jones to stop gossiping about her fellow employees
    B. refer the matter to the District Commander for investigation
    C. take disciplinary action against agent Smith
    D. investigate the matter and get all the facts from both agents

27. During their probationary period, parking enforcement and traffic control agents are informed of deficiencies in their performance.
This practice is 27.____

    A. *good,* chiefly because agents learn where they need to improve
    B. *good,* chiefly because agents can defend themselves against false charges
    C. *poor,* chiefly because agents may become easily discouraged
    D. *poor,* chiefly because any improvement in performance is likely to be temporary

28. Of the following, the MOST practical method of providing on-the-job training for newly assigned enforcement agents who have just completed the course at the training division is for the senior to 28.____

    A. assign each new agent to go out on patrol with a more experienced agent until the new agent learns the job
    B. have the new agents accompany the senior on patrol for about two weeks
    C. accompany the new agents on patrol for the first half of their tour each day, but let them patrol on their own for the last half
    D. give each agent his own patrol area to cover alone, thus letting him learn the job by doing it

29. A senior enforcement agent should generally give an *oral* order rather than a *written* order to subordinates when 29.____

    A. a precise record of the instructions given in the order is required
    B. the subordinates must refresh their memories from time to time to properly carry out the order

C. the order is a very complicated one
D. the order involves a routine activity which the subordinates have performed properly in the past

30. The one of the following which is NOT a valid principle for a supervisor to keep in mind when talking to a subordinate about his performance is: 30.____

A. People frequently know when they deserve criticism
B. Supervisors should be prepared to offer suggestions to subordinates about how to improve their work
C. Good points should be discussed before bad points
D. Magnifying a subordinate's faults will get him to improve faster

31. In many organizations information travels quickly through the "grapevine". 31.____
Following are three statements concerning the "grapevine":
I. Information an enforcement agent does not want to tell her supervisor may reach the supervisor through the grapevine.
II. A supervisor can often do her job better by knowing the information that travels through the grapevine.
III. A supervisor can depend on the grapevine as a way to get accurate information from the enforcement agents on her staff.
Which one of the following correctly classifies the above statements into those which are generally CORRECT and those which are NOT?

A. II is correct, but I and III are not
B. III is correct, but I and II are not
C. I and II are correct, but III is not
D. I and III are correct, but II is not

32. The Traffic Control Bureau has received a letter of complaint from a member of the public about an enforcement agent. Preliminary investigation shows that the complaint appears to be unjustified and that the subordinate is completely innocent. 32.____
Of the following, it would generally be MOST appropriate for the agent's supervisor to

A. proceed no further since the complaint is unjustified
B. transfer the subordinate to another patrol assignment to prevent possible contact with the same member of the public
C. make no note of the complaint on a complaint record form because any entry in the files could harm the subordinate's career
D. complete a thorough investigation of the matter and fill out a complaint record form

33. Following are three statements concerning supervision: 33.____
I. A supervisor knows he is doing a good job if his subordinates depend upon him to make every decision
II. A supervisor who delegates authority to his subordinates soon finds that his subordinates begin to resent him.
III. Giving credit for good work is frequently an effective method of getting subordinates to work harder.
Which one of the following correctly classifies the above statements into those that are CORRECT and those that are NOT?

A. I and II are correct, but III is not
B. II and III are correct, but I is not

C. II is correct, but I and III are not
D. III is correct, but I and II are not

34. Preparing supervisors to carry out their training responsibilities is the most effective training activity that can be carried on. 34.____
Applying this principle to senior enforcement agents would be

A. *undesirable,* chiefly because adequate training is given to all enforcement agents at the training division
B. *undesirable,* chiefly because training supervisors is costly and inefficient
C. *desirable,* chiefly because training of subordinates by supervisors who are trained to teach is generaly helpful
D. *desirable,* chiefly because it gives the seniors an added job function

35. Training senior enforcement agents to take over the job of the District Commander when the District Commander is absent is *generally* 35.____

A. *desirable*, chiefly because it increases staff flexibility and the district's readiness to handle emergencies
B. *desirable*, chiefly because it enables seniors to pass promotion examinations
C. *undesirable*, chiefly because errors made by the seniors during such training cannot be corrected
D. *undesirable,* chiefly because Department of Traffic regulations forbid seniors from performing the District Commander's job

36. Following are three statements concerning on-the-job training: 36.____
I. On-the-job training is rarely used as a method of training employees.
II. On-the-job training is often carried on with little or no planning.
III. On-the-job training is often less expensive than other types of training.
Which one of the following BEST classifies the above statements into those that are CORRECT and those that are NOT?

A. I is correct, but II and III are not
B. II is correct, but I and III are not
C. I and II are correct, but III is not
D. II and III are correct, but I is not

37. The one of the following that is the MOST appropriate action for a senior enforcement agent to take when criticizing a subordinate for carelessness in making out summonses is to 37.____

A. make the subordinate feel ashamed of his work
B. direct his criticism at specific mistakes made by the subordinate
C. focus his comments on the subordinate's overall job performance
D. tell the subordinate that his carelessness shows that he is unable to handle the job

38. Of the following, the LEAST appropriate action for a supervisor to take in preparing a disciplinary case against a subordinate is to 38.____

A. keep careful records of each incident in which the subordinate has been guilty of misconduct or incompetency, even though immediate disciplinary action may not be necessary
B. discuss with the employee each incident of misconduct as it occurs so the employee knows where he stands
C. accept memoranda from any other employees who may have been witnesses to acts of misconduct
D. keep the subordinate's personnel file confidential so that he is unaware of the evidence being gathered against him

39. Traffic control agents on duty at intersections should be instructed by their supervisors to do all of the following EXCEPT 39.____

A. stand in the center of the intersection of two-way streets
B. turn in the direction in which traffic is moving
C. direct turning vehicles to complete their turns behind him
D. move from place to place within an intersection of a one-way street, as traffic conditions change

40. The one of the following which is NOT an acceptable reason for taking disciplinary action against a subordinate guilty of serious violations of the rules is that 40.____

A. the supervisor can "let off steam" against subordinates who break rules frequently
B. a subordinate whose work continues to be unsatisfactory may be terminated
C. a subordinate may be encouraged to improve his work
D. an example is set for other employees

KEY (CORRECT ANSWERS)

1. A	11. B	21. B	31. C
2. A	12. C	22. D	32. D
3. B	13. B	23. A	33. D
4. D	14. B	24. C	34. C
5. D	15. B	25. B	35. A
6. A	16. C	26. D	36. D
7. D	17. B	27. A	37. B
8. C	18. B	28. A	38. D
9. D	19. D	29. D	39. C
10. A	20. C	30. D	40. A

EXAMINATION SECTION
TEST 1

DIRECTIONS: Each question or incomplete statement is followed by several suggested answers or completions. Select the one that BEST answers the question or completes the statement. *PRINT THE LETTER OF THE CORRECT ANSWER IN THE SPACE AT THE RIGHT.*

1. Of the following, the factor affecting employee morale which the immediate supervisor is LEAST able to control is 1.____

   A. handling of grievances
   B. fair and impartial treatment of subordinates
   C. general personnel rules and regulations
   D. accident prevention

2. When one of your agents does outstanding work, you should 2.____

   A. explain to your other agents that you expect the same kind of work from them
   B. praise him for his work so that he will know it is appreciated
   C. say nothing because other agents may think you are showing favoritism
   D. show him how his work can be improved even more so that he will not sit back

3. For you as a supervisor to consider a suggestion from a probationary agent for improving a procedure would be 3.____

   A. *poor* practice, because this agent is too new on the job to know much about it
   B. *good* practice, because you may be able to share credit for the suggestion
   C. *poor* practice, because it may hurt the morale of the older employees
   D. *good* practice, because the suggestion may be worthwhile

4. If you find you must criticize the work of one of your enforcement agents, it would be BEST for you to 4.____

   A. mention the good points in his work as well as the faults
   B. caution him that he will receive an unsatisfactory performance report unless his work improves
   C. compare his work to that of the other agents you supervise
   D. apologize for making the criticism

5. As a senior enforcement agent, which one of the following matters would it be BEST for you to talk over with your supervisor before you take final action? 5.____

   A. One of the agents you supervise continues to disregard your instructions repeatedly in spite of repeated warnings.
   B. One of your agents tells you he wants to discuss a personal problem.
   C. A probationary agent tells you he does not understand a procedure.
   D. One of your agents tells you he disagrees with the way you rate his work.

6. If one of your subordinates asks you a question about a department rule and you do not know the answer, you should tell him that 6.____

   A. he should try to get the information himself
   B. you do not have the answer, but you will get it for him as soon as you can

C. he should ask you the question again a week from now
D. he should put the question in writing

7. If, as a senior agent, you realize that you have been unfair in criticizing one of your subordinates, the BEST action for you to take is to 7.____

A. say nothing but overlook some error made by this agent in the future
B. be frank and tell the agent that you are sorry for the mistake you made
C. let the agent know in some indirect way, without admitting your mistake, that you realize he was not at fault
D. say nothing but be more careful about criticizing subordinates in the future

8. Of the following, the MOST important reason for a supervisor to write an accident report as soon as possible after an accident has happened is to 8.____

A. make sure that important facts about the accident are not forgotten
B. avoid delay in getting compensation for the injured person
C. get adequate medical treatment for the injured person
D. keep department accident statistics up to date

9. In any matter which may require disciplinary action, the FIRST responsibility of the supervisor is to 9.____

A. decide what penalty should be applied for the offense
B. refer the matter to a higher authority for complete investigation
C. place the interests of the department above those of the employee
D. investigate the matter fully to get all the facts

10. Suppose you find it necessary to criticize one of the enforcement agents you supervise. You should 10.____

A. send an official letter to his home
B. speak to him about the matter privately
C. speak to him at a staff meeting
D. ask another enforcement agent who is friendly with him to talk to him about the matter

11. Some of your subordinates have been coming to you with complaints you feel are unimportant.
For you to hear their stories out is 11.____

A. *poor* practice; you should spend your time on more important matters
B. *good* practice; this will increase your popularity with your subordinates
C. *poor* practice; subordinates should learn to come to you only with major grievances
D. *good* practice; it may prevent minor complaints from developing into major grievances

12. Suppose that not one of a group of employees has turned in an idea to the employees' suggestion system during the past year.
The MOST probable reason for this situation is that the 12.____

A. supervisor of these employees is not doing enough to encourage them to take part in this program
B. employees in this group are not able to develop any good ideas
C. money awards given for suggestions used are not high enough to make employees interested
D. methods and procedures of operation do not need improvement

13. For you as a supervisor to give each of your subordinates *exactly the same* type of supervision is 13.____

A. *advisable,* because doing this insures fair and impartial treatment of each individual
B. *not advisable,* because each person is different and there is no one supervisory procedure for dealing with individuals that applies in every case
C. *advisable,* because once a supervisor learns how to deal with a subordinate who brings a problem to him, he can handle another subordinate with this problem in the same way
D. *not advisable,* because individuals like to think that they are receiving better treatment than others

14. In evaluating personnel, a supervisor should keep in mind that the MOST important objective of performance evaluations is to 14.____

A. encourage employees to compete for higher performance ratings
B. give recognition to employees who perform well
C. help employees improve their work
D. discipline employees who perform poorly

15. A subordinate tells you that he is having trouble concentrating on his work due to a personal problem at home. 15.____
Of the following, it would be BEST for you to

A. refer him to a community service agency
B. listen quietly to the story, because he may just need a sympathetic ear
C. tell him that you cannot help him because the problem is not job-related
D. ask him some questions about the nature of the problem and tell him how you would handle it

16. To do a good job of performance evaluation, it is BEST for a supervisor to 16.____

A. measure the employee's performance against standard performance requirements
B. compare the employee's performance to that of another employee doing similar work
C. leave out any consideration of the employee's personal traits
D. give greatest weight to instances of unusually good or unusually poor performance

17. It is particularly important that disciplinary actions be equitable as between individuals. 17.____
This statement implies that

A. punishment applied in disciplinary actions should be lenient
B. proposed disciplinary actions should be reviewed by higher authority

C. subordinates should have an opportunity to present their stories before penalties are applied
D. penalties for violations of the rules should be standardized and consistently applied

18. Assume that an agency has an established procedure for handling employee grievances. An employee in this agency comes to his immediate supervisor with a grievance. The supervisor investigates the matter and makes a decision. However, the employee is not satisfied with the decision made by the supervisor. 18.____
The BEST action for the supervisor to take is to

A. tell the employee he will review the matter further
B. remind the employee that he is the supervisor and the employee must act in accordance with his decision
C. explain to the employee how he can carry his complaint forward to the next step in the grievance procedure
D. tell the employee he will consult with his own superiors on the matter

19. Of the following, the CHIEF purpose of a probationary period for a new employee is to allow time for 19.____

A. finding out whether the selection processes are satisfactory
B. determining the fitness of the employee to continue in the job
C. the employee to decide whether he wants a permanent appointment
D. the employee to make adjustments in his home circumstances made necessary by the job

20. Of the following, the subject that would be LEAST important to include in a *break-in* program for new enforcement agents is 20.____

A. explanation of rules, regulations, and policies of the agency
B. instruction in the agency's history and programs
C. explanation of the importance of the new employees' own particular job
D. explanation of the duties and responsibilities of the parking meter collectors who collect the parking meter fees

21. Suppose a new enforcement agent under your supervision seems slow to learn and is making mistakes in writing summonses. 21.____
Your FIRST action should be to

A. pass this information on to the district commander
B. reprimand the agent so he will not repeat these mistakes
C. find out whether this agent understands your instructions
D. note these facts for future reference when writing up the monthly performance evaluation

22. In training new enforcement agents to do a certain job, it would be LEAST desirable for you to 22.____

A. demonstrate how the job is done, step by step
B. encourage the agents to ask questions if they aren't clear about any point
C. tell them about the various mistakes other agents have made in doing this job
D. have the agents do the job, explaining to you what they are doing and why

23. One of the agents under your supervision is resentful when you ask her to remove her jangling bracelets before she starts on patrol. 23.____
Of the following, the BEST explanation you can give her for the rule against wearing such jewelry while on duty is that

A. the jewelry may create a safety hazard
B. employees must give up certain personal liberties if they want to keep their jobs
C. agents cannot perform their duties as efficiently if they wear distracting jewelry
D. citizens may receive an unfavorable impression of the department

24. Of the following, the LEAST important reason for having a department handbook and a bureau standard operating procedure is to 24.____

A. help in training new employees
B. provide a source of reference for department and bureau rules and procedures
C. prevent errors in work by providing clear guidelines
D. make the supervisor's job easy

25. On inspecting your squad prior to patrol, you note an enforcement agent improperly and unacceptably uniformed. The FIRST action you should take is to 25.____

A. call the enforcement agent aside and insist on immediate correction if possible
B. notify the district commander right away
C. have the enforcement agent submit a memorandum explaining the reason for the improper uniform
D. permit the enforcement agent to proceed on patrol but warn him not to let this happen again

KEY (CORRECT ANSWERS)

1.	C	11.	D
2.	B	12.	A
3.	D	13.	B
4.	A	14.	C
5.	A	15.	B
6.	B	16.	A
7.	B	17.	D
8.	A	18.	C
9.	D	19.	B
10.	B	20.	D

21. C
22. C
23. D
24. D
25. A

TEST 2

DIRECTIONS: Each question or incomplete statement is followed by several suggested answers or completions. Select the one that BEST answers the question or completes the statement. *PRINT THE LETTER OF THE CORRECT ANSWER IN THE SPACE AT THE RIGHT.*

1. An enforcement agent is just preparing to write a summons for double parking when the driver of the vehicle returns to nove the car. 1.____
   For this enforcement agent to continue on patrol without issuing the summons is

   A. *advisable,* since he had not started to write the summons and, therefore, should extend this courtesy to the citizen
   B. *inadvisable,* since it is the agent's duty to issue the summons
   C. *advisable,* since the driver may abuse or assault him if he issues the summons
   D. *inadvisable,* since it may lead the driver to think he can get away with other parking violations

2. For enforcement agents on duty to give street directions to the public when asked for them is 2.____

   A. *good* practice, because the agents are best qualified to know all the streets in their district
   B. *poor* practice, because this may delay them in covering their assigned areas fully
   C. *good* practice, because this helps to establish a good relationship between the public and the department
   D. *poor* practice, because police officers are better qualified to give such information

3. The MAIN reason for having the department of traffic give out publicity about the work of the bureau of enforcement is to 3.____

   A. justify increased money for the department in future budgets
   B. show the public the need for better salaries for employees of this very important bureau
   C. free the top officials of the department from the pressures of special interest groups
   D. inform the public about the work and problems of this bureau so that they will better understand and comply with its regulations

4. When you are training new enforcement agents, you should instruct them that if a motorist is loud and rude to them, they should 4.____

   A. say nothing and continue on patrol
   B. call a policeman and have the motorist arrested
   C. shout right back in the same manner
   D. hide their badge and refuse to give their number

5. While you are checking an area, a motorist in a private car complains to you that an agent issued a summons to him for double parking but that a passenger car parked right behind him did not get a summons. 5.____
   The BEST action for you to take is to tell him

A. to call the main office
B. to give you all the information and you will investigate the matter
C. that it was probably just an oversight and you will speak to the agent
D. that whether or not the other driver got a summons is not his business

6. Rules of the bureau of enforcement require that summonses are to be issued for parking violations even when 6._____

A. there is no sign
B. the vehicles are fire engines or ambulances
C. the car has DPL plates
D. the car has a PBA card

7. When a plate number on a state permit and the plate on the car do not agree, the enforcement agent should 7._____

A. notify the district commander to advise the state office
B. report the matter to the state office immediately by phone
C. note all the information on the appropriate form
D. notify the bureau chief at the main office

8. On checking your patrol, you find one of your agents off-post. Your FIRST action should be to 8._____

A. reprimand him and send him to his proper post
B. prepare a memorandum to the district commander
C. ask the agent to prepare a memorandum
D. enter the incident on his form and on yours

9. What is the CORRECT procedure an enforcement agent should follow to report a defective off-street meter? 9._____

A. Report on Optical Scanning Card
B. Report on the appropriate form
C. Make note on summons
D. Make an oral report to the senior agent

10. When an agent on patrol observes a vehicle on violation on the opposite side of the street, he should 10._____

A. cross immediately and issue a summons
B. walk to the nearest crosswalk and go back to issue the summons
C. continue on patrol
D. note violation on the appropriate form

11. A parking privilege extended to a driver displaying an SVI card is permission to park 11._____

A. at meters free
B. in No Standing areas
C. at bus stops
D. in DPL spaces

12. If an enforcement agent sees a badly damaged on-street meter, the CORRECT procedure for the agent to follow is to 12._____

A. note the location of the meter on the appropriate form
B. prepare an Optical Scanning Card and submit it on return from patrol

C. ignore it since damaged meters are common and are not within the range of an agent's duties
D. make a note and call the main office

13. Form Enf. 63 should be used by enforcement agents to report 13.____

A. defective on-street meters
B. lost summonses
C. summons refusals
D. possible stolen vehicles

14. From the enforcement agent's viewpoint, the MOST important result of the establishment of the parking violations bureau is that 14.____

A. enforcement is more rapid and efficient
B. agents rarely have had to testify on tickets issued since
C. collection of fines has been speeded up
D. policemen are able to devote more of their time to fighting crime

15. Double parking is permitted by any 15.____

A. commercial vehicle that is quickly loading or unloading alongside a curb where parking is permitted
B. vehicle with a person at the wheel
C. vehicle that is quickly loading or unloading
D. vehicle with MD plates

16. Unmarked police cars displaying green or blue enameled plaques should be tagged only when 16.____

A. parked at a meter on violation
B. parked at a hydrant
C. parked in a bus stop
D. double parked

17. Foreign consuls are issued distinctive license plates which include the letters FC. Which one of the following is a foreign consul plate? 17.____

A. 1237 FC B. FC 1237 C. 12 FC 37 D. 9 FCA

18. Which of the following is a Sunday holiday according to city traffic regulations? 18.____

A. Lincoln's Birthday B. Labor Day
C. Columbus Day D. Veterans' Day

19. While checking the agency copies of summonses, you discover that part of the serial number is missing on one summons.
The CORRECT action for you to take is to 19.____

A. notify the district commander
B. destroy the copy and make out another
C. determine the correct number and insert it in ink
D. have the enforcement agent prepare a memorandum of explanation

20. A form must be submitted by an employee of the bureau of enforcement for any absence EXCEPT 20.____

A. a city civil service job interview
B. vacation days listed on the approved annual leave schedule
C. emergency leave
D. time off for overtime

21. Suppose you get a flat tire at 3:00 P.M. while on tour in a department vehicle. The CORRECT action you should take is to 21.____

A. ask the communications center to send the A.A.A.
B. leave the car at the curb and phone the district office
C. use a local garage to fix the flat and get a bill in duplicate
D. use the car radio to call the department for assistance

22. A supervisor is giving instructions to the agents under his supervision on the proper procedures to follow if assaulted while on patrol. Which one of the following statements should NOT be made by the supervisor to his subordinates? 22.____

A. Make a citizen's arrest of the assailant
B. Obtain police assistance, if required
C. Notify the district commander
D. Obtain medical care if necessary

23. The 6:30 A.M. - 2:30 P.M. tour is always scheduled from Monday through Friday because 23.____

A. the inconvenient hours deserve a bonus of weekends off
B. the Police Department is able to give more time to enforcement of traffic regulations on Saturday mornings
C. an important traffic regulation to be enforced is in effect from Monday through Friday only
D. cars are not available on Saturday

24. You are operating a department vehicle with the two-way radio on. As you approach a construction site, you see a posted warning that blasting is in progress. According to standard operating procedure of the bureau of enforcement, the CORRECT action for you to take is to 24.____

A. immediately turn off the radio
B. report the exact location of the blasting area to the communications center
C. keep the radio on, but not use the microphone
D. leave the neighborhood of the construction site at once

25. Of the following, the factor MOST likely to cause lowered morale among enforcement agents is 25.____

A. lack of higher salaries
B. necessity for working rotating shifts
C. abuse from citizens whom they have summonsed
D. working in *paired* areas

26. If a citizen accuses an enforcement agent on patrol of damaging his car, the agent should tell him to make his complaint to the 26.____

   A. finance administration
   B. main office of the department of traffic
   C. police department
   D. office of the comptrolle

27. The parking violations bureau requires that summonses forwarded to them be separated according to 27.____

   A. violation codes
   B. make of the vehicles
   C. type of registration of the vehicles
   D. police precincts in which the violations occurred

28. When pleading *Not Guilty* by mail to a parking violation, a motorist must select a hearing date. 28.____
The date the motorist may choose is any ______ days of the offense.

   A. weekday within 30
   B. weekday within 31 to 40
   C. day except Sunday within 60
   D. weekday within 60

29. If meters are to be installed in an area where four banks are located, the MOST suitable type to use would be ______ hour meters. 29.____

   A. 4 B. 1 C. 2 D. 3

30. Which one of these is NOT a part of the Transportation Administration? 30.____

   A. Department of Highways
   B. Department of Marine and Aviation
   C. Department of Traffic
   D. Bridge and Tunnel Authority

KEY (CORRECT ANSWERS)

1. A
2. C
3. D
4. A
5. B

6. D
7. B
8. D
9. B
10. C

11. A
12. B
13. D
14. B
15. A

16. C
17. A
18. B
19. C
20. B

21. C
22. A
23. C
24. C
25. C

26. D
27. D
28. B
29. A
30. D

TEST 3

DIRECTIONS: Each question or incomplete statement is followed by several suggested answers or completions. Select the one that BEST answers the question or completes the statement. *PRINT THE LETTER OF THE CORRECT ANSWER IN THE SPACE AT THE RIGHT.*

Questions 1-4.

DIRECTIONS: Questions 1 through 4 are to be answered ONLY according to the information given in the paragraph below.

Abandoned cars — with tires gone, chrome stripped away, and windows smashed — have become a common sight on the city's streets. In 2000, more than 72,000 were deposited at curbs by owners who never came back, an increase of 15,000 from the year before and more than 30 times the number abandoned a decade ago. In January 2001, the city Protection Administrator asked the State Legislature to pass a law requiring a buyer of a new automobile to deposit $100 and an owner of an automobile at the time the law takes effect to deposit $50 with the State Department of Motor Vehicles. In return, they would be given a certificate of deposit that would be passed to each succeeding owner. The final owner would get the deposit money back if he could present proof that he has disposed of his car in an environmentally acceptable manner. The Legislature has given no indication that it planned to rush ahead on the matter.

1. The number of cars abandoned in city streets in 1999 was MOST NEARLY 1.____

   A. 2,500 B. 12,000 C. 27,500 D. 57,000

2. The proposed law would require a person who owned a car bought before the law was passed to deposit 2.____

   A. $100 with the State Department of Motor Vehicles
   B. $50 with the Environmental Protection Administration
   C. $100 with the State Legislature
   D. $50 with the State Department of Motor Vehicles

3. The proposed law would require the State to return the deposit money ONLY when the 3.____

   A. original owner of the car shows proof that he sold it
   B. last owner of the car shows proof that he got rid of the car in a satisfactory way
   C. owner of a car shows proof that he has transferred the certificate of deposit to the next owner
   D. last owner of a car returns the certificate of deposit

4. The MAIN idea or theme of the above article is that 4.____

   A. a proposed new law would make it necessary for car owners in the State to pay additional taxes
   B. the State Legislature is against a proposed law to require deposits from automobile owners to prevent them from abandoning their cars
   C. the city is trying to find a solution for the increasing number of cars abandoned on its streets

D. to pay for the removal of abandoned cars, the city's Environmental Protection Administrator has asked the State to fine automobile owners who abandon their vehicles

Questions 5-9.

DIRECTIONS: Questions 5 through 9 are to be answered ONLY according to the information given in the paragraph below.

Safety belts provide protection for the passengers of a vehicle by preventing them from crashing around inside if the vehicle is involved in a collision. They operate on the principle similar to that used in the packaging of fragile items. You become a part of the vehicle package, and you are kept from being tossed about inside if the vehicle is suddenly decelerated. Many injury-causing collisions at low speeds, for example at city intersections, could have been injury-free if the occupants had fastened their safety belts. There is a double advantage to the driver in that it not only protects him from harm, but prevents him from being yanked away from the wheel, thereby permitting him to maintain control of the car. Since without seat belts the risk of injury is about 50% greater, and the risk of death is about 30% greater, the New York State Vehicle and Traffic Law provides that a motor vehicle manufactured or assembled after June 30, 1964 and designated as a 1965 or later model should have two safety belts for the front seat. It also provides that a motor vehicle manufactured after June 30, 1966 and designated as a 1967 or later model should have at least one safety belt for the rear seat for each passenger for which the rear seat of such vehicle was designed.

5. The principle on which seat belts work is that 5.____

A. a car and its driver and passengers are fragile
B. a person fastened to the car will not be thrown around when the car slows down suddenly
C. the driver and passengers of a car that is suddenly decelerated will be thrown forward
D. the driver and passengers of an automobile should be packaged the way fragile items are packaged

6. We can assume from the above passage that safety belts should be worn at all times because you can NEVER tell when 6.____

A. a car will be forced to turn off onto another road
B. it will be necessary to shift into low gear to go up a hill
C. you will have to speed up to pass another car
D. a car may have to come to a sudden stop

7. Besides preventing injury, an additional benefit from the use of safety belts is that 7.____

A. collisions are fewer
B. damage to the car is kept down
C. the car can be kept under control
D. the number of accidents at city intersections is reduced

8. The risk of death in car accidents for people who don't use safety belts is 8.____

A. 30% greater than the risk of injury
B. 30% greater than for those who do use them

C. 50% less than the risk of injury
D. 50% greater than for those who use them

9. In the State, the number and location of safety belts required by law in a 1966 model car is two safety belts in the front seat 9.____

A. only
B. and one safety belt in the back seat
C. and one safety belt for each person sitting in the back seat
D. and three safety belts in the back seat of a 5-passenger car

10. Of the following, the MOST important reason for a supervisor to prepare good written reports is that 10.____

A. a supervisor is rated on the quality of his reports
B. decisions are often made on the basis of the reports
C. such reports take less time for superiors to review
D. such reports demonstrate efficiency of department operations

11. Of the following, the BEST test of a good report is whether it 11.____

A. provides the information needed
B. shows the good sense of the writer
C. is prepared according to a proper format
D. is grammatical and neat

12. When a supervisor writes a report, he can BEST show that he has an understanding of the subject of the report by 12.____

A. including necessary facts and omitting non-essential details
B. using statistical data
C. giving his conclusions but not the data on which they are based
D. using a technical vocabulary

13. Suppose you and another supervisor on the same level are assigned to work together on a report. You disagree strongly with one of the recommendations the other supervisor wants to include in the report but you cannot change his views. 13.____
Of the following, it would be BEST that

A. you refuse to accept responsibility for the report
B. you ask that someone else be assigned to this project to replace you
C. each of you state his own ideas about this recommendation in the report
D. you give in to the other supervisor's opinion for the sake of harmony

14. Standardized forms are often provided for submitting reports. 14.____
Of the following, the MOST important advantage of using standardized forms for reports is that

A. they take less time to prepare than individually written reports
B. the person making the report can omit information he considers unimportant
C. the responsibility for preparing these reports can be turned over to subordinates
D. necessary information is less likely to be omitte

15. A report which may BEST be classed as a periodic report is one which 15.____

A. requires the same type of information at regular intervals
B. contains detailed information which is to be retained in permanent records
C. is prepared whenever a special situation occurs
D. lists information in graphic form

16. When you drive so that you look ahead to possible mistakes by other drivers and prepare to take preventive action to make up for their mistakes, you are driving 16.____

A. offensively
B. aggressively
C. defensively
D. recklessly

17. The BEST reason for turning off the ignition of a motor vehicle when the gas tank is being filled is that, if this is not done, 17.____

A. the carburetor may be damaged by the introduction of cold gasoline
B. the fumes from the exhaust may overcome the person filling the tank
C. an air block may develop in the vacuum feed line
D. a spark from the electrical system may make the fumes of gasoline catch fire

18. If your car pulls to one side and you are not braking, it is probably a sign of 18.____

A. worn-out shock absorbers
B. worn rear tires
C. unevenly distributed weight in the car
D. worn or improperly adjusted steering mechanism

19. Almost 40 percent of the motor vehicle accidents in the state are rear end collisions. The use of proper following distances can prevent many of these accidents. The RECOMMENDED following distances (space between your car and the car in front) is 19.____

A. one foot for each mile per hour of speed of your car
B. two car lengths (about 40 feet) when traveling 30 miles per hour
C. one car length (about 20 feet) for each ten miles per hour of speed of your car
D. 60 feet at 60 miles per hour

20. The basic rule of driving conduct at an intersection is the rule of right-of-way. According to this rule, 20.____

A. vehicles entering a traffic circle have right-of-way over those already in it
B. pedestrians in crosswalks have right-of-way only if the traffic signal is in their favor
C. at an intersection with no traffic control device, the car on your right has the privilege of going first
D. a car turning left has the right-of-way over a vehicle going straight ahead

21. When you are being passed by another car, you should 21.____

A. slow down and stay to your left
B. slow down and stay to your right
C. keep your normal speed so as not to confuse the driver of the other car
D. keep your normal speed but move to the right

22. The flashing red signal on a traffic light has basically the SAME meaning for motorists as a 22.____

A. steady yellow signal on a traffic light
B. yield sign
C. stop sign
D. red arrow signal on a traffic light

23. When driving, after you pass a car, you should immediately signal your return to the right lane and then swing back into this lane when 23.____

A. you can see the car's front bumper in your rearview mirror
B. the car you are passing has signaled that it is safe to return to the right lane
C. the car you are passing is out of sight
D. you can see pavement in front of the car just passed as you look quickly over your shoulder

24. The type of street marking that cannot be crossed by traffic going in either direction except for a left turn into or out of a driveway or alley is a 24.____

A. single solid white line
B. double broken white line with white edges
C. single solid yellow line with a parallel broken white line
D. double solid yellow line

25. A state traffic sign with a down-pointed triangle would MOST likely warn the driver to 25.____

A. yield
B. detour
C. stop
D. keep right except to pass

KEY (CORRECT ANSWERS)

1.	A	11.	A
2.	D	12.	A
3.	B	13.	C
4.	C	14.	D
5.	B	15.	A
6.	D	16.	C
7.	C	17.	D
8.	B	18.	D
9.	A	19.	C
10.	B	20.	C

21. B
22. C
23. A
24. D
25. A

EXAMINATION SECTION
TEST 1

DIRECTIONS: Each question or incomplete statement is followed by several suggested answers or completions. Select the one that BEST answers the question or completes the statement. *PRINT THE LETTER OF THE CORRECT ANSWER IN THE SPACE AT THE RIGHT.*

1. An employee of the bureau who has used up all his sick leave submits a form requesting that a Monday absence be changed to sick leave. 1.____
The MOST appropriate action for the district commander to take is to

   A. recommend that the absence be charged *Sick - No Pay*
   B. recommend that the absence be charged to annual leave
   C. approve a request for advance sick time to be prepared by the employee
   D. forward the employee's form without approval

2. Unless exempted by administrative direction, it is a policy of the bureau of enforcement that all records, other than summons stubs and field patrol reports, are to be 2.____

   A. kept indefinitely
   B. destroyed after three years
   C. destroyed after five years
   D. destroyed only when directed

3. The collection of parking meter funds is the responsibility of the 3.____

   A. transportation administration
   B. comptroller's office
   C. finance administration
   D. municipal services administration

4. If a citizen accuses an enforcement agent on patrol of damaging his car, the agent should tell him to make his complaint to the 4.____

   A. office of the comptroller
   B. main office of the department of traffic
   C. police department
   D. finance administration

5. The 6:30 A.M. - 2:30 P.M. tour is always scheduled from Monday through Friday because 5.____

   A. the inconvenient hours deserve a bonus of weekends off
   B. the Police Department is able to give more time to enforcement of traffic regulations on Saturday mornings
   C. an important traffic regulation to be enforced is in effect from Monday through Friday only
   D. cars are not available on Saturday

6. If a supervising enforcement agent feels there are reasons why it would be desirable to change patrols in order to cover an area not previously patrolled, he should 6.____

A. recommend the change to the principal enforcement agent after consulting with the senior agents
B. have the senior agents submit written reports on the desirability of the change
C. conduct a 30-day test of the proposed patrol
D. send a memorandum to the main office of the bureau

7. You are operating a department vehicle with the two-way radio on. As you approach a construction site, you see a posted warning that blasting is in progress. According to standard operating procedure of the bureau of enforcement, the CORRECT action for you to take is to 7.____

A. immediately turn off the radio
B. report the exact location of the blasting area to the communications center
C. keep the radio on, but not use the microphone
D. leave the neighborhood of the construction site at once

8. If meters are to be installed in an area where four banks are located, the MOST suitable type to use would be ______ hour meters. 8.____

A. 1/2 B. 1 C. 2 D. 3

9. The parking violations bureau requires that summonses forwarded to them be separated according to 9.____

A. violation codes
B. make of the vehicles
C. type of registration of the vehicles
D. police precincts in which the violations occurred

10. The flashing red signal on a traffic light has basically the same meaning for motorists as a 10.____

A. steady yellow signal on a traffic light
B. yield sign
C. stop sign
D. red arrow signal on a traffic light

11. The settlement of all traffic offenses formerly handled by the Criminal Court is now shared by the Transportation Administration (PVB) and the 11.____

A. State Department of Motor Vehicles
B. Criminal Court
C. Police Department plus the State Department of Motor Vehicles
D. State Department of Motor Vehicles plus the Criminal Court

12. The penalties that can be imposed for a violation of traffic rules and regulations in the city are set forth in the 12.____

A. City Charter
B. State Vehicle and Traffic Law
C. Administrative Code
D. City Traffic Regulations

13. Parking summonses are NOT issued by the 13.____

A. Bureau of Franchises
B. Fire Department
C. Port Authority
D. Department of Highways

14. Which one of these is NOT a part of the Transportation Administration? 14.____

A. Department of Highways
B. Department of Marine and Aviation
C. Department of Traffic
D. Triborough Bridge and Tunnel Authority

15. All moving violations of traffic regulations in the city are handled by the 15.____

A. Transportation Administration (PVB)
B. State Department of Motor Vehicles (Administrative Adjudication Bureau)
C. Criminal Court
D. Traffic Court

16. The MOST widely used type of safety warning signs manufactured by the traffic department's bureau of signs and markings are the ______ signs. 16.____

A. school crossing
B. lane-squeeze
C. curve
D. turn

Questions 17-22.

DIRECTIONS: Questions 17 through 22 are to be answered ONLY according to the information given in the paragraph below.

Perhaps the strongest argument the mass transit backer has is the advantage in efficiency that mass transit has over the automobile in the urban traffic picture. It has been estimated that given comparable location and construction conditions, the subway can carry four times as many passengers per hour and cost half as much to build as urban highways. Yet public apathy regarding the mass transportation movement in the 1960's resulted in the building of more roads. Planned to provide 42,000 miles of highways in the period from 1956-72, including 7500 miles within cities, the Federal Highway System project is now about two-thirds completed. The Highway Trust Fund supplies 90 percent of the cost of the System, with state and local-sources putting up the rest of the money. By contrast, a municipality has had to put up the bulk of the cost of a rapid transit system. Although the System and its Trust Fund have come under attack in the past few years from environmentalists and groups opposed to the continued building of urban freeways - considered to be the most expensive, destructive, and inefficient segments of the System - a move by them to get the Trust Fund transformed into a general transportation fund at the expiration of the present program seems to be headed nowhere.

17. Given similar building conditions and location, a city that builds a subway instead of a highway can expect to receive for each dollar spent ______ as much transport value. 17.____

A. half
B. twice
C. four times
D. eight times

18. The general attitude of the public in the past ten years toward the mass transportation movement has been 18.____

A. favorable
B. indifferent
C. enthusiastic
D. unfriendly

19. The number of miles of highways still to be completed in the Federal Highway System project is MOST NEARLY 19.____

A. 2,500
B. 5,000
C. 14,000
D. 28,000

20. What do certain groups who object to some features of the Federal Highway System program want to do with the Highway Trust Fund after its expiration date? 20.____

A. Extend it in order to complete the project
B. Change it so that the money can be used for all types of transportation
C. End it even if the project is not completed
D. Change it so that the money will be used only for urban freeways

21. Which one of the following statements is a valid conclusion based on the facts in the above passage? 21.____

A. The advantage of greater efficiency is the only argument that supporters of the mass transportation movement can offer.
B. It was easier for cities to build roads rather than mass transit systems in the last 15 years because of the large financial contribution made by the Federal government.
C. Mass transit systems cause as much congestion and air pollution in cities as automobiles.
D. The Highway Trust Fund will become a general transportation fund.

22. The MAIN idea or theme of the above passage is that the 22.____

A. cost of the Federal Highway System is shared by the federal, state, and local governments
B. public is against spending money for building mass transportation facilities in the cities
C. cities would benefit more from expansion and improvement of their mass transit systems than from the building of more highways
D. building of mass transportation facilities has been slowed by the Highway Trust Fund

23. To which one of the following problems should you, as a supervising agent, give LOWEST priority during a very busy work period? 23.____

A. A letter of complaint from an angry citizen has been referred from the mayor's office.
B. The director of the bureau wants you to investigate and report on the advisability of introducing a new filing system at some future date.
C. The senior enforcement agents have a grievance they wish to discuss with you.
D. An agent has violated a departmental rule and disciplinary action is required.

24. Of the following duties of a supervising enforcement agent, the one that it would be LEAST desirable to delegate to a senior enforcement agent is 24.____

   A. contacting local police precincts for information
   B. checking of records on which reports to superiors are based
   C. speaking to enforcement agents about some new department regulations
   D. reorganization of office and field staff

25. During a certain three-month period, the bureau of enforcement issued 239,788 summonses. Of these, 37,900 were issued between the hours of 12 Noon and 1 P.M.; 33,350 were issued between 1 P.M. and 2 P.M.; and 23,334 were issued between 2 P.M. and 3 P.M. 25.____
What percentage of the total number of summonses issued during this three-month period was issued between 1 P.M. and 3 P.M.?

   A. 22% B. 24% C. 26% D. 28%

KEY (CORRECT ANSWERS)

1.	A	11.	D
2.	B	12.	A
3.	C	13.	D
4.	A	14.	D
5.	C	15.	B
6.	A	16.	A
7.	C	17.	D
8.	A	18.	B
9.	D	19.	C
10.	C	20.	B

21. B
22. C
23. B
24. D
25. B

TEST 2

DIRECTIONS: Each question or incomplete statement is followed by several suggested answers or completions. Select the one that BEST answers the question or completes the statement. *PRINT THE LETTER OF THE CORRECT ANSWER IN THE SPACE AT THE RIGHT.*

Questions 1-6.

DIRECTIONS: Questions 1 through 6 are to be answered SOLELY on the basis of the information given in the paragraph below.

The use of role-playing as a training technique was developed during the past decade by social scientists, particularly psychologists, who have been active in training experiments. Originally, this technique was applied by clinical psychologists who discovered that a patient appears to gain understanding of an emotionally disturbing situation when encouraged to act out roles in that situation. As applied in government and business organizations, the purpose of role-playing is to aid employees to understand certain work problems involving interpersonal relations and to enable observers to evaluate various reactions to them. Thus, for example, on the problem of handling grievances, two individuals from the group might be selected to act out extemporaneously the parts of subordinate and supervisor. When this situation is enacted by various pairs among the class and the techniques and results are discussed, the members of the group are presumed to reach conclusions about the most effective means of handling similar situations. Often the use of role reversal, where participants take parts different from their actual work roles, assists individuals to gain more insight into other people's problems and viewpoints. Although role-playing can be a rewarding training device, the trainer must be aware of his responsibilities. If this technique is to be successful, thorough briefing of both actors and observers as to the situation in question, the participants' roles, and what to look for, is essential.

1. The role-playing technique was FIRST used for the purpose of 1.____

   A. measuring the effectiveness of training programs
   B. training supervisors in business organizations
   C. treating emotionally disturbed patients
   D. handling employee grievances

2. When role-playing is used in private business as a training device, the CHIEF aim is to 2.____

   A. develop better relations between supervisor and subordinate in the handling of grievances
   B. come up with a solution to a specific problem that has arisen
   C. determine the training needs of the group
   D. increase employee understanding of the human relation factors in work situations

3. From the above passage, it is MOST reasonable to conclude that when role-playing is used, it is preferable to have the roles acted out by 3.____

   A. only one set of actors
   B. no more than two sets of actors
   C. several different sets of actors
   D. the trainer or trainers of the group

4. Based on the above passage, a trainer using the technique of role reversal in a problem of first-line supervision should assign a senior enforcement agent to play the part of a(n) 4.____

   A. enforcement agent
   B. senior enforcement agent
   C. principal enforcement agent
   D. angry citizen

5. It can be inferred from the above passage that a *limitation* of role-play as a training method is that 5.____

   A. many work situations do not lend themselves to role-play
   B. employees are not experienced enough as actors to play the roles realistically
   C. only trainers who have psychological training can use it successfully
   D. participants who are observing and not acting do not benefit from it

6. To obtain good results from the use of role-play in training, a trainer should give participants 6.____

   A. a minimum of information about the situation so that they can act spontaneously
   B. scripts which illustrate the best method for handling the situation
   C. a complete explanation of the problem and the roles to be acted out
   D. a summary of work problems which involve interpersonal relations

7. Of the following, the MOST important reason for a supervisor to prepare *good* written reports is that 7.____

   A. a supervisor is rated on the quality of his reports
   B. decisions are often made on the basis of the reports
   C. such reports take less time for superiors to review
   D. such reports demonstrate efficiency of department operations

8. Of the following, the BEST test of a *good* report is whether it 8.____

   A. provides the information needed
   B. shows the good sense of the writer
   C. is prepared according to a proper format
   D. is grammatical and neat

9. When a supervisor writes a report, he can BEST show that he has an understanding of the subject of the report by 9.____

   A. including necessary facts and omitting non-essential details
   B. using statistical data
   C. giving his conclusions but not the data on which they are based
   D. using a technical vocabulary

10. Suppose you and another supervisor on the same level are assigned to work together on a report. You disagree strongly with one of the recommendations the other supervisor wants to include in the report but you cannot change his views.
Of the following, it would be BEST that 10.____

   A. you refuse to accept responsibility for the report
   B. you ask that someone else be assigned to this project to replace you

C. each of you state his own ideas about this recommendation in the report
D. you give in to the other supervisor's opinion for the sake of harmony

11. Standardized forms are often provided for submitting reports. 11.___
Of the following, the MOST important advantage of using standardized forms for reports is that

A. they take less time to prepare than individually written reports
B. necessary information is less likely to be omitted
C. the responsibility for preparing these reports can be delegated to subordinates
D. the person making the report can omit information he considers unimportant

12. A report which may BEST be classed as a *periodic* report is one which 12.___

A. requires the same type of information at regular intervals
B. contains detailed information which is to be retained in permanent records
C. is prepared whenever a special situation occurs
D. lists information in graphic form

13. Which one of the following is NOT an important reason for keeping accurate records in an office? 13.___

A. Facts will be on hand when decisions have to be made.
B. The basis for past actions can be determined.
C. Information needed by other bureaus can be furnished.
D. Filing is easier when records are properly made out.

14. Suppose you are preparing to write a report recommending a change in a certain procedure. You learn that another supervisor made a report a few years ago suggesting a change in this same procedure, but that no action was taken. 14.___
Of the following, it would be MOST desirable for you to

A. avoid reading the other supervisor's report, so that you will write with a more up-to-date point of view
B. make no recommendation, since management seems to be against any change in the procedure
C. read the other report before you write your report, to see what bearing it may have on your recommendations
D. avoid including in your report any information that can be obtained by referring to the other report

15. If a report you are preparing to your superior is going to be a very long one, it would be DESIRABLE to include a summary of your basic conclusions 15.___

A. at the end of the report
B. at the beginning of the report
C. in a separate memorandum
D. right after you present the supporting data

16. Suppose that some bureau and department policies must be very frequently applied by your subordinates while others rarely come into use. 16.____
As a supervising enforcement agent, a GOOD technique for you to use in fulfilling your responsibility of seeing to it that policies are adhered to is to

A. ask the director of the bureau to issue to all employees an explanation in writing of all policies
B. review with your subordinates every week those policies which have daily application
C. follow up on and explain at regular intervals the application of those policies which are not used very often by your subordinates
D. recommend to your superiors that policies rarely used be changed or dropped

17. The BASIC purpose behind the principle of delegation of authority is to 17.____

A. give the supervisor who is delegating a chance to acquire skills in higher level functions
B. free the supervisor from routine tasks in order that he may do the important parts of his job
C. prevent supervisors from overstepping the lines of authority which have been established
D. place the work delegated in the hands of those employees who can perform it best

18. A district commander can BEST assist management in long-range planning for the bureau of enforcement by 18.____

A. reporting to his superiors any changing conditions in the district
B. maintaining a neat and efficiently run office
C. scheduling patrols so that areas with a high rate of non-compliance get more intensive coverage
D. properly training new personnel assigned to his district

19. Suppose that new quarters have been rented for your district office. 19.____
Of the following, the LEAST important factor to be considered in planning the layout of the office is the

A. need for screening confidential activities from unauthorized persons
B. relative importance of the various types of work
C. areas of noise concentration
D. convenience with which communication between sections of the office can be achieved

20. Of the following, the MOST basic effect of organizing a department so that lines of authority are clearly defined and duties are specifically assigned is to 20.____

A. increase the need for close supervision
B. decrease the initiative of subordinates
C. lessen the possibility of duplication of work
D. increase the responsibilities of supervisory personnel

21. An accepted management principle is that decisions should be delegated to the lowest point in the organization at which they can be made effectively. The one of the following which is MOST likely to be a result of the application of this principle is that 21.____

A. no factors will be overlooked in making decisions
B. prompt action will follow the making of decisions
C. decisions will be made more rapidly
D. coordination of decisions that are made will be simplified

22. Suppose you are a supervisor and need some guidance from a higher authority. In which one of the following situations would it be PERMISSIBLE for you to bypass the regular upward channels of communication in the chain of command? 22.____

A. In an emergency when your superior is not available
B. When it is not essential to get a quick reply
C. When you feel your immediate superior is not understanding of the situation
D. When you want to obtain information that you think your superior does not have

23. Of the following, the CHIEF limitation of the organization chart as it is generally used in business and government is that the chart 23.____

A. makes lines of responsibility and authority undesirably definite and formal
B. is often out of date as soon as it is completed
C. does not show human factors and informal working relationships
D. is usually too complicated

24. The *span of control* for any supervisor is the 24.____

A. *number* of tasks he is expected to perform himself
B. *total* office space he and his subordinates occupy
C. *amount* of work he is responsible for getting out
D. *number* of subordinates he can supervise effectively

25. Of the following duties performed by a supervising enforcement agent, which would be considered a LINE function rather than a STAFF function? 25.____

A. Evaluation of office personnel
B. Recommendations for disciplinary action
C. Initiating budget requests for replacement of equipment
D. Inspections, at irregular times, of conditions and staff in the field

KEY (CORRECT ANSWERS)

1. C
2. D
3. C
4. A
5. A
6. C
7. B
8. A
9. A
10. C
11. B
12. A
13. D
14. C
15. B
16. C
17. B
18. A
19. B
20. C
21. B
22. A
23. C
24. D
25. D

READING COMPREHENSION
UNDERSTANDING AND INTERPRETING WRITTEN MATERIAL

EXAMINATION SECTION

TEST 1

DIRECTIONS: Each question or incomplete statement is followed by several suggested answers or completions. Select the one that BEST answers the question or completes the statement. *PRINT THE LETTER OF THE CORRECT ANSWER IN THE SPACE AT THE RIGHT.*

Questions 1-5.

DIRECTIONS: Questions 1 through 5 are to be answered SOLELY on the basis of the following passage.

Stopping, standing, and parking of motor vehicles is regulated by law to keep the public highways open for a smooth flow of traffic, and to keep stopped vehicles from blocking intersections, driveways, signs, fire hydrants, and other areas that must be kept clear. These established regulations apply in all situations, unless otherwise indicated by signs. Other local restrictions are posted in the areas to which they apply. Three examples of these other types of restrictions, which may apply singly or in combination with one another, are:

NO STOPPING: This means that a driver may not stop a vehicle for any purpose except when necessary to avoid interference with other vehicles, or in compliance with directions of a police officer or signal.

NO STANDING: This means that a driver may stop a vehicle only temporarily to actually receive or discharge passengers.

NO PARKING: This means that a driver may stop a vehicle only temporarily to actually load or unload merchandise or passengers. When stopped, it is advisable to turn on warning flashers if equipped with them. However, one should never use a directional signal for this purpose, because it may confuse the other drivers. Some NO PARKING signs prohibit parking between certain hours on certain days. For example, the sign may read NO PARKING 8 A.M. TO 11 A.M. MONDAY, WEDNESDAY, FRIDAY. These signs are usually utilized on streets where cleaning operations take place on alternate days.

1. The parking regulation that applies to fire hydrants is an example of _____ regulations. 1.____
   A. local B. established C. posted D. temporary

2. When stopped in a NO PARKING zone, it is ADVISABLE to 2.____
   A. turn on the right directional signal to indicate to other drivers that you will remain stopped
   B. turn on the left directional signal to indicate to other drivers that you may be leaving the curb after a period of time

C. turn on the warning flashers if your car is equipped with them
D. put the vehicle in reverse so that the backup lights will be on to warn approaching cars that you have temporarily stopped

3. You may stop a vehicle temporarily to discharge passengers in an area under the restriction of a _____ zone. 3.____
A. NO STOPPING – NO STANDING
B. NO STANDING – NO PARKING
C. NO PARKING – NO STOPPING
D. NO STOPPING – NO STANDING – NO PARKING

4. A sign reads NO PARKING 8 A.M. TO 11 A.M., MONDAY, WEDNESDAY, FRIDAY. 4.____
Based on this sign, a parking enforcement agent would issue a summons to a car that is parked on a _____ at _____ A.M.
A. Tuesday; 9:30
B. Wednesday; 12:00
C. Friday; 10:30
D. Saturday; 8:00

5. NO PARKING signs prohibiting parking between certain hours, on certain days, are USUALLY utilized on streets where 5.____
A. vehicles frequently take on and discharge passengers
B. cleaning operations take place on alternate days
C. NO STOPPING signs have been ignored
D. commercial vehicles take on and unload merchandise

Questions 6-15.

DIRECTIONS: Questions 6 through 15 are to be answered SOLELY on the basis of the following passage.

Parking Enforcement Agents in Iron City work three shifts. The first shift is from 10 A.M. to 6 P.M. The second shift is 6 P.M. to 2 A.M. The third shift is from 2 A.M. to 10 A.M. Each shift at the Central Office employs three people who patrol the surrounding area. Parking Enforcement Agents have one hour off per shift for lunch.

Starting on Tuesday, Agents Fred Black, Mary Evans, and Thomas Hart worked the first shift. Harold Wilson and Mary Wood worked the second shift. The third agent for the second shift was ill. Thomas Hart worked the second shift in addition to his regular first shift, and thus earned overtime pay. Mike Brown, Anne Hill, and Jeff Smith worked the third shift.

On his first shift, Agent Thomas Hart wrote 11 summonses for meter violations, 15 summonses for double parking, and 13 summonses for parking in a no-standing zone. On his second shift, Thomas Hart wrote 21 summonses for double parking, 13 summonses for meter violations, and 15 summonses for parking in a no-standing zone.

6. On Tuesday, Agent Mary Wood was on duty from 6.____
A. 6 A.M. to 2 P.M.
B. 10 A.M. to 6 P.M.
C. 2 A.M. to 6 P.M.
D. 6 P.M. to 2 A.M.

7. How many Parking Enforcement Agents normally work from 6 P.M. to 2 A.M.? 7.____
   A. One B. Two C. Three D. Four

8. The number of Parking Enforcement Agents who ACTUALLY worked the second shift on Tuesday was 8.____
   A. one B. two C. three D. four

9. Among the three successive shifts which started on Tuesday, the total number of DIFFERENT Parking Enforcement Agents who actually reported for duty was 9.____
   A. 7 B. 8 C. 9 D. 10

10. The total number of summonses Agent Hart wrote during the FIRST shift he worked was 10.____
    A. 11 B. 13 C. 39 D. 49

11. Agent Hill was scheduled to finish her shift at 11.____
    A. 10 A.M. B. 6 P.M. C. 10 P.M. D. 2 A.M.

12. Parking Enforcement Agents have one hour off per shift. The TOTAL hours actually worked by Agent Evans on Tuesday was _____ hours. 12.____
    A. 8 B. 7½ C. 7 D. 6½

13. The TOTAL number of summonses Agent Hart wrote for meter violations was 13.____
    A. 15 B. 24 C. 26 D. 34

14. During both his shifts, Agent Hart wrote the MOST summonses for 14.____
    A. meter violations
    B. standing in a no-parking zone
    C. double parking
    D. parking in a no-standing zone

15. The TOTAL number of summonses Agent Hart wrote during his two shifts was 15.____
    A. 28 B. 48 C. 68 D. 88

Questions 16-22.

DIRECTIONS: Questions 16 through 22 are to be answered SOLELY on the basis of the following passage.

The parking meter was designed 30 years ago primarily as a mechanism to assist in reducing overtime parking at the curb, to increase parking turnover, and to facilitate enforcement of parking regulations. That the meter has accomplished these basic functions is attested to by its use in an increasing number of cities.

A recent survey of cities in the United States indicates that overtime parking was reduced 75% or more in 47% of the cities surveyed, and to a lesser degree in 43% of the cities surveyed, making a total of 90% of the cities surveyed where the parking meter was found to be effective in reducing overtime parking at the curb.

A side effect of the reduction in overtime parking is the increase in parking turnover. Approximately 89% of the places surveyed found meters useful in this respect. Meters also encourage even spacing of cars at the curb. Unmetered curb parking is often so irregular that it wastes space or makes parking and departure difficult.

The effectiveness of parking meters, in the final analysis, rests upon the enforcement of regulations by squads of enforcement agents who will diligently patrol the metered area. The task of checking parking time is made easier with meters, since violations can be checked from a moving vehicle or by visual sightings of an agent on foot patrol, and the laborious process of chalking tires is greatly reduced. It is reported that, after meters have been installed, it takes on the average only 25% of the time formerly required to patrol the same area.

The fact that a parker activates a mechanism that immediately begins to count time, that will indicate exactly when the parking time has expired, and that will advertise such fact by showing a red flag, tends to make a parker more conscious of his parking responsibilities than the hit and miss system of possible detection by a patrolman.

16. According to the above passage, when the parking meter was introduced, one of its major purposes was NOT to — 16.____
    - A. cut down overtime curb parking
    - B. make curb parking available to more parkers
    - C. bring in revenue from parking fees
    - D. make it easier to enforce parking regulations

17. In the cities surveyed, how effective was the installation of parking meters in cutting down overtime parking? — 17.____
    - A. It was effective to some degree in all of the cities surveyed.
    - B. It was ineffective in only one out of every ten cities surveyed.
    - C. It reduced overtime parking at least 75% in most cities surveyed.
    - D. There was only a small reduction in overtime parking in 43% of the cities surveyed.

18. When overtime parking is reduced by the installation of parking meters, an accompanying result is — 18.____
    - A. an increase in the amount of parking space
    - B. the use of the available parking spaces by more cars
    - C. the faster movement of traffic
    - D. a decrease in the number of squads required to enforce traffic regulations

19. According to the above passage, on streets which have parking meters, as compared with streets which are unmetered, — 19.____
    - A. there is less waste of parking space
    - B. parking is more difficult
    - C. parking time limits are irregular
    - D. drivers waste more time looking for an empty parking space

20. According to the above passage, the use of parking meters will NOT be effective unless 20.____
   A. parking areas are patrolled in automobiles
   B. it is combined with the chalking of tires
   C. the public cooperates
   D. there is strict enforcement of parking regulations

21. According to the above passage, one reason why there is greater compliance with parking regulations when parking time is regulated by meters rather than by a foot patrolman chalking tires is that 21.____
   A. overtime parking becomes glaringly evident to everyone
   B. the parker is himself responsible for operating the timing mechanism
   C. there is no personal relationship between parker and enforcing officer
   D. the timing of elapsed parking time is accurate

22. In the last paragraph of the above passage, the words *a parker activates a mechanism* refers to the fact that a motorist 22.____
   A. starts the timing device of the meter working
   B. parks his car
   C. checks whether the meter is working
   D. starts the engine of his car

Questions 23-25.

DIRECTIONS: Questions 6 through 15 are to be answered SOLELY on the basis of the information given in the following passage.

When markings upon the curb or the pavement of a street designate parking space, no person shall stand or park a vehicle in such designated parking space so that any part of such vehicle occupies more than one such space or protrudes beyond the markings designating such a space, except that a vehicle which is a size too large to be parked within a single designated parking space shall be parked with the front bumper at the front of the space with the rear of the vehicle extending as little as possible into the adjoining space to the rear, or vice-versa.

23. The regulation quoted above applies to parking at any 23.____
   A. curb or pavement
   B. metered spaces
   C. street where parking is permitted
   D. parking spaces with marked boundaries

24. The regulation quoted above prohibits the occupying of more than one indicated parking space by 24.____
   A. any vehicle
   B. large vehicles
   C. small vehicles
   D. vehicles in spaces partially occupied

25. In the regulation quoted above, the term *vice-versa* refers to a vehicle of a size too large parked with 25.____
    A. front bumper flush with front of parking space it occupies
    B. front of vehicle extending into front of parking space
    C. rear bumper flush with rear of parking space it occupies
    D. rear of vehicle protruding into adjoining parking space

---

KEY (CORRECT ANSWERS)

1. B
2. C
3. B
4. C
5. B

6. D
7. C
8. C
9. B
10. C

11. A
12. C
13. B
14. C
15. D

16. C
17. B
18. B
19. A
20. D

21. A
22. A
23. D
24. C
25. C

TEST 2

DIRECTIONS: Each question or incomplete statement is followed by several suggested answers or completions. Select the one that BEST answers the question or completes the statement. *PRINT THE LETTER OF THE CORRECT ANSWER IN THE SPACE AT THE RIGHT.*

Questions 1-5.

DIRECTIONS: Questions 1 through 5 are to be answered SOLELY on the basis of the following bulletin on SCHOOL ELIGIBILITY CARDS.

SCHOOL ELIGIBILITY CARDS

All bus operators are responsible for the proper use of School Eligibility Cards for reduced fares on their buses. These cards are issued to elementary and high school students. Such cards are good for the entire year from September 13 to June 28, and are issued subject to the following conditions:

A. The card is to be used by the student whose name appears on the face of the card, and only on days when school is in session. If offered by any other person, it will be taken away by the bus operator, and full fare will be collected from the person presenting the card.

B. The card will allow the student to ride on the particular bus indicated on the face of the card for a fare of fifty cents between 6 A.M. and 7 P.M. The fare of 50 cents must be deposited in the fare box by the student after the card is shown to the bus operator.

C. The student, after paying the 50 cent fare, is entitled to the same transfer privileges as other passengers.

D. The card will be taken away if altered or misused, and the student will not be given a new card for a period of five school months.

E. The card is not good unless all entries on the card are made by the teacher and the card is signed by the teacher.

1. If a student's School Eligibility Card is taken away by a bus operator because of misuse, the student will 1.____
   A. never be issued a new card because of this misuse
   B. not be issued a new card until he pays for the old one
   C. be eligible for a new card after five school months
   D. be eligible for a new card if he gets a note from his teacher

2. A bus operator should take away a School Eligibility Card if it is presented 2.____
   A. at 9 A.M. before school opens
   B. at 3 P.M. after school opens
   C. by a college student
   D. more than twice a day

3. A bus operator should permit a student to ride at reduced fare if he presents his School Eligibility Card at 3.____
   A. 8:00 A.M. on Sunday
   B. 8 A.M. on Monday
   C. 8:00 A.M. on Saturday
   D. 8:00 P.M. on Wednesday

4. If a student presents a School Eligibility Card, pays a 50 cent fare, and asks for a transfer, the bus operator should 4.____
   A. tell the student that during school hours he may not get a transfer
   B. tell him to use his School Eligibility Card instead
   C. give him a transfer if other passengers can get them free
   D. tell him he must pay the full dollar fare to get one

5. According to the above bulletin, School Eligibility Cards are NOT good on 5.____
   A. September 15
   B. October 26
   C. February 23
   D. June 30

Questions 6-12.

DIRECTIONS: Questions 6 through 12 are to be answered SOLELY on the basis of the following passage on the EXTRACT OF RULES FOR SYSTEM PICK FOR BUS OPERATORS.

<u>EXTRACT OF RULES FOR SYSTEM PICK FOR BUS OPERATORS</u>

Operators picking up an early run (one ending before 9:00 P.M., including all time allowances) on weekdays must pick an early run on Saturday and Sunday.

No operator will be allowed to pick on the extra list unless he desires to transfer to a depot where all runs, tricks, etc. have been picked.

After an operator finishes picking and the monitor has entered the operator's name for the run on the picking board, no change of run will be permitted. Erasures and other signs of mutilation will not be permitted on the picking board.

It is planned to permit about 100 operators in the picking room at one time, but the time allowed for any one person to pick will not exceed five minutes. If for any reason you cannot attend, you may submit a preference slip or be represented by proxy.

An operator inactive because of sickness, injury, etc. for sixty days prior to his pick assignment must present a certificate from a doctor stating he may return to duty not later than two weeks after date of pick.

Your cooperation is requested. Please be on hand to pick at your designated time, and leave picking room promptly when you have finished picking.

6. The rules apply to a pick of 6.____
   A. Saturday and Sunday
   B. depot extra
   C. weekday
   D. system

7. An operator picking an early run on weekdays 7.____
   A. cannot be off on Saturdays or Sundays
   B. must submit a preference slip
   C. will be assigned to the extra list on other days
   D. must pick an early run on Saturday and Sunday

8. According to the rules, an operator 8.____
   A. will be in the picking room alone while designating his choice
   B. must wait in the picking room after making his choice until all runs have been chosen
   C. is informed that he may pick his run at any time he wishes to on pick day
   D. may have someone else pick for him if he cannot be present on the day of the pick

9. In order to pick on the extra list, an operator MUST 9.____
   A. present a doctor's certificate
   B. have been inactive for sixty days
   C. appear at the picking room in person
   D. be willing to transfer to a terminal where all the runs have been picked

10. Once a bus operator picks a run and his name has been entered by the monitor, he 10.____
   A. must accept the run picked as no changes will be permitted
   B. can change his mind if the choice was made by proxy
   C. may ask the monitor to erase his pick if the next man has not yet picked
   D. can swap runs with another operator but only after sixty days

11. An operator making his pick after having been out sick for three months must 11.____
   A. pick on the extra list
   B. present a doctor's certificate to the monitor
   C. wait two weeks before returning to duty
   D. pick an early run or trick

12. The rules state that 12.____
   A. only 100 operators can pick in any one day
   B. cooperation is demanded, and a penalty will be imposed on any operator who is uncooperative
   C. a preference slip must be signed by the monitor
   D. an operator must make his pick within 5 minutes time

Questions 13-20.

DIRECTIONS: Questions 13 through 20 are to be answered SOLELY on the basis of the following passage on LOST PROPERTY.

LOST PROPERTY

When a passenger turns over a piece of lost property to a porter, or when a porter finds a lost article, he shall turn it in to the most convenient office equipped with a Lost Property bag and shall obtain a receipt therefor from the employee responsible for handling lost property. The responsible employee must forward articles of great value, such as expensive jewelry or large sums of money, to the Lost Property Office by special messenger as soon as possible and notify the Desk Trainmaster. The responsible employee must turn over all firearms to the Transit Police, take a proper receipt, and notify the Lost Property Office as soon as possible.

Perishable property, such as food products not in cans or boxes and requiring refrigeration, should be sold at the terminal by the terminal supervisor after holding for 8 hours, and the money forwarded to the Administrative Office; if the property is not sold, it should be destroyed and a record made on the lost property form.

13. A porter MUST turn over a lost umbrella at the _____ office. 13.____
    A. desk trainmaster's B. lost property
    C. transit police D. most convenient

14. A porter who finds a pistol on a station should take it to the _____ office. 14.____
    A. transit police B. lost property
    C. administrative D. most convenient

15. The Lost Property Office is mentioned 15.____
    A. once B. twice C. three times D. four times

16. If a porter finds a carton of canned peas, he should 16.____
    A. sell it B. destroy it C. keep it D. turn it in

17. If a porter finds a burlap bag containing about 15 pounds of fresh fish, he should 17.____
    A. sell it B. destroy it C. keep it D. turn it in

18. A porter must get a receipt for a lost article to prove that he 18.____
    A. found it B. received it
    C. turned it in D. knows what it is

19. A special messenger is NOT required to be used for a 19.____
    A. bag of 10 dollar bills B. silver-handled pistol
    C. gold candlestick D. genuine pearl necklace

20. A porter finding a box of flowers with a tag showing the addressee should 20.____
    A. deliver it B. turn it in
    C. telephone addressee D. take it to the Lost Property Office

Questions 21-25.

DIRECTIONS: Questions 21 through 25 are to be answered SOLELY on the basis of the following passage on BUS RADIO TRANSMISSION CODE.

BUS RADIO TRANSMISSION CODE

Buses are equipped with a 2-way radio system to aid the bus operator in the performance of his job. It is used primarily to transmit information to the Radio Dispatcher located in the Central Radio Operations Center. To assist the bus operator in the transmission of information without loss of time or possible confusion, the following Code is used:

Code Red Tag:	To be used only in extreme emergency, such as police assistance in the event of a hold-up, assault, serious vandalism, etc. The bus operator transmitting a Red Tag Alert shall have priority over all other incoming calls. All other bus operators shall stand by until Dispatcher gives order to resume normal operations.
Code 1:	Collision involving a bus.
Code 2:	Passenger injured on board bus.
Code 3:	Disabled bus.
Code 4:	Bus blocked by fire apparatus, other vehicle, parade, etc.

21. If a bus operator observes a mugging taking place on his bus, he should radio a Code 21.____
    A. 1 B. 2 C. 3 D. 4

22. If a passenger trips and hurts himself on a bus, the bus operator should radio a Code 22.____
    A. 1 B. 2 C. 3 D. 4

23. If a bus is blocked by a street demonstration of marching adults, the bus operator should radio a Code 23.____
    A. 1 B. 2 C. 4 D. Red Tag

24. While a bus operator is reporting an injury to a passenger who fell and hurt his leg on the bus, a second bus operator interrupts this radio conversation with a Code Red Tag. 24.____
    The FIRST bus operator should
    A. continue with his message so that the passenger may be aided quickly
    B. repeat his message since the interruption may have scrambled his voice
    C. immediately stop talking
    D. ask the second bus operator to wait until he has completed his message

25. If a bus engine stalls and cannot be restarted, the bus operator should radio a Code 25.____
    A. 1 B. 2 C. 3 D. Red Tag

KEY (CORRECT ANSWERS)

1.	C	11.	B
2.	C	12.	D
3.	B	13.	D
4.	C	14.	D
5.	D	15.	B
6.	D	16.	D
7.	D	17.	D
8.	D	18.	C
9.	D	19.	B
10.	A	20.	B

21.	D
22.	B
23.	C
24.	C
25.	C

POLICE SCIENCE NOTES.

POLICE TRAFFIC SERVICES

Goal

The police traffic services goal is to effect the safe and efficient movement of persons and goods on publicly traveled highways. "Safety" and "efficiency" are often competing functions because attempts to maximize safety must usually be made at the expense of efficiency; conversely, to maximize efficiency may minimize safety.

General Responsibility Areas

To accomplish the traffic services goal the police encourage cooperation among all groups and agencies interested and responsible for traffic safety, but they must also act directly in their four general responsibility areas.

Pedestrian

The pedestrian is a major problem to the police in their efforts to achieve the safe and efficient movement of vehicles, persons and goods. Pedestrians are highly represented (in many cities half of those killed are pedestrians) in the fatality experience of urban areas, and during the daylight or business hours are principal contributors to traffic conflict and congestion. More than one study in recent years have shown that the pedestrian is more often at fault in causing the accident in which he has become involved then is the driver who has hit him.

Police/pedestrian responsibilities include participation in training and information programs aimed at pedestrians from pre-school ages to senior citizens.

Driver

Of the four responsibility areas, the driver is of prime concern to the police in terms of traffic safety, the one requiring the most attention because of his most complex problems. The driver's unique combination of skills, attitudes and motivations, coupled with his operation of a heavy mobile machine which can inflict tremendous damage and injury, are many times inadequate to the demands required for safe vehicle operation. Be it because of heavy intoxication or mere daydreaming, drivers may make errors which can be, and often are, tremendously costly to himself and others.

The police responsibilities relative to drivers include driver training and education, public information programs of a general nature, driver licensing, promotion and enforcement of legislation, and the promulgation of reasonable and uniform operational policies, vehicle equipment regulations.

Vehicle

Unsafe vehicle condition is a constant, inherent potential for accidents, therefore, vehicle inspection programs should be and are considered as an essential part of any highway safety program. The police should incorporate inspection programs into their routine stops and patrol operations to reduce the number of defective vehicles on the road.

Facility

The police should promote an active program designed to improve the facility upon or over which traffic units move through the highway transportation system. Highway design defects and other dangerous conditions of both temporary and permanent nature should be actively identified and reported to the appropriate agency for correction. Police should maintain very close association with traffic and highway engineers.*

The police contribute importantly to the engineering function by providing engineers with the information collected from accidents and with operational records of traffic congestion. In turn, the police should look to the engineer for appropriate advice and information to assist them in their basic traffic-related activities.

---

*Traffic engineers are responsible for designing systems to move traffic efficiently with safety, coordinated signals, one way streets, off street parking, traffic control and direction signs and signals, etc. Highway engineers are responsible for designing and building the highways; for construction.

Traffic Safety Missions

A coordinated effort to accomplish a comprehensive traffic safety program requires activity in five areas, the traffic safety missions.

Traffic Supervision Mission

Police traffic supervision is primarily concerned with four basic line functions: collision investigation, law enforcement, traffic direction and control, and general motorist services. These activities are intended to reduce collisions through prevention programs, provide for the safety and convenience of highway users, and assist the motoring public through provision of needed services on the highway system.

Information Mission

The foremost activity performed to accomplish this mission is that of keeping adequate traffic records. This includes the tasks of file maintenance, retrieval and response, analysis and processing, dissemination of information required, and quality control. A primary task is the development and operation of adequate methods for communication information to the line officers. The entire success of the enforcement program depends on how well the supervisors and officers of the operating divisions are informed.

The information mission must be capable of identifying problem drivers, pointing out high accident locations, assisting officials in drafting laws and policies by revealing problem areas, identifying areas in which research is needed, and providing information essential to the training and retraining of drivers.

Public Information and Safety Education Mission

The measures of success registered by a highway safety program will be determined by the amount of public support it receives. It is necessary, therefore, that community support be developed through an effective public information and safety education mission. The mission activities will include: informing the public about traffic accidents, explaining to the community the various traffic safety measures taken by the department, providing individual drivers, pedestrians and cyclists with information they need to protect themselves and others against accidents, and convincing all citizens of the need for each of them to meet this personal responsibility to drive, walk and cycle safely.

Communication Mission

The task of the communications mission is to maintain an effective flow of pertinent information and demands to all agency personnel so that the achievements of all other missions will be expedited. The entire force must be considered as a part of the communication mission. Each officer is an observer and participant and is expected to communicate, through appropriate media, every observation that will be of use to the attainment of agency objectives.

Management Mission

The management mission is that of assuring that the organization functions efficiently toward the accomplishment of agency objectives. Included are the management tasks of planning, organizing, staffing, directing, coordinating, reporting and budgeting.

Definitions

Traffic

Traffic is anything which moves on a public highway for the purpose of transporting persons and materials; it is a human–directed movement. Each driver and his vehicle, cyclist and his cycle, pedestrian, herdsman and his flock, equestrian and his horse, etc., is a traffic unit which, together with other traffic units, constitute the whole of traffic on a highway. Traffic does not include units such as road graders and pavement spreaders as they are used in road repair or construction because they are not on the highway for the purpose of transportation, nor are wild or loose animals traffic units because they are not under human control.

Traffic Control Signal

A traffic control signal is a mechanical device which signals traffic units to stop or proceed alternatively and periodically. The common red, amber and green signal is a traffic control signal.

Traffic Control Sign

A traffic control sign is a sign which conveys mandatory or warning messages to persons which require or recommend actions appropriate to the message conveyed by the sign. Stop signs, no parking signs, curve warning signs, etc., are traffic control signs.

Traffic Control Device

A traffic control device is any device or material which directs, controls or aids traffic flow on a highway. Examples of traffic control devices are lines designating traffic lanes, roadway centers, and passing or no-passing zones, reflectorized paddles at roadside, curbings to channelize traffic flow, ridges in pavement surface which cause tire hum to convey warning, etc.

Point Control

Point control is the control and direction of traffic by an officer through the use of standard gestures and audible signals for the purpose of stopping, starting or changing the direction of traffic units to facilitate traffic flow.

Police Traffic Law Enforcement

Police traffic law enforcement is the totality of actions taken by police officers in their efforts to prevent, apprehend, and process through the criminal justice system, those persons who are traffic law offenders. Enforcement can take the form of verbal warnings, written warnings, citations or summonses, physical arrests followed by incarceration, or administrative sanctions aimed at revoking or restricting driver or vehicle licensing.

Police Traffic Law Enforcement Efforts

"Presence Plust Contact" are the key words describing effective police efforts toward traffic accident reduction. It would be difficult to find a motorist who does not recheck his driving operation when he becomes aware of the presence of an officer in his immediate vicinity. This is the reason traffic experts advocate the use of marked and highly visible police vehicles for traffic law enforcement. What is more difficult to assess is the duration of the "halo effect"—careful and lawful driving in the suspected presence of officers. Hardest to evaluate is the effectiveness of enforcement contacts by officers in reducing accidents and violations on the part of those violators who are actually apprehended. Various enforcement programs over the years have proved successful in accident and violation reduction, but the proportional operation of presence and contact on motorists' behavior has escaped precise measurement.

Traffic law enforcement actions taken by officers vary according to the seriousness of the violation and what is permitted by statute and departmental police. *Physical arrest*—taking violators into custody—is reserved for the more serious offenses, when it appears unlikely that the offender will not voluntarily appear before a judicial officer, or when the hazardous driving may continue upon immediate release. Dependent upon the jurisdiction, serious violations are cause for incarceration by statutory requirement, departmental policy, or the arresting officer's discretion.

A *summons* or *citation* is a document issued by officers to violators for less serious offenses. It is a notification to the defendant both of the offense with which he will be charged and of where, when, and before which judicial agency the matter will be heard. The vast majority of traffic violations are handled by this method because it is the most efficient procedure for the offenders and the agencies within the criminal justice system.

The *written warning*, while not permitted or advocated in all jurisdictions, is the third enforcement action utilized by enforcement officers. This procedure is followed when the violation is not serious and/or when the motorist's faulty operation appears to be one which will not be repeated. While written warnings can be issued for either rules of the road or faulty equipment violations, their use as a corrective measure with a built-in follow-up procedure for defective equipment is more common.

Verbal warning is the fourth common enforcement action. Used in situations similar to that under which written warnings are issued, the verbal warning is different in that no official documentation is made of the incident, the driver's record is not affected, and there is no action to ascertain whether or not the problem is corrected. The threat of negative sanctions is minimized, the purpose being more to educate and correct the unlawful or unsafe conduct which had been observed. In fact, it has been suggested that this type of contact should be termed something akin to "driver improvement discussion" or "officer's educational effort" to more effectively point up its purpose.

Administrative sanction is the fifth enforcement action available to the police. This type of procedure involves the notification of an administrative agency with quasi-judicial authority that a driver or vehicle owner has failed to meet legal requirements which subjects him to sanctions against his driver, vehicle or other license or permit. The most common action in this category is that of driver license suspension under implied consent laws.

Regarding enforcement, the police must attempt to achieve in the public's mind that traffic laws and departmental policies are reasonable and necessary, that the police are omnipresent, that violations will be observed, that enforcement action will be taken, and that necessary corrective actions by the courts and administrative agencies will be swift and sufficient to assure appropriate future compliance. The objective to be achieved is that of *voluntary* compliance on the part of the community of highway users so that direct enforcement contacts will no longer be necessary except in unusual cases.

An effective police program for traffic safety and control aims for both accident reduction and public acceptance. The enforcement methods available to the police should be judiciously and artfully applied so that the end result is the greatest reduction in violations at the least possible economic and social cost—an efficient operation directed at specific goals.

Heavy Volume Traffic Movement and Emergency Conditions

The efficient movement of heavy volume traffic requires advance planning. The main difference between moving traffic to or from a sports event and during a disaster emergency is that in the latter case the knowledge of the persons involved that their lives (rather than their time) may be at stake subjects them to possible panic, which leads to hysterical loss of control. The outcome depends upon the effectiveness of the planning and training of personnel prior to the need for controlling such mass movements.

Disasters require that persons and traffic be diverted or removed from the danger areas. This is the responsibility of the police. Ways must be kept open to accommodate all types of traffic, including emergency vehicles and personnel which have priority. Anything which blocks or impedes traffic flow during a true emergency must be reported to superiors immediately and corrected or removed. The usual method of using a tow truck may not be available, therefore, whatever is required should be requested of supervisors or commanders, including permission to upset vehicles and roll them off the roadway.

The traffic control responsibilities of the auxiliary police during emergencies will depend upon the provisions of the emergency plans, and these will have been developed in the light of the locally prevailing conditions. However, controls will be designed to accomplish one of two objectives, either persons will be diverted from areas of danger or they will be assisted in movement away from hazardous areas toward a shelter or other place of safety. In a situation wherein the plan is to move people to a nearby shelter, officers will be ordered to eliminate vehicular traffic so that the full use of the highway is retained for pedestrian use. Where circumstances dictate the mass evacuation of an area, both vehicular and foot traffic will be permitted, although officers will attempt to utilize vehicles' capacities to their utmost in order to expedite rapid evacuation. The traffic control plan will usually provide that officers be placed on point control assignments at major intersections or at any other position from which they can most efficiently effect the mass movement of traffic. Any delay of traffic movement during emergencies requires police attention and control. Bottlenecks must be immediately eliminated or reduced to provide swift and efficient movement of traffic.

Under circumstances where an area is closed to all or into which only rescue teams or officials are permitted, all avenues through which the public may enter must be covered by an officer. The positions or posts should be individually numbered so that supervisors may direct officers to these posts, and both he and the assigned officers are aware of the precise location of assignment.

Point Control

When an officer* is directing traffic it is necessary that the people using the highway know he is there for that purpose and that the officer knows and utilizes standardized, appropriate gestures and audible signals to stop, start, and turn traffic.

To indicate that the officer is present for the purpose of directing traffic he should: position himself so that he can be seen clearly by all, usually in the center of an intersection or street; stand straight with weight equally distributed on both feet; allow hands and arms to hang easily at his sides except when gesturing; stand facing or with his back to traffic which he has stopped and with his side toward traffic he has directed to move.

To stop traffic the officer should first extend his arm and index finger toward and look directly at the person to be stopped until that person is aware or it can be reasonably assumed that he is aware of the officer's gesture. Second, the pointing hand is raised at the wrist so that its palm is toward the person to be stopped, and the palm is held in this position until the person is observed to stop. To stop traffic from both directions on a two-way street the procedure is then repeated for traffic coming from the other direction while continuing to maintain the raised arm and palm toward the traffic previously stopped. (Illustrations 1-4.)

To start traffic the officer should first stand with shoulder and side toward the traffic to be started, extend his arm and index finger toward and look directly at the person to be started until that person is aware or it can be reasonably assumed that he is aware of the officer's gesture. Second, with palm up, the pointing arm is swung from the elbow, only, through a vertical semi-circle until the hand is adjacent to the chin. If necessary this gesture is repeated until traffic begins to move. To start traffic from both directions on a two-way

*Under some circumstances two officers are necessary for the control of some heavily traveled points, complicated and unusual intersections, or one-way movement in alternate directions around an obstruction. In these cases one of the officers will initiate all changes in traffic flow and direction and the other will assist. The purpose accomplished by this procedure is the prevention of confusion on the part of the traffic units being directed.

street, the procedure is then repeated for traffic coming from the other direction. (Illustrations 5 and 6.)

Right turning drivers usually effect their turns without the necessity of being directed by the officer. When directing a right turn becomes necessary, the officer should proceed as follows: if the driver is approaching from the officer's right side his extended right arm and index finger and gaze are first directed toward the driver, followed by swinging the extended arm and index finger in the direction of the driver's intended turn (Illustrations 7-9); if the driver is approaching from the officer's left side, either the same procedure may be followed utilizing the left arm extended or the extended left forearm may be raised to a vertical position from the elbow while closing the fingers so that the remaining extended thumb points in the direction of the driver's intended turn.

Left turning drivers should not be directed to effect their movement while the officer is also directing oncoming traffic to proceed. Therefore, the officer should either direct opposing vehicles to start while avoiding left turn gestures directed at turning drivers, which will lead them to complete their turn only when there is a gap in the concoming traffic, or to stop or hold oncoming drivers, after which the left turning driver can be directed into his turn. The officer's right side and arm should be toward the oncoming traffic, and the left side and arm should be toward the left turning driver. After stopping oncoming traffic by using the right arm and hand, the right hand should remain in the halt gesture, then the extended left arm and index finger and officer's gaze is directed toward the driver who intends to effect a left turn. When the left turning driver's attention has been gained, the extended left arm and index finger are swung to point in the direction the driver intends to go. (Illustrations 10-12.)

In order to clear the lane occupied by a driver who intends to make a left turn, but cannot because of oncoming traffic, he can be directed into the intersection and stopped adjacent to the officer's position until the left turn can be safely completed. The driver should be directed into the intersection by pointing toward him with the extended arm and index finger which is then swung to point at the position at which the officer wishes the driver to stop and wait for clearing traffic. In the alternative, the driver may be directed to move with one arm and hand gesture while the other arm and hand are utilized to point to the position at which the driver is to stop. (Illustration 13.) After the driver is positioned within the intersection, the officer may either halt oncoming traffic and direct the completion of the turn or permit the driver to effect the turn during a natural break in the oncoming traffic.

Signalling Aids

The whistle is used to get the attention of drivers and pedestrians. It is used as follows:

1. *One Long* blast with a STOP signal.
2. *Two short* blasts with the GO signal.
3. *Several short* blasts to get the attention of a driver or pedestrian who does not respond to a given signal.

The whistle should be used judiciously. It should not be used to indicate frustration, but the volume should be just that sufficient to be heard by those whose attention is required. Therefore, whistle blasts directed at pedestrians should be moderate in volume. The whistle should be used only to indicate stop, go, or to gain attention, and when its purpose has been achieved the officer should cease sounding the whistle. If the whistle is utilized continuously it ceases to hold meaning for drivers and pedestrians.

The voice is seldom used in directing traffic. Arm gestures and the whistle are usually sufficient. There are numerous reasons why verbal commands are not used. Verbal orders are not easy to give or understand and often lead to misinterpretations which are dangerous. An order which is shouted can antagonize the motorist.

Occasionally a driver or pedestrian will not understand the officer's directions. When this happens the officer should move reasonably close to the person and politely and briefly explain his directions. No officer shall exhibit loss of temper by shouting or otherwise indicate antagonism toward those who do not understand or who do not wish to obey the officer's directions.

The baton is confusing unless properly used. *To stop* a driver with the baton, the officer should face the oncoming traffic, hold the baton in the right hand, bend the right elbow, hold the baton vertically, then swing the baton from left to right through an arc of approximately 45 degrees. (Illustration 14.)

The go signal and the *left turn* direction are the same gestures as those previously described except that the baton acts as an extension of the hand and index finger. (Illustrations 15 and 16.)

Signals and directions given with the aid of the baton should be exaggerated and often need to be repeated because of the poor visibility existing. The baton's light should be turned off when it is not being actively utilized to give directions.

A flashlight can be used to halt traffic. To stop traffic slowly swing the beam of the light across the path of oncoming traffic. The beam from the flashlight strikes the pavement as an elongated spot of light. After the driver has stopped arm signals may be given in the usual manner, the vehicle's headlights providing illumination. (Illustrations 17 and 18.)

Illustration No. 1
Point

Illustration No. 2
Stop

Illustration No. 3
Point

Illustration No. 4
Stop

Illustration No. 5
Pointing

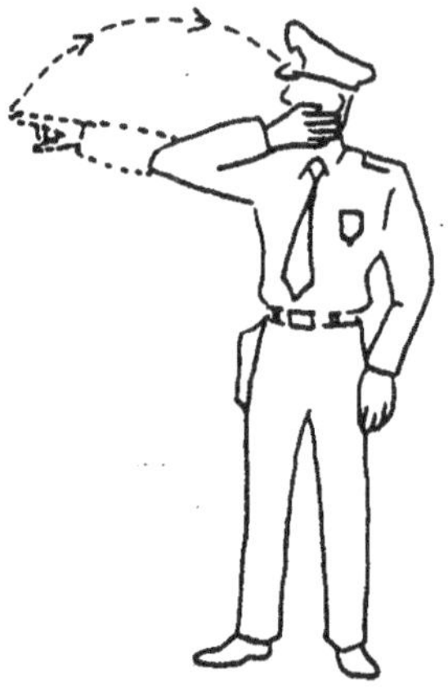

Illustration No. 6
Starting

Illustration No. 7
Point at the driver

Illustration No. 8
Arm Swing

Illustration No. 9
Point where driver
is to go

Illustration No. 10
Halt opposing traffic
with right hand

Illustration No. 11
Hold opposing traffic
and point to turning
driver

Illustration No. 12
Give turn signal with
left hand

Illustration No. 13
Direct driver into
intersection

Illustration No. 14
Stop signal

Illustration No. 15
Go signal

Illustration No. 16
Left turn

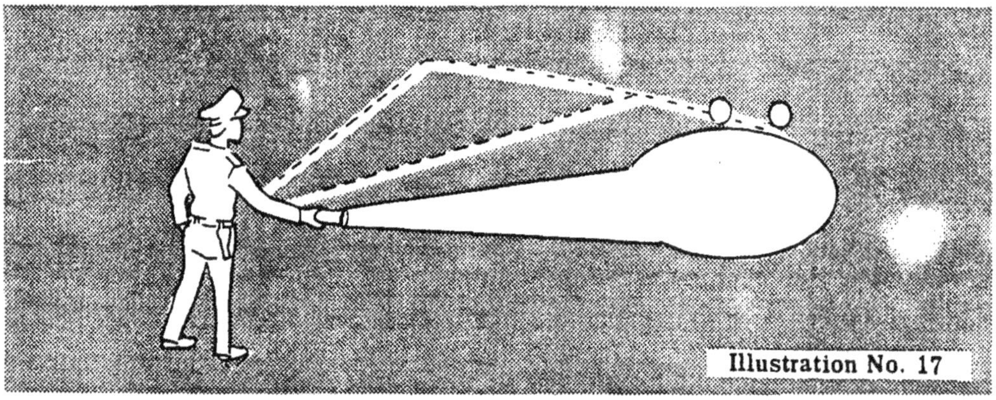

Illustration No. 17

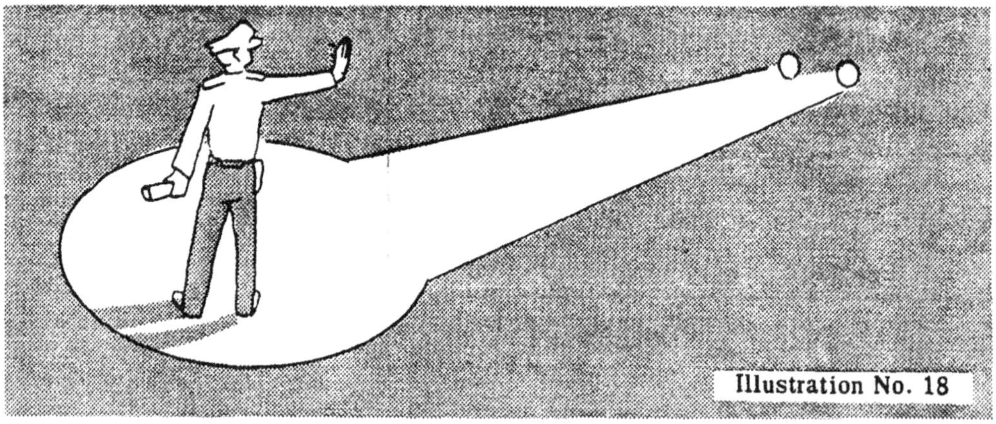

Illustration No. 18

PHILOSOPHY, PRINCIPLES, PRACTICES, AND TECHNICS
OF
SUPERVISION, ADMINISTRATION, MANAGEMENT, AND ORGANIZATION

TABLE OF CONTENTS

	Page
MEANING OF SUPERVISION	1
THE OLD AND THE NEW SUPERVISION	1
THE EIGHT (8) BASIC PRINCIPLES OF THE NEW SUPERVISION	1
I. Principle of Responsibility	1
II. Principle of Authority	2
III. Principle of Self-Growth	2
IV. Principle of Individual Worth	2
V. Principle of Creative Leadership	2
VI. Principle of Success and Failure	2
VII. Principle of Science	3
VIII. Principle of Cooperation	3
WHAT IS ADMINISTRATION?	3
I. Practices Commonly Classed as "Supervisory"	3
II. Practices Commonly Classed as "Administrative"	3
III. Practices Commonly Classed as Both "Supervisory" and "Administrative"	4
RESPONSIBILITIES OF THE SUPERVISOR	4
COMPETENCIES OF THE SUPERVISOR	4
THE PROFESSIONAL SUPERVISOR-EMPLOYEE RELATIONSHIP	4
MINI-TEXT IN SUPERVISION, ADMINISTRATION, MANAGEMENT, AND ORGANIZATION	5
I. Brief Highlights	5
A. Levels of Management	6
B. What the Supervisor Must Learn	6
C. A Definition of Supervision	6
D. Elements of the Team Concept	6
E. Principles of Organization	6
F. The Four Important Parts of Every Job	7
G. Principles of Delegation	7
H. Principles of Effective Communications	7
I. Principles of Work Improvement	7
J. Areas of Job Improvement	7
K. Seven Key Points in Making Improvements	8

L. Corrective Techniques for Job Improvement 8
M. A Planning Checklist 8
N. Five Characteristics of Good Directions 9
O. Types of Directions 9
P. Controls 9
Q. Orienting the New Employee 9
R. Checklist for Orienting New Employees 9
S. Principles of Learning 10
T. Causes of Poor Performance 10
U. Four Major Steps in On-the-Job Instructions 10
V. Employees Want Five Things 10
W. Some Don'ts in Regard to Praise 11
X. How to Gain Your Workers' Confidence 11
Y. Sources of Employee Problems 11
Z. The Supervisor's Key to Discipline 11
AA. Five Important Processes of Management 12
BB. When the Supervisor Fails to Plan 12
CC. Fourteen General Principles of Management 12
DD. Change 12

II. Brief Topical Summaries 13
A. Who/What is the Supervisor? 13
B. The Sociology of Work 13
C. Principles and Practices of Supervision 14
D. Dynamic Leadership 14
E. Processes for Solving Problems 15
F. Training for Results 15
G. Health, Safety, and Accident Prevention 16
H. Equal Employment Opportunity 16
I. Improving Communications 16
J. Self-Development 17
K. Teaching and Training 17
1. The Teaching Process 17
a. Preparation 17
b. Presentation 18
c. Summary 18
d. Application 18
e. Evaluation 18
2. Teaching Methods 18
a. Lecture 18
b. Discussion 18
c. Demonstration 19
d. Performance 19
e. Which Method to Use 19

PHILOSOPHY, PRINCIPLES, PRACTICES, AND TECHNICS
OF
SUPERVISION, ADMINISTRATION, MANAGEMENT, AND ORGANIZATION

MEANING OF SUPERVISION

The extension of the democratic philosophy has been accompanied by an extension in the scope of supervision. Modern leaders and supervisors no longer think of supervision in the narrow sense of being confined chiefly to visiting employees, supplying materials, or rating the staff. They regard supervision as being intimately related to all the concerned agencies of society, they speak of the supervisor's function in terms of "growth," rather than the "improvement" of employees.

This modern concept of supervision may be defined as follows: Supervision is leadership and the development of leadership within groups which are cooperatively engaged in inspection, research, training, guidance, and evaluation.

THE OLD AND THE NEW SUPERVISION

TRADITIONAL
1. Inspection
2. Focused on the employee
3. Visitation
4. Random and haphazard
5. Imposed and authoritarian
6. One person usually

MODERN
1. Study and analysis
2. Focused on aims, materials, methods, supervisors, employees, environment
3. Demonstrations, intervisitation, workshops, directed reading, bulletins, etc.
4. Definitely organized and planned (scientific)
5. Cooperative and democratic
6. Many persons involved (creative)

THE EIGHT (8) BASIC PRINCIPLES OF THE NEW SUPERVISION

I. Principle of Responsibility
Authority to act and responsibility for acting must be joined.
  A. If you give responsibility, give authority.
  B. Define employee duties clearly.
  C. Protect employees from criticism by others.
  D. Recognize the rights as well as obligations of employees.
  E. Achieve the aims of a democratic society insofar as it is possible within the area of your work.
  F. Establish a situation favorable to training and learning.
  G. Accept ultimate responsibility for everything done in your section, unit, office, division, department.
  H. Good administration and good supervision are inseparable.

II. Principle of Authority
The success of the supervisor is measured by the extent to which the power of authority is not used.
A. Exercise simplicity and informality in supervision
B. Use the simplest machinery of supervision
C. If it is good for the organization as a whole, it is probably justified.
D. Seldom be arbitrary or authoritative.
E. Do not base your work on the power of position or of personality.
F. Permit and encourage the free expression of opinions.

III. Principle of Self-Growth
The success of the supervisor is measured by the extent to which, and the speed with which, he is no longer needed.
A. Base criticism on principles, not on specifics.
B. Point out higher activities to employees.
C. Train for self-thinking by employees to meet new situations.
D. Stimulate initiative, self-reliance, and individual responsibility
E. Concentrate on stimulating the growth of employees rather than on removing defects.

IV. Principle of Individual Worth
Respect for the individual is a paramount consideration in supervision.
A. Be human and sympathetic in dealing with employees.
B. Don't nag about things to be done.
C. Recognize the individual differences among employees and seek opportunities to permit best expression of each personality.

V. Principle of Creative Leadership
The best supervision is that which is not apparent to the employee.
A. Stimulate, don't drive employees to creative action.
B. Emphasize doing good things.
C. Encourage employees to do what they do best.
D. Do not be too greatly concerned with details of subject or method.
E. Do not be concerned exclusively with immediate problems and activities.
F. Reveal higher activities and make them both desired and maximally possible.
G. Determine procedures in the light of each situation but see that these are derived from a sound basic philosophy.
H. Aid, inspire, and lead so as to liberate the creative spirit latent in all good employees.

VI. Principle of Success and Failure
There are no unsuccessful employees, only unsuccessful supervisors who have failed to give proper leadership.
A. Adapt suggestions to the capacities, attitudes, and prejudices of employees.
B. Be gradual, be progressive, be persistent.
C. Help the employee find the general principle; have the employee apply his own problem to the general principle.
D. Give adequate appreciation for good work and honest effort.
E. Anticipate employee difficulties and help to prevent them.
F. Encourage employees to do the desirable things they will do anyway.
G. Judge your supervision by the results it secures.

VII. Principle of Science
Successful supervision is scientific, objective, and experimental. It is based on facts, not on prejudices.
A. Be cumulative in results.
B. Never divorce your suggestions from the goals of training.
C. Don't be impatient of results.
D. Keep all matters on a professional, not a personal, level.
E. Do not be concerned exclusively with immediate problems and activities.
F. Use objective means of determining achievement and rating where possible.

VIII. Principle of Cooperation
Supervision is a cooperative enterprise between supervisor and employee.
A. Begin with conditions as they are.
B. Ask opinions of all involved when formulating policies.
C. Organization is as good as its weakest link.
D. Let employees help to determine policies and department programs.
E. Be approachable and accessible—physically and mentally.
F. Develop pleasant social relationships.

WHAT IS ADMINISTRATION

Administration is concerned with providing the environment, the material facilities, and the operational procedures that will promote the maximum growth and development of supervisors and employees. (Organization is an aspect and a concomitant of administration.)

There is no sharp line of demarcation between supervision and administration; these functions are intimately interrelated and, often, overlapping. They are complementary activities.

I. Practices Commonly Classed as "Supervisory"
A. Conducting employees' conferences
B. Visiting sections, units, offices, divisions, departments
C. Arranging for demonstrations
D. Examining plans
E. Suggesting professional reading
F. Interpreting bulletins
G. Recommending in-service training courses
H. Encouraging experimentation
I. Appraising employee morale
J. Providing for intervisitation

II. Practices Commonly Classified as "Administrative"
A. Management of the office
B. Arrangement of schedules for extra duties
C. Assignment of rooms or areas
D. Distribution of supplies
E. Keeping records and reports
F. Care of audio-visual materials
G. Keeping inventory records
H. Checking record cards and books

I. Programming special activities
J. Checking on the attendance and punctuality of employees

III. Practices Commonly Classified as Both "Supervisory" and "Administrative"
   A. Program construction
   B. Testing or evaluating outcomes
   C. Personnel accounting
   D. Ordering instructional materials

RESPONSIBILITIES OF THE SUPERVISOR

A person employed in a supervisory capacity must constantly be able to improve his own efficiency and ability. He represent the employer to the employees and only continuous self-examination can make him a capable supervisor.

Leadership and training are the supervisor's responsibility. An efficient working unit is one in which the employees work with the supervisor. It is his job to bring out the best in his employees. He must always be relaxed, courteous, and calm in his association with his employees. Their feelings are important, and a harsh attitude does not develop the most efficient employees.

COMPETENCES OF THE SUPERVISOR

I. Complete knowledge of the duties and responsibilities of his position.
II. To be able to organize a job, plan ahead, and carry through.
III. To have self-confidence and initiative.
IV. To be able to handle the unexpected situation and make quick decisions.
V. To be able to properly train subordinates in the positions they are best suited for.
VI. To be able to keep good human relations among his subordinates.
VII. To be able to keep good human relations between his subordinates and himself and to earn their respect and trust.

THE PROFESSIONAL SUPERVISOR-EMPLOYEE RELATIONSHIP

There are two kinds of efficiency: one kind is only apparent and is produced in organizations through the exercise of mere discipline; this is but a simulation of the second, or true, efficiency which springs from spontaneous cooperation. If you are a manager, no matter how great or small your responsibility, it is your job, in the final analysis, to create and develop this involuntary cooperation among the people whom you supervise. For, no matter how powerful a combination of money, machines, and materials a company may have, this is a dead and sterile thing without a team of willing, thinking, and articulate people to guide it.

The following 21 points are presented as indicative of the exemplary basic relationship that should exist between supervisor and employee:

1. Each person wants to be liked and respected by his fellow employee and wants to be treated with consideration and respect by his superior.
2. The most competent employee will make an error. However, in a unit where good relations exist between the supervisor and his employees, tenseness and fear do not exist. Thus, errors are not hidden or covered up, and the efficiency of a unit is not impaired.

3. Subordinates resent rules, regulations, or orders that are unreasonable or unexplained.
4. Subordinates are quick to resent unfairness, harshness, injustices, and favoritism.
5. An employee will accept responsibility if he knows that he will be complimented for a job well done, and not too harshly chastised for failure; that his supervisor will check the cause of the failure, and, if it was the supervisor's fault, he will assume the blame therefore. If it was the employee's fault, his supervisor will explain the correct method or means of handling the responsibility.
6. An employee wants to receive credit for a suggestion he has made, that is used. If a suggestion cannot be used, the employee is entitled to an explanation. The supervisor should not say "no" and close the subject.
7. Fear and worry slow up a worker's ability. Poor working environment can impair his physical and mental health. A good supervisor avoids forceful methods, threats, and arguments to get a job done.
8. A forceful supervisor is able to train his employees individually and as a team, and is able to motivate them in the proper channels.
9. A mature supervisor is able to properly evaluate his subordinates and to keep them happy and satisfied.
10. A sensitive supervisor will never patronize his subordinates.
11. A worthy supervisor will respect his employees' confidences.
12. Definite and clear-cut responsibilities should be assigned to each executive.
13. Responsibility should always be coupled with corresponding authority.
14. No change should be made in the scope or responsibilities of a position without a definite understanding to that effect on the part of all persons concerned.
15. No executive or employee, occupying a single position in the organization, should be subject to definite orders from more than one source.
16. Orders should never be given to subordinates over the head of a responsible executive. Rather than do this, the officer in question should be supplanted.
17. Criticisms of subordinates should, whoever possible, be made privately, and in no case should a subordinate be criticized in the presence of executives or employees of equal or lower rank.
18. No dispute or difference between executives or employees as to authority or responsibilities should be considered too trivial for prompt and careful adjudication.
19. Promotions, wage changes, and disciplinary action should always be approved by the executive immediately superior to the one directly responsible.
20. No executive or employee should ever be required, or expected, to be at the same time an assistant to, and critic of, another.
21. Any executive whose work is subject to regular inspection should, wherever practicable, be given the assistance and facilities necessary to enable him to maintain an independent check of the quality of his work.

MINI-TEXT IN SUPERVISION, ADMINISTRATION, MANAGEMENT, AND ORGANIZATION

I. Brief Highlights

Listed concisely and sequentially are major headings and important data in the field for quick recall and review.

A. Levels of Management

Any organization of some size has several levels of management. In terms of a ladder, the levels are:

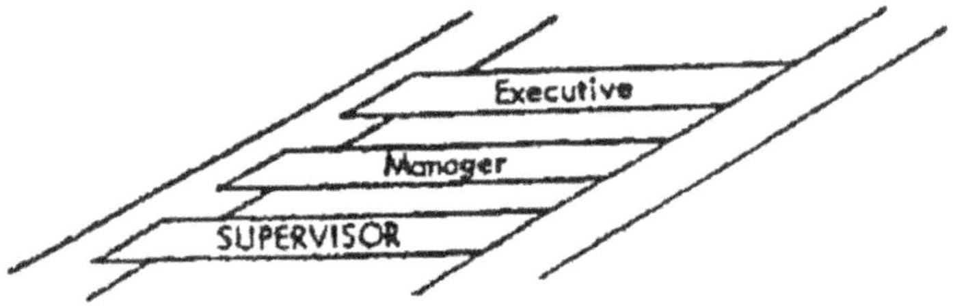

The first level is very important because it is the beginning point of management leadership.

B. What the Supervisor Must Learn

A supervisor must learn to:

1. Deal with people and their differences
2. Get the job done through people
3. Recognize the problems when they exist
4. Overcome obstacles to good performance
5. Evaluate the performance of people
6. Check his own performance in terms of accomplishment

C. A Definition of Supervisor

The term supervisor means any individual having authority, in the interests of the employer, to hire, transfer, suspend, lay-off, recall, promote, discharge, assign, reward, or discipline other employees or responsibility to direct them, or to adjust their grievances, or effectively to recommend such action, if, in connection with the foregoing, exercise of such authority is not of a merely routine or clerical nature but requires the use of independent judgment.

D. Elements of the Team Concept

What is involved in teamwork? The component parts are:

1. Members
2. A leader
3. Goals
4. Plans
5. Cooperation
6. Spirit

E. Principles of Organization

1. A team member must know what his job is.
2. Be sure that the nature and scope of a job are understood.
3. Authority and responsibility should be carefully spelled out.
4. A supervisor should be permitted to make the maximum number of decisions affecting his employees.
5. Employees should report to only one supervisor.
6. A supervisor should direct only as many employees as he can handle effectively.
7. An organization plan should be flexible.

8. Inspection and performance of work should be separate.
9. Organizational problems should receive immediate attention.
10. Assign work in line with ability and experience.

F. The Four Important Parts of Every Job
   1. Inherent in every job is the *accountability* for results.
   2. A second set of factors in every job is *responsibilities*.
   3. Along with duties and responsibilities one must have the *authority* to act within certain limits without obtaining permission to proceed.
   4. No job exists in a vacuum. The supervisor is surrounded by key *relationships*.

G. Principles of Delegation
   Where work is delegated for the first time, the supervisor should think in terms of these questions:
   1. Who is best qualified to do this?
   2. Can an employee improve his abilities by doing this?
   3. How long should an employee spend on this?
   4. Are there any special problems for which he will need guidance?
   5. How broad a delegation can I make?

H. Principles of Effective Communications
   1. Determine the media.
   2. To whom directed?
   3. Identification and source authority.
   4. Is communication understood?

I. Principles of Work Improvement
   1. Most people usually do only the work which is assigned to them.
   2. Workers are likely to fit assigned work into the time available to perform it.
   3. A good workload usually stimulates output.
   4. People usually do their best work when they know that results will be reviewed or inspected.
   5. Employees usually feel that someone else is responsible for conditions of work, workplace layout, job methods, type of tools/equipment, and other such factors.
   6. Employees are usually defensive about their job security.
   7. Employees have natural resistance to change.
   8. Employees can support or destroy a supervisor.
   9. A supervisor usually earns the respect of his people through his personal example of diligence and efficiency.

J. Areas of Job Improvement
   The areas of job improvement are quite numerous, but the most common ones which a supervisor can identify and utilize are:
   1. Departmental layout
   2. Flow of work
   3. Workplace layout
   4. Utilization of manpower
   5. Work methods
   6. Materials handling

7. Utilization
8. Motion economy

K. Seven Key Points in Making Improvements
1. Select the job to be improved
2. Study how it is being done now
3. Question the present method
4. Determine actions to be taken
5. Chart proposed method
6. Get approval and apply
7. Solicit worker participation

I. Corrective Techniques of Job Improvement

Specific Problems
1. Size of workload
2. Inability to meet schedules
3. Strain and fatigue
4. Improper use of men and skills
5. Waste, poor quality, unsafe conditions
6. Bottleneck conditions that hinder output
7. Poor utilization of equipment and machine
8. Efficiency and productivity of labor

General Improvement
1. Departmental layout
2. Flow of work
3. Work plan layout
4. Utilization of manpower
5. Work methods
6. Materials handling
7. Utilization of equipment
8. Motion economy

Corrective Techniques
1. Study with scale model
2. Flow chart study
3. Motion analysis
4. Comparison of units produced to standard allowance
5. Methods analysis
6. Flow chart and equipment study
7. Down time vs. running time
8. Motion analysis

M. A Planning Checklist
1. Objectives
2. Controls
3. Delegations
4. Communications
5. Resources
6. Manpower

7. Equipment
8. Supplies and materials
9. Utilization of time
10. Safety
11. Money
12. Work
13. Timing of improvements

N. Five Characteristics of Good Directions

In order to get results, directions must be:

1. Possible of accomplishment
2. Agreeable with worker interests
3. Related to mission
4. Planned and complete
5. Unmistakably clear

O. Types of Directions

1. Demands or direct orders
2. Requests
3. Suggestion or implication
4. volunteering

P. Controls

A typical listing of the overall areas in which the supervisor should establish controls might be:

1. Manpower
2. Materials
3. Quality of work
4. Quantity of work
5. Time
6. Space
7. Money
8. Methods

Q. Orienting the New Employee

1. Prepare for him
2. Welcome the new employee
3. Orientation for the job
4. Follow-up

R. Checklist for Orienting New Employees

	Yes	No
1. Do you appreciate the feelings of new employees when they first report for work?	___	___
2. Are you aware of the fact that the new employee must make a big adjustment to his job?	___	___
3. Have you given him good reasons for liking the job and the organization?	___	___
4. Have you prepared for his first day on the job?	___	___
5. Did you welcome him cordially and make him feel needed?	___	___

		Yes	No
6.	Did you establish rapport with him so that he feels free to talk and discuss matters with you?	___	___
7.	Did you explain his job to him and his relationship to you?	___	___
8.	Does he know that his work will be evaluated periodically on a basis that is fair and objective?	___	___
9.	Did you introduce him to his fellow workers in such a way that they are likely to accept him?	___	___
10.	Does he know what employee benefits he will receive?	___	___
11.	Does he understand the importance of being on the job and what to do if he must leave his duty station?	___	___
12.	Has he been impressed with the importance of accident prevention and safe practice?	___	___
13.	Does he generally know his way around the department?	___	___
14.	Is he under the guidance of a sponsor who will teach the right way of doing things?	___	___
15.	Do you plan to follow-up so that he will continue to adjust successfully to his job?	___	___

S. Principles of Learning
1. Motivation
2. Demonstration or explanation
3. Practice

T. Causes of Poor Performance
1. Improper training for job
2. Wrong tools
3. Inadequate directions
4. Lack of supervisory follow-up
5. Poor communications
6. Lack of standards of performance
7. Wrong work habits
8. Low morale
9. Other

U. Four Major Steps in On-The-Job Instruction
1. Prepare the worker
2. Present the operation
3. Tryout performance
4. Follow-up

V. Employees Want Five Things
1. Security
2. Opportunity
3. Recognition
4. Inclusion
5. Expression

W. Some Don'ts in Regard to Praise
1. Don't praise a person for something he hasn't done.
2. Don't praise a person unless you can be sincere.
3. Don't be sparing in praise just because your superior withholds it from you.
4. Don't let too much time elapse between good performance and recognition of it

X. How to Gain Your Workers' Confidence
Methods of developing confidence include such things as:
1. Knowing the interests, habits, hobbies of employees
2. Admitting your own inadequacies
3. Sharing and telling of confidence in others
4. Supporting people when they are in trouble
5. Delegating matters that can be well handled
6. Being frank and straightforward about problems and working conditions
7. Encouraging others to bring their problems to you
8. Taking action on problems which impede worker progress

Y. Sources of Employee Problems
On-the-job causes might be such things as:
1. A feeling that favoritism is exercised in assignments
2. Assignment of overtime
3. An undue amount of supervision
4. Changing methods or systems
5. Stealing of ideas or trade secrets
6. Lack of interest in job
7. Threat of reduction in force
8. Ignorance or lack of communications
9. Poor equipment
10. Lack of knowing how supervisor feels toward employee
11. Shift assignments

Off-the-job problems might have to do with:
1. Health
2. Finances
3. Housing
4. Family

Z. The Supervisor's Key to Discipline
There are several key points about discipline which the supervisor should keep in mind:
1. Job discipline is one of the disciplines of life and is directed by the supervisor.
2. It is more important to correct an employee fault than to fix blame for it.
3. Employee performance is affected by problems both on the job and off.
4. Sudden or abrupt changes in behavior can be indications of important employee problems.
5. Problems should be dealt with as soon as possible after they are identified.
6. The attitude of the supervisor may have more to do with solving problems than the techniques of problem solving.
7. Correction of employee behavior should be resorted to only after the supervisor is sure that training or counseling will not be helpful.

8. Be sure to document your disciplinary actions.
9. Make sure that you are disciplining on the basis of facts rather than personal feelings.
10. Take each disciplinary step in order, being careful not to make snap judgments, or decisions based on impatience.

AA. Five Important Processes of Management
1. Planning
2. Organizing
3. Scheduling
4. Controlling
5. Motivating

BB. When the Supervisor Fails to Plan
1. Supervisor creates impression of not knowing his job
2. May lead to excessive overtime
3. Job runs itself—supervisor lacks control
4. Deadlines and appointments missed
5. Parts of the work go undone
6. Work interrupted by emergencies
7. Sets a bad example
8. Uneven workload creates peaks and valleys
9. Too much time on minor details at expense of more important tasks

CC. Fourteen General Principles of Management
1. Division of work
2. Authority and responsibility
3. Discipline
4. Unity of command
5. Unity of direction
6. Subordination of individual interest to general interest
7. Remuneration of personnel
8. Centralization
9. Scalar chain
10. Order
11. Equity
12. Stability of tenure of personnel
13. Initiative
14. Esprit de corps

DD. Change

Bringing about change is perhaps attempted more often, and yet less well understood, than anything else the supervisor does. How do people generally react to change? (People tend to resist change that is imposed upon them by other individuals or circumstances.

Change is characteristic of every situation. It is a part of every real endeavor where the efforts of people are concerned.

1. Why do people resist change?
   People may resist change because of:
   a. Fear of the unknown
   b. Implied criticism
   c. Unpleasant experiences in the past
   d. Fear of loss of status
   e. Threat to the ego
   f. Fear of loss of economic stability

2. How can we best overcome the resistance to change?
   In initiating change, take these steps:
   a. Get ready to sell
   b. Identify sources of help
   c. Anticipate objections
   d. Sell benefits
   e. Listen in depth
   f. Follow up

II. Brief Topical Summaries

A. Who/What is the Supervisor?
   1. The supervisor is often called the "highest level employee and the lowest level manager."
   2. A supervisor is a member of both management and the work group. He acts as a bridge between the two.
   3. Most problems in supervision are in the area of human relations, or people problems.
   4. Employees expect: Respect, opportunity to learn and to advance, and a sense of belonging, and so forth.
   5. Supervisors are responsible for directing people and organizing work. Planning is of paramount importance.
   6. A position description is a set of duties and responsibilities inherent to a given position.
   7. It is important to keep the position description up-to-date and to provide each employee with his own copy.

B. The Sociology of Work
   1. People are alike in many ways; however, each individual is unique.
   2. The supervisor is challenged in getting to know employee differences. Acquiring skills in evaluating individuals is an asset.
   3. Maintaining meaningful working relationships in the organization is of great importance.
   4. The supervisor has an obligation to help individuals to develop to their fullest potential.
   5. Job rotation on a planned basis helps to build versatility and to maintain interest and enthusiasm in work groups.
   6. Cross training (job rotation) provides backup skills.

7. The supervisor can help reduce tension by maintaining a sense of humor, providing guidance to employees, and by making reasonable and timely decisions. Employees respond favorably to working under reasonably predictable circumstances.
8. Change is characteristic of all managerial behavior. The supervisor must adjust to changes in procedures, new methods, technological changes, and to a number of new and sometimes challenging situations.
9. To overcome the natural tendency for people to resist change, the supervisor should become more skillful in initiating change.

C. Principles and Practices of Supervision

1. Employees should be required to answer to only one superior.
2. A supervisor can effectively direct only a limited number of employees, depending upon the complexity, variety, and proximity of the jobs involved.
3. The organizational chart presents the organization in graphic form. It reflects lines of authority and responsibility as well as interrelationships of units within the organization.
4. Distribution of work can be improved through an analysis using the "Work Distribution Chart."
5. The "Work Distribution Chart" reflects the division of work within a unit in understandable form.
6. When related tasks are given to an employee, he has a better chance of increasing his skills through training.
7. The individual who is given the responsibility for tasks must also be given the appropriate authority to insure adequate results.
8. The supervisor should delegate repetitive, routine work. Preparation of recurring reports, maintaining leave and attendance records are some examples.
9. Good discipline is essential to good task performance. Discipline is reflected in the actions of employees on the job in the absence of supervision.
10. Disciplinary action may have to be taken when the positive aspects of discipline have failed. Reprimand, warning, and suspension are examples of disciplinary action.
11. If a situation calls for a reprimand, be sure it is deserved and remember it is to be done in private.

D. Dynamic Leadership

1. A style is a personal method or manner of exerting influence.
2. Authoritarian leaders often see themselves as the source of power and authority.
3. The democratic leader often perceives the group as the source of authority and power.
4. Supervisors tend to do better when using the pattern of leadership that is most natural for them.
5. Social scientists suggest that the effective supervisor use the leadership style that best fits the problem or circumstances involved.
6. All four styles—telling, selling, consulting, joining—have their place. Using one does not preclude using the other at another time.

7. The theory X point of view assumes that the average person dislikes work, will avoid it whenever possible, and must be coerced to achieve organizational objectives.
8. The theory Y point of view assumes that the average person considers work to be a natural as play, and, when the individual is committed, he requires little supervision or direction to accomplish desired objectives.
9. The leader's basic assumptions concerning human behavior and human nature affect his actions, decisions, and other managerial practices.
10. Dissatisfaction among employees is often present, but difficult to isolate. The supervisor should seek to weaken dissatisfaction by keeping promises, being sincere and considerate, keeping employees informed, and so forth.
11. Constructive suggestions should be encouraged during the natural progress of the work.

E. Processes for Solving Problems

1. People find their daily tasks more meaningful and satisfying when they can improve them.
2. The causes of problems, or the key factors, are often hidden in the background. Ability to solve problems often involves the ability to isolate them from their backgrounds. There is some substance to the cliché that some persons "can't see the forest for the trees."
3. New procedures are often developed from old ones. Problems should be broken down into manageable parts. New ideas can be adapted from old one.
4. People think differently in problem-solving situations. Using a logical, patterned approach is often useful. One approach found to be useful includes these steps:
   a. Define the problem
   b. Establish objectives
   c. Get the facts
   d. Weigh and decide
   e. Take action
   f. Evaluate action

F. Training for Results

1. Participants respond best when they feel training is important to them.
2. The supervisor has responsibility for the training and development of those who report to him.
3. When training is delegated to others, great care must be exercised to insure the trainer has knowledge, aptitude, and interest for his work as a trainer.
4. Training (learning) of some type goes on continually. The most successful supervisor makes certain the learning contributes in a productive manner to operational goals.
5. New employees are particularly susceptible to training. Older employees facing new job situations require specific training, as well as having need for development and growth opportunities.
6. Training needs require continuous monitoring.
7. The training officer of an agency is a professional with a responsibility to assist supervisors in solving training problems.

8. Many of the self-development steps important to the supervisor's own growth are equally important to the development of peers and subordinates. Knowledge of these is important when the supervisor consults with others on development and growth opportunities.

G. Health, Safety, and Accident Prevention
   1. Management-minded supervisors take appropriate measures to assist employees in maintaining health and in assuring safe practices in the work environment.
   2. Effective safety training and practices help to avoid injury and accidents.
   3. Safety should be a management goal. All infractions of safety which are observed should be corrected without exception.
   4. Employees' safety attitude, training and instruction, provision of safe tools and equipment, supervision, and leadership are considered highly important factors which contribute to safety and which can be influenced directly by supervisors.
   5. When accidents do occur, they should be investigated promptly for very important reasons, including the fact that information which is gained can be used to prevent accidents in the future.

H. Equal Employment Opportunity
   1. The supervisor should endeavor to treat all employees fairly, without regard to religion, race, sex, or national origin.
   2. Groups tend to reflect the attitude of the leader. Prejudice can be detected even in very subtle form. Supervisors must strive to create a feeling of mutual respect and confidence in every employee.
   3. Complete utilization of all human resources is a national goal. Equitable consideration should be accorded women in the work force, minority-group members, the physically and mentally handicapped, and the older employee. The important question is: "Who can do the job?"
   4. Training opportunities, recognition for performance, overtime assignments, promotional opportunities, and all other personnel actions are to be handled on an equitable basis.

I. Improving Communications
   1. Communications is achieving understanding between the sender and the receiver of a message. It also means sharing information—the creation of understanding.
   2. Communication is basic to all human activity. Words are means of conveying meanings; however, real meanings are in people.
   3. There are very practical differences in the effectiveness of one-way, impersonal, and two-way communications. Words spoken face-to-face are better understood. Telephone conversations are effective, but lack the rapport of person-to-person exchanges. The whole person communicates.
   4. Cooperation and communication in an organization go hand in hand. When there is a mutual respect between people, spelling out rules and procedures for communicating is unnecessary.
   5. There are several barriers to effective communications. These include failure to listen with respect and understanding, lack of skill in feedback, and misinterpreting the meanings of words used by the speaker. It is also common

practice to listen to what we want to hear, and tune out things we do not want to hear.

6. Communication is management's chief problem. The supervisor should accept the challenge to communicate more effectively and to improve interagency and intra-agency communications.
7. The supervisor may often plan for and conduct meetings. The planning phase is critical and may determine the success or the failure of a meeting.
8. Speaking before groups usually requires extra effort. Stage fright may never disappear completely, but it can be controlled.

J. Self-Development

1. Every employee is responsible for his own self-development.
2. Toastmaster and toastmistress clubs offer opportunities to improve skills in oral communications.
3. Planning for one's own self-development is of vital importance. Supervisors know their own strengths and limitations better than anyone else.
4. Many opportunities are open to aid the supervisor in his developmental efforts, including job assignments; training opportunities, both governmental and non-governmental—to include universities and professional conferences and seminars.
5. Programmed instruction offers a means of studying at one's own rate.
6. Where difficulties may arise from a supervisor's being away from his work for training, he may participate in televised home study or correspondence courses to meet his self-development needs.

K. Teaching and Training

1. The Teaching Process

   Teaching is encouraging and guiding the learning activities of students toward established goals. In most cases this process consists of five steps: preparation, presentation, summarization, evaluation, and application.

   a. Preparation

      Preparation is two-fold in nature; that of the supervisor and the employee. Preparation by the supervisor is absolutely essential to success. He must know what, when, where, how, and whom he will teach. Some of the factors that should be considered are:

      1) The objectives
      2) The materials needed
      3) The methods to be used
      4) Employee participation
      5) Employee interest
      6) Training aids
      7) Evaluation
      8) Summarization

      Employee preparation consists in preparing the employee to receive the material. Probably the most important single factor in the preparation of the employee is arousing and maintaining his interest. He must know the objectives of the training, why he is there, how the material can be used, and its importance to him.

b. Presentation
In presentation, have a carefully designed plan and follow it. The plan should be accurate and complete, yet flexible enough to meet situations as they arise. The method of presentation will be determined by the particular situation and objectives.

c. Summary
A summary should be made at the end of every training unit and program. In addition, there may be internal summaries depending on the nature of the material being taught. The important thing is that the trainee must always be able to understand how each part of the new material relates to the whole.

d. Application
The supervisor must arrange work so the employee will be given a chance to apply new knowledge or skills while the material is still clear in his mind and interest is high. The trainee does not really know whether he has learned the material until he has been given a chance to apply it. If the material is not applied, it loses most of its value.

e. Evaluation
The purpose of all training is to promote learning. To determine whether the training has been a success or failure, the supervisor must evaluate this learning.
In the broadest sense, evaluation includes all the devices, methods, skills, and techniques used by the supervisor to keep himself and the employees informed as to their progress toward the objectives they are pursuing. The extent to which the employee has mastered the knowledge, skills, and abilities, or changed his attitudes, as determined by the program objectives, is the extent to which instruction has succeeded or failed.
Evaluation should not be confined to the end of the lesson, day, or program but should be used continuously. We shall note later the way this relates to the rest of the teaching process.

2. Teaching Methods
A teaching method is a pattern of identifiable student and instructor activity used in presenting training material.
All supervisors are faced with the problem of deciding which method should be used at a given time.

a. Lecture
The lecture is direct oral presentation of material by the supervisor. The present trend is to place less emphasis on the trainer's activity and more on that of the trainee.

b. Discussion
Teaching by discussion or conference involves using questions and other techniques to arouse interest and focus attention upon certain areas, and by doing so creating a learning situation. This can be one of the most

valuable methods because it gives the employees an opportunity to express their ideas and pool their knowledge.

c. Demonstration
The demonstration is used to teach how something works or how to do something. It can be used to show a principle or what the results of a series of actions will be. A well-staged demonstration is particularly effective because it shows proper methods of performance in a realistic manner.

d. Performance
Performance is one of the most fundamental of all learning techniques or teaching methods. The trainee may be able to tell how a specific operation should be performed but he cannot be sure he knows how to perform the operation until he has done so.
As with all methods, there are certain advantages and disadvantages to each method.

e. Which Method to Use
Moreover, there are other methods and techniques of teaching. It is difficult to use any method without other methods entering into it. In any learning situation, a combination of methods is usually more effective than any one method alone.

Finally, evaluation must be integrated into the other aspects of the teaching-learning process.

It must be used in the motivation of the trainees; it must be used to assist in developing understanding during the training; and it must be related to employee application of the results of training.

This is distinctly the role of the supervisor.

www.ingramcontent.com/pod-product-compliance
Lightning Source LLC
Chambersburg PA
CBHW081815300426
44116CB00014B/2367
* 9 7 8 1 7 9 9 3 0 2 1 5 5 *